Human remains found in manhole, 1983

FEBRUARY 8

On 8 February 1983, a drains maintenance engineer found decomposed human flesh in a manhole outside a house in north London. The discovery was reported to the police and led to the questioning of Dennis Nilsen, a thirty-seven-year-old civil servant working for the Manpower Services Commission. Nilsen confessed that he was the person responsible, and revealed the whereabouts of further remains. He said that he had killed sixteen people.

Also by James Bland:

TRUE CRIME DIARY

TRUE CRIME
Diary

VOLUME 2

James Bland

Futura

A Futura Book

First published in Great Britain in 1989
by Futura Publications, a Division of
Macdonald & Co (Publishers) Ltd
London & Sydney

ISBN 0 7088 4214 3

Typeset by Leaper & Gard Ltd, Bristol, England
Reproduced, printed and bound in Great Britain by
Hazell Watson & Viney Limited
Member of BPCC plc
Aylesbury, Bucks, England

Futura Publications
A Division of
Macdonald & Co (Publishers) Ltd
66–73 Shoe Lane
London EC4P 4AB
A member of Maxwell Pergamon Publishing Corporation plc

CONTENTS

Preface   7

January   9
February   39
March   73
April   102
May   132
June   162
July   190
August   219
September   251
October   284
November   316
December   348

CONTENTS

Preface

January
February
March
April
May
June
July
August
September
October
November
December

PREFACE

This second volume of *True Crime Diary* follows the same formula as the first in presenting a large collection of modern murder stories as a book of anniversaries. The contents include cases of all types and from many countries, and while some are already famous, others are virtually unknown.

As before, I have sought to recount these stories in a brief and straightforward manner, pointing out the significance of particular cases, though without advancing any theories of my own.

All in all, I feel justified in suggesting that those who liked Volume One will be equally pleased with its sequel. Beyond that, however, I will make no claims for it, and leave readers to decide its merits for themselves.

J.B.

Murder of Leon Beron, 1911

On the morning of 1 January 1911, a policeman found the body of Leon Beron, a forty-eight-year-old Russian Jew, hidden among furze bushes on Clapham Common, south-west London. He had been struck on the head with a blunt instrument, then — when he was already dead — stabbed in the chest three times. There were also a number of superficial cuts on his face, including one shaped roughly like the letter S on each cheek. But it seemed that robbery had been the motive for the crime, for a gold watch and about twenty sovereigns (£20) were missing from the body.

Beron, a widower, owned nine little houses in Stepney, east London, but lived in a room above a shop in the same district. It was learnt that on the previous evening he had left a local kosher restaurant in the company of Stinie Morrison, a professional burglar aged about thirty who had served five prison sentences, totalling twelve years. Morrison, also a Russian Jew, was missing from his lodgings; he had told his landlady that he was going to Paris. He was, however, arrested at another East End restaurant on 8 January and taken to Leman Street police station.

The arrest was made ostensibly because Morrison — a convict on parole who had been out of prison only a short while — had failed to notify the police of his change of address. But he knew that this was not the only reason, and soon after his arrival at the police station he made the mistake of saying to Detective Inspector Frederick Wensley, 'You have accused me of a serious crime. You have accused me of murder!' At that stage, it was afterwards alleged, no mention had been made of Beron's death. But the police officers concerned were certain of Morrison's guilt.

Two witnesses claimed to have seen him in Beron's company during the early hours of 1 January: one of these was the driver of a hansom-cab, who said that he had driven them to Clapham from Whitechapel — a distance of six miles — after picking them up about 2 a.m. A second cab-driver said that he had picked Morrison up near the common between 2.30 and 3.00 a.m. (about the time of Beron's death), and driven him to Kennington, south London. A third cab-driver — this one had a taxi — claimed to have picked Morrison and another man up in Kennington at 3.30 a.m. Stinie Morrison, a very tall, handsome man, was brought to trial at the Old Bailey on 6 March, charged with Beron's murder.

The prosecution's case was based largely on circumstantial evidence, much of which was confused. A number of volatile East End characters, mainly aliens, appeared as witnesses, facing the court in a less than awe-struck manner. The prisoner stood throughout the nine-day trial with one hand on his hip, observing the proceedings disdainfully.

The S-shaped cuts on the dead man's cheeks were the subject of some speculation: it was suggested by the defence that Beron had been a police spy and that he had given information about the anarchists responsible for the Houndsditch Murders (see 3 January). It was also suggested that Beron's brother Solomon, who went mad during the closing speech for the defence and had to be taken away to a lunatic asylum, might have committed the murder himself. But the jury decided that Morrison was guilty and he was sentenced to death. This sentence was afterwards commuted to life imprisonment.

Accustomed though he was to being in prison, Stinie Morrison now found his existence intolerable.

He frequently protested his innocence, and in 1916, on hearing that one of the police officers responsible for his conviction had been killed in a Zeppelin raid, he smiled grimly and remarked, 'Now I believe in Providence!' However, the news proved not to be much of a consolation to him, and he finally starved himself to death in January 1921.

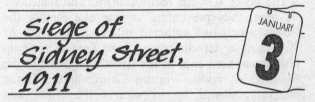

Siege of Sidney Street, 1911

JANUARY 3

Britain's most famous gun battle took place on 3 January 1911, when police officers tried to arrest two men trapped in a tenement building in Sidney Street, between Commercial Road and Whitechapel Road, in the East End of London.

The men, Fritz Svaars and Jacob Vogel, were members of a group of Russian anarchists. On 16 December previously they, in company with twelve comrades, had taken part in an attempted robbery at a jeweller's shop in Houndsditch, during the course of which three police officers had been shot dead and two others wounded. Their presence in a second-floor room occupied by Mrs Betsy Gershon had been reported by an informer on 2 January, and the building had been surrounded in the hope that they could be taken by surprise as they left. But after waiting for many hours in vain the police decided on a different course of action.

Early in the morning, with the help of the landlady, they managed to get Mrs Gershon out of the building without arousing suspicion; they then began evacuating the rest of the rooms. The anarchists remained out of sight until dawn, when police attracted their attention by throwing stones at the window. There were fifty police officers on the scene at this stage, fifteen of them armed with revolvers and four with rifles, and it was thought that such an impressive display of strength might induce the two fugitives to surrender. Instead, they opened fire, wounding a detective sergeant, and before long there were bullets ricocheting in all directions.

The police sent for reinforcements and sealed off the area, thus preventing anyone else joining the crowds which had gathered to watch the fray. At 10.15 a.m. a detachment of Scots Guards took up positions at both ends of the street and joined in the shooting. At noon, Winston Churchill, the Home Secretary, turned up to witness the battle and suggested that a cannon should be brought along, to blow in the front of the building. This proposal, unusual as it seemed to the police, was taken to the War Office and a troop of the Royal Horse Artillery was sent. Before it reached Sidney Street, however, smoke was seen coming from a top-floor window. Within half an hour the building was on fire.

The shooting continued as the blaze spread downwards, driving the anarchists before it. The fire brigade arrived but was not allowed to put out the fire. Eventually one of the men was killed by a rifle bullet; the other then fought on alone until the building collapsed around him.

The battle had lasted over six hours, with some of the spectators being hit by bullets. The firemen, when they were finally allowed to put out the fire, sustained a number of casualties before managing to get it under control. The affair led to much criticism of the government, particularly over the use of troops.

Of the others who had taken part in the Houndsditch crime, George Gardstein, the leader, had already died as a result of being accidently shot by another Russian, and several more had been arrested but were later acquited. The rest were never caught.

Disappearance of Mona Tinsley, 1937

JANUARY 5

At half past nine on the night of 5 January 1937, Nottinghamshire police were informed of the disappearance of a ten-year-old schoolgirl, Mona Tinsley, of 11, Thoresby Avenue, Newark. She had failed to arrive home after coming out of school — a twenty-minute walk away — at four o'clock that afternoon, and her parents had no idea what had become of her. The police began to investigate and the following day learnt that the missing girl had been seen with a man at Newark bus station soon after leaving the school. It was then clear that she had been abducted.

A few hours after receiving this report police officers went to see Frederick Nodder, a motor mechanic living in a semi-detached house near the village of Hayton, three and a half miles from Retford. Nodder, who had lodged with Mona's parents for three weeks in 1935, was known to them as Frederick Hudson and to their children as 'Uncle Fred'. He had been seen waiting outside Mona's school the previous afternoon, but denied knowing anything of her whereabouts.

Nodder was a married man who had left his wife. As he was wanted for non-payment of an affiliation order, he was taken into custody and charged accord-

13

ingly. It was found that he had taken Mona Tinsley by bus from Newark to Retford, a distance of about twenty miles, on 5 January, and also that the missing girl had been seen standing at the back door of his house at noon the following day.

After being identified by several witnesses, Nodder made a statement, admitting that he had seen Mona coming out of school on the day of her disappearance. He said that she had wanted to go to Sheffield to see her aunt, who had just had a baby, and that he — a friend of the aunt's — had taken her to stay overnight at his house. The next day he had taken her to Worksop and left her to travel the rest of the way to Sheffield on her own. The latter part of this statement could not be corroborated and was not believed. On 10 January Frederick Nodder was charged with abduction.

The police widened their search, going over waste ground and dumps and dragging rivers and canals, but found no trace of the missing girl. Nodder came up for trial in March at the Warwick Assizes in Birmingham and was found guilty. The judge, like everyone else, was certain that he had murdered the child and, in passing sentence, said: 'What you did with that little girl, what became of her, only you know. It may be that time will reveal the dreadful secret which you carry in your breast.' He sentenced Nodder to seven years' penal servitude — a term which he was not to complete.

Three months afterwards, on 6 June, a family boating party found Mona Tinsley's body floating on the River Idle, over twenty miles from Newark. She had been strangled. After further investigation Nodder was charged with her murder.

When he was brought to trial on this charge at the Nottingham Assizes in November, he pleaded not guilty and stuck to the story he had told earlier. But once again he was not believed, and the judge, in passing sentence of death, told him: 'Justice has slowly but surely overtaken you.'

Nodder, aged forty-four, was hanged at Lincoln Prison on 30 December 1937.

Death of Evelyn Foster 1931

During the late evening of 6 January 1931, an Otterburn bus crew making a return journey from Newcastle found a blazing car about seventy yards from the road at a desolate stretch of the Northumberland moor called Wolf's Neck. Stopping to investigate, they found Evelyn Foster, their employer's twenty-nine-year-old unmarried daughter, lying nearby with severe burns, having apparently met with an accident while driving the firm's new Hudson taxi. The bus crew took her to Otterburn at great speed, but she died shortly afterwards in the presence of her parents and family doctor. Before doing so, however, she managed to make a statement in which she claimed to be the victim of a frightful crime.

She said that she had been driving home when she was stopped at Ellishaw, not far from Otterburn, by a short, stocky man wearing an overcoat and bowler hat, who asked to be taken to Ponteland, in the direction of Newcastle. She agreed to take him, but before they reached Ponteland the man started to make advances towards her and she had to stop the car in order to fight him off. But the man then dealt her several blows, as a result of which she lost consciousness, and when she recovered she found that he had taken her place in the driving-seat and was driving the car back towards Otterburn.

At Wolf's Neck, she continued, he suddenly took the car off the road, driving it over a bank with a steep drop before bringing it to a halt on the rough ground; he then got out and set fire to it while she was still inside. She managed to drag herself free of it in time to see her assailant leave the scene in another car which had just drawn up at the roadside, but was unable to move any further and had to remain by the burning car until the bus crew found her.

Evelyn's story horrified the inhabitants of Otterburn, and they waited impatiently for news that the murderer had been apprehended. But they waited in vain, for the police were unable to trace the man in the bowler hat, or anyone else who had seen him. Moreover, they soon began to doubt whether Evelyn's story was entirely true.

A pathologist, after examining the body, reported to the coroner's inquest early in February that the deceased had died of shock caused by external burns, and that she had been sitting in the car for some time after the fire had started. But he also said that he had found no bruises or cuts consistent with the blows she claimed to have received, and this, together with other findings reported at the inquest, led the coroner to raise the question of whether Evelyn Foster could have started the fire herself — perhaps for the purpose of claiming insurance money — and caused her own death by accident.

The suggestion, though bitterly resented by Evelyn's family and friends, was evidently discussed at length by the jury, for it took them two hours to arrive at a verdict of wilful murder. The police afterwards issued a statement, declaring themselves satisfied that the short, stocky man did not exist.

The case remains officially unsolved and continues to be the subject of speculation.

Shooting of Dieter Poeschke. 1974

On the afternoon of 7 January 1974, Hans Appel, the thirty-four-year-old owner of a large construction company, and his wife's brother Dieter Poeschke, a garage mechanic aged twenty-one, were driving through the streets of Frankfurt. They were on friendly terms, and Poeschke was giving Appel a lift because his own car was out of service. Neither of them could have had any inkling of the tragedy which was about to occur.

Appel was preoccupied with his wife Renate, who was ten years younger than himself. He and she had both been married before, both had children by their earlier marriages, and Renate had since borne Appel a daughter. But then, in 1973, Renate's other brother Juergen, a former prisoner in East Germany who had been granted an amnesty, arrived in Frankfurt and moved into their home as a lodger.

Although the three adults and the children all got on well together for a while, it was not long before Appel's daughter Claudia, aged six, let him into a secret. 'Mummy and Uncle Juergen were in bed all afternoon,' she said one evening. 'They were naked!'

Hans Appel, a devoted husband, was shocked. At first he wondered whether Juergen, who had been separated from the rest of the family for sixteen years, really was Renate's brother or just a lover pretending to be. But a check with the immigration authorities was enough to dispel the suspicion, convincing him that Renate and Juergen had been committing incest.

Appel confronted them both, telling them that he

17

knew of their relationship, and when neither tried to deny it, he ordered Juergen out of the house. Juergen promptly left, taking Renate with him, and they went to live with Dieter and his wife in their two-room apartment in Sachsenhausen.

But, disgusted as he was with his wife's behaviour, Appel still loved her and wanted her back. He tried to persuade her to return with offers of jewellery and a fur coat — and when she refused he became desperate and bought himself a gun.

Suddenly, while they were in the car, he decided to confide in Dieter, and find out his opinion of what was going on. He therefore asked him if he believed that Juergen and Renate had been committing incest. Astonished by the question, Dieter then revealed that he and Juergen *both* practised incest with Renate 'all the time'!

On hearing this while he was already in a state of turmoil, Appel could stand no more. He pulled the gun from his pocket, shot and wounded Dieter, then brought the car to a halt, swerving onto the pavement. The door opened, and the wounded man fell out, but as he tried to get to his feet, Appel shot him twice more at close range and this time killed him. He then got out of the car himself and walked away from the scene.

When interviewed by the police, Appel admitted being the person responsible and the whole sordid truth emerged. He was tried in July 1974 and sent to prison for twenty-one months, but this sentence was set aside on appeal. Renate and Juergen went on living together after charges of incest against them had been dropped.

Execution of Bywaters and Thompson, 1923

On 9 January 1923, Frederick Bywaters, aged twenty, and Edith Thompson, twenty-eight, were hanged for the murder of Edith's husband in October the previous year. The case was a sensational one, and there were many protests at the executions being carried out. Reports that Edith was drugged and carried to the scaffold in a stupor provided opponents of the death penalty with a good deal of propaganda during the decades which followed.

Percy Thompson, aged thirty-two, was a shipping clerk in London, where his wife also worked as a manageress for a firm of wholesale milliners. Married in 1915, they had no children and lived uneventful lives until Edith began an affair with Bywaters, a merchant seaman, in 1921. Thereafter, though she remained with her husband and tried to keep up appearances, she saw him only as an obstacle to her happiness. Her life became one of surreptitious meetings when Bywaters was on leave and constant yearning for him when he was at sea.

On the night of the murder the Thompsons were walking towards their home in Kensington Gardens, Ilford, after visiting a London theatre, when Bywaters confronted them in the street. There was an argument between the two men, followed by a struggle, then Bywaters stabbed Percy several times with a knife before running off into the darkness. Percy Thompson died from a haemorrhage as he lay on the pavement.

Edith made a false statement to police, claiming that the crime had been committed by a stranger, but her association with Bywaters came to light and soon they were arrested. Edith then admitted that Bywaters had killed her husband, and Bywaters finally confessed his guilt. Though both of them claimed that Edith had had no part in the crime, letters found in Bywaters' possession suggested otherwise. The two prisoners were brought up for trial at the Old Bailey on 6 December 1922, both pleading not guilty.

Edith's letters, many of which were produced as evidence, contained many references to poison and innuendoes about attempts made by herself to kill her husband — on one occasion by putting powdered glass in his porridge. Though evidence was given of the complete absence both of poison and of glass from the victim's body, these references were interpreted as proof that she was guilty of collusion in a premeditated act.

Bywaters claimed that there had been no premeditation. He said that he had lain in wait for the Thompsons that night, not to kill Percy but to force him to leave Edith. He said that he had not produced his knife until Percy threatened to shoot him and appeared to be taking a gun from his pocket.

Edith Thompson gave evidence against the advice of her counsel, saying that she had not wanted to kill her husband. She explained the incriminating references in her letters by saying that she wanted Bywaters to think that she would do anything to keep him to herself.

The judge, in his summing-up, disregarded evidence in Edith's favour, laying stress upon her adultery, which disgusted him.

The case gave rise to many plays and books, F. Tennyson Jesse's novel, *A Pin to See the Peepshow*, being the most famous of them.

Discovery of Vivian Messiter's body, 1929

JANUARY
10

On the morning of 10 January 1929, the decomposing body of Vivian Messiter, a representative of the Wolfe's Head Oil Company, was discovered at the company's depot in Southampton. He had been beaten to death with a hammer, the attack leaving the nearest wall and a stack of boxes spattered with blood; he had also been robbed. The depot had been found padlocked on the outside after his disappearance at the end of the previous October and had remained so until the company authorized another of its employees to break in and take possession of it. The murder weapon — without fingerprints — was found at the scene of the crime.

Messiter, aged fifty-seven, had lived in lodgings and was known never to see anyone except on business. He had had no contact with any of his surviving relatives for months, and none of them was able to provide any clue to the identity of his murderer. However, a blank receipt book from which the first nine pages had been torn was found among the dead man's records, and pressure marks on the tenth page showed that the ninth had acknowledged payment for an oil sale to a company afterwards found to be fictitious. It therefore appeared that somebody had been obtaining commission on sales which had not taken place.

The handwriting on the receipt proved to be that of a W.F. Thomas, whose signature had been found on a scrap of paper left in the depot. A letter from the same person, this time signing himself William F. Thomas, was found at Messiter's lodgings; it had been written on 23 October 1928, in reply to an advertisement in the local press for a salesman, and gave the address of a lodging house in Cranbury Avenue, Southampton.

Thomas was not to be found at the lodging house; he had left it on 3 November 1928, after staying only two weeks, and a forwarding address which he had given to the landlady proved to be non-existent. It was later discovered that he had moved to the village of Downton, about fifteen miles away, on the day of his departure, to begin working as a motor mechanic for a building contractor named Mitchell. He had remained in that employment for seven weeks, then disappeared after stealing the firm's wages, totalling £130.

William F. Thomas was found to be an alias of William Henry Podmore, a petty criminal from the Midlands who had served several short prison sentences and was wanted for car and motor-cycle frauds in Manchester. Traced to a small hotel in London, he told police that he had worked for Messiter for two days, delivering oil and repairing and testing his car, but denied having made the entry in the receipt book and claimed to know nothing about the murder.

The police did not feel that they had a strong enough case to charge him with murder; he was therefore taken to Manchester where, on 29 January, he was convicted of the car and motor-cycle frauds and sent to prison for six months. Upon his release, he was arrested at the prison gates and charged with the offence committed in Downton — for which he was given another six-month sentence.

By the time this sentence had been served, the police had enough evidence for a murder charge, Podmore having confessed the crime to two fellow-prisoners. So, when he left Wandsworth Prison on 17 December, he was again arrested.

Brought to trial in Winchester the following March, he continued to declare that he was innocent. He was, however, convicted, the jury being satisfied that he had murdered Vivian Messiter because his fraudulent claims had been discovered. He was hanged on 22 April 1930, at the age of twenty-nine.

Execution of John Gilbert Graham, 1957

JANUARY
11

John Gilbert Graham, who was executed in Colorado on 11 January 1957, was a mass murderer responsible for the deaths of forty-four people in a plane crash on 1 November 1955. A young married man with two small children, he had caused the accident with a time-bomb while his mother, Mrs Daisy King, was one of the plane's passengers. The crime had been committed for the sake of money.

Graham, at the time of the murders, was twenty-three years old. He and his mother ran a drive-in restaurant together in Denver, and Mrs King, who had been widowed twice, lived with him and his family. He had much to gain from his mother's death, for she was a rich woman as a result of having inherited an estate valued at $150,000 from her second husband.

He also expected to benefit from a flight insurance policy which he had taken out on her life just before she boarded the plane.

Mrs King was on the first leg of a journey to Spenard, Alaska, to visit her daughter, Helen Ruth Hablutzel (Graham's half-sister), when the time-bomb, which had been placed in her luggage, went off. The plane, having left the airport in Denver only a few minutes earlier, crashed in a field, causing a second explosion. There were no survivors.

Graham had a criminal record for forgery and bootlegging; he also had experience of logging and construction jobs, from which he was thought likely to have gained a knowledge of explosives. Moreover, it was learnt that he and his mother had frequently quarrelled over money. After prolonged questioning Graham made a confession which he later retracted.

His trial, for the murder of Mrs King, began in April 1956 and was watched by millions of television viewers. The jury's verdict was returned on 4 May.

Graham later made a second confession, but showed no remorse for all the deaths which he had caused. At his execution, which took place in the gas chamber of the state penitentiary, he appeared to be as indifferent to his own fate as he had been to that of his victims.

Matricide in South Africa, 1925

JANUARY
13

During the early evening of 13 January 1925, Petrus Hauptfleisch, a drunken middle-aged slaughterer, ran from his home in Richmond, Cape Province, screaming that his sixty-seven-year-old mother had been 'burnt in the kitchen fire'. Mrs Hauptfleisch, a widow, was found dead, lying on her side on the brick-built stove in the kitchen. Her body was half naked and badly burned, and some of her clothes lay scattered on the floor.

When the doctor arrived, Hauptfleisch — who had moved the body in the meantime — claimed that his mother had been cleaning the chimney by burning it out with petrol, and had accidentally burnt herself to death. But the doctor, who had known Mrs Hauptfleisch for over twenty years, did not believe this. He knew that she was far too cautious to try to clean the chimney in such a dangerous manner, and also that she was not the sort of person to walk about the house improperly dressed.

Afterwards, on examining her body, he found postmortem lividity indicating that Mrs Hauptfleisch had died while lying on her back and that she had remained in that position for an hour or more after death. This, together with the discovery of evidence of suffocation, led to Hauptfleisch being arrested and charged with his mother's murder a few days later. He was brought to trial in Cape Town in September the same year.

Hauptfleisch was an ex-farmer who had served as a soldier in the First World War. His wife had left him, taking their small son, because she could not tolerate his heavy drinking. His mother, with whom he had lived ever since, was known to have been frightened of him for the same reason. Only a month before her death she had had to take refuge with a neighbour because her son, in a drunken rage, had threatened to stone her.

At his trial it was contended that Hauptfleisch had asphyxiated his mother as she lay on her bed. Later, to make it appear that she had died in an accident, he had placed her body on the kitchen stove, doused it with petrol and set fire to it. Hauptfleisch denied all this, but did not give a good impression of himself. He was found guilty and sentenced to death.

Though a further examination of his mother's body produced the same results as the first, Hauptfleisch continued to maintain that he was innocent. However, he was hanged on 23 December 1925.

Discovery of Elizabeth Short's body, 1947

JANUARY
15

On the morning of 15 January 1947, the body of a young woman was found on a vacant lot in a suburb of Los Angeles. It had been shockingly mutilated — among other things, it had been cut into two pieces at the waist, and the letters B and D had been carved on one of the thighs. More dreadful still was the finding by pathologists that most of the victim's injuries had been inflicted while she was still alive. Her death had taken place only a short while before the gruesome discovery was made.

A fingerprint check by the FBI revealed that the body was that of Elizabeth Short, aged twenty-two, from Medford, Massachusetts, who had a record for juvenile delinquency. But Mrs Phoebe Short, Elizabeth's mother, was unable to make a positive identification because the mutilations had made the body unrecognizable.

It emerged that Elizabeth Short had been very attractive, but unhappy, drunken and promiscuous. She had left home at seventeen to go to Miami — where she was found to be in need of care and protection — and had later worked in Hollywood as a film extra. She was known in Hollywood as the 'Black Dahlia', having established an image of herself by dressing entirely in black — which was also the colour

26

of her hair. But since then she had worked as a waitress in San Diego.

A letter produced by Phoebe Short gave her daughter's San Diego address, but the police found that she had left it, without luggage, six days before the discovery of her body. A man with whom she had been seen about the same time was interviewed, and said that on the day in question he had driven her to the Biltmore Hotel in Los Angeles, where she claimed that she was going to meet her sister; he had not seen or heard from her afterwards. It was also learnt that she had been seen in the company of another woman two or three days before her death. But what had happened to her after that nobody seemed to know.

No trace of her clothing or any other of her possessions had been found at the vacant lot, and a search of drains and sewers failed to produce a single garment which could be identified as having belonged to her.

The newspaper accounts of the case led to many false confessions — one of them from a woman who stated: 'The Black Dahlia stole my man, so I killed her and cut her up!' But these claims were easily discounted, as details of the mutilations had not been published.

A Los Angeles newspaper received through the post an envelope with a message in pasted-up letters on the outside: 'Here are Dahlia's belongings. Letter will follow.' The envelope contained Elizabeth Short's birth certificate, address book and social security card, and as the address book had one page missing, it was assumed that this had borne the name of the sender — perhaps her murderer. But no further communication was received from this person, and fingerprints found on the envelope did not match any in the FBI files.

Eventually an army corporal who claimed to have known the victim was arrested as a suspect. Bloodstains were found on his clothes and his locker

27

contained newspaper cuttings about the crime. Moreover, he boasted: 'When I get drunk I get rough with women!' On closer examination, however, he was found to be a mentally unbalanced man who had had no connection with the murder.

No further progress was made on the case, and the crime remains unsolved. The motive for the murder has never been discovered.

Murder of Dr. Bernd Servé, 1953

JANUARY
17

On the night of 17 January 1953, Dr Bernd Servé, a lawyer, and a youth of nineteen named Adolf Hüllecremer were sitting in a stationary car in a quiet road leading north out of Düsseldorf when they were attacked by two men wearing masks, one of them armed with a gun. Servé was shot dead, the bullet entering his body below the left jaw and leaving an exit wound in his right temple; Hüllecremer was battered over the head but only lost consciousness momentarily. Both victims were then robbed, and an unsuccessful attempt was made to start the car before the attackers left the scene.

The crime was still unsolved on 28 November 1955, when Friedhelm Behre, a twenty-six-year-old baker, and his girlfriend Thea Kürmann, aged twenty-three, were found dead on the outskirts of Kalkum, a small town near Düsseldorf, four weeks after being reported missing. In this case both victims had been battered with a blunt instrument but died from drowning after their car had been driven into a gravel pit filled with water. Like Servé and Hüllecremer, the couple had been robbed, but it was not at first realized that there was a connection between the two crimes.

Ten weeks later, on 7 February 1956, another couple, Peter Falkenberg, a professional driver aged twenty-six, and Hildegard Wassing, a twenty-year-old typist, were reported missing. Falkenberg's car, with blood inside it, was found abandoned the following day, and on 9 February the couple's charred bodies were discovered in a burnt-out hayrick in the village of Ilverich, just outside Düsseldorf. Both had been battered over the head with a heavy instrument, but Falkenberg had also been shot at close range, the bullet following the same unusual path as in Dr Servé's case. The girl had been raped.

There was almost another of these 'Doubles Murders', as they were called, in a wood at Meerer-busch — also near Düsseldorf — on 4 May the same year, when two men disturbed a courting couple and held them at gunpoint. On this occasion, after the man had been forced to hand over his wallet, the girl suddenly ran off, screaming for help. Although one of the gunmen caught and began to attack her, passers-by arrived on the scene and the two culprits fled.

A few weeks after that, on 10 June, a man was apprehended by an armed forest ranger, who had noticed him behaving suspiciously in the same wood. Werner Boost, a twenty-eight-year-old family man who worked in a factory, admitted owning a loaded gun which had been found at the spot, saying that he used it for hunting animals. But his arrest led to the discovery of various stolen articles, including a tent, a motor-cycle, more guns and some jewellery, in the same area.

A further gun, and parts of yet another, were found in his house in Düsseldorf — together with jars of cyanide, sulphur and saltpetre — and inquiries revealed that he was an expert marksman, able to hit a target without removing the gun from a holster worn at his waist. This was regarded as significant, as Dr Servé and Peter Falkenberg were believed to have been shot in this manner.

Though suspected of having been involved in the murders, Werner was at first charged only with a trespassing offence — for which he was sent to prison for six months — but it was later found that since his arrest his wife had been receiving money from Franz Lorbach, one of his fellow factory-workers. Viewing this with suspicion, police carried out a search of Lorbach's home, and more stolen articles were discovered.

Lorbach, who had served a prison term himself for poaching, told police officers that he had received the articles in question from Boost, but had not realized that they were stolen. He was arrested and eventually, in February 1957, made a statement in which he accused Boost of the murders and admitted to having been his accomplice on the night Dr Servé was killed. Boost, he said, was a maniac who had made him commit crimes by hypnotizing him, and had also given him pep pills and a 'truth serum'. He had lived in fear of him for four years.

It was learnt that Boost, the illegitimate son of a country girl, had settled in Düsseldorf in 1950 — having previously lived in East Germany, where he had made his living by illegally escorting parties of refugees to the West. He was suspected of having committed a number of murders in the border zone at this time, but no charges were brought against him in connection with them.

Besides being able to use a gun with deadly accuracy, Boost was an expert in unarmed combat, and knew how to mix and prepare poisons. According to Lorbach, he had been experimenting with drugs and chemicals in the hope of finding new ways of killing people, and was also responsible for crimes against other courting couples, in which the men had been robbed and the women raped. On such occasions, having raped the woman himself, he would try to persuade his companion to do the same.

Brought to trial in 1959, Boost was sentenced to life imprisonment for the murders of Dr Servé and the two courting couples, and Lorbach, who had given evidence against him, was given a six-year sentence for his own part in the first of these crimes. Having served his sentence, however, Lorbach found himself a job and managed to put the past behind him. In 1965, he visited the police officer responsible for his arrest, to express his gratitude for the help which that officer had given him.

Murder of Shari Hull 1981

JANUARY
18

In a suburb of Salem, Oregon, on the evening of 18 January 1981, Shari Hull and Lisa Garcia, both aged twenty, were about to leave an office building which they had just been cleaning when a man appeared there, taking them by surprise. He forced them, at gunpoint, to undress and take part in a number of sexual acts, then made them lie face down on the floor while he shot them in the head — Shari three times and Lisa twice. Finally, he left the building, no doubt under the impression that they were dead.

Both girls were, in fact, still alive, and Lisa Garcia was conscious. Having outwitted her attacker by breathing as shallowly as possible, she dragged herself to the office telephone and called the police. Though

Shari died shortly afterwards, Lisa survived and was later to see the man responsible brought to trial. In the meantime, however, she was found to have contracted herpes from him.

The suburb in which the crimes had been committed was close to the I-5 freeway, and Lisa's description of the killer was similar to those given of a man wanted in connection with a number of robberies and sex crimes which had taken place along that freeway during the previous few weeks. Having already feared that this man would sooner or later resort to murder, police were now in no doubt that he had done so. But there were to be further murders, as well as many other attacks, along the I-5 before he was captured.

On 3 February a fireman's home near Redding, California, was broken into and his wife and stepdaughter murdered, the stepdaughter having first been raped. Then, on 15 February, a teenage girl was shot dead in Beaverton, a suburb of Portland — about forty miles from Salem — apparently after admitting the killer to her home.

It was an investigation among all the known acquaintances of this last victim which brought Randall Brent Woodfield, a thirty-year-old bartender in the same suburb, to the attention of the police. Randy Woodfield, who had only known the victim slightly, was found to have a record of minor sex offences and to have served part of a ten-year sentence for robbery before being released on parole in July 1979. A search of his home and car led to the discovery of evidence connecting him, not with the latest murder, but with the crimes against Shari Hull and Lisa Garcia. He was accordingly arrested and charged with murder and attempted murder.

At the time of his trial, in June 1981, the murder weapon had not been discovered. But there was a great deal of evidence against him, including the testimony of Lisa Garcia, who identified him with certainty as her attacker. Woodfield remained detached and unemotional throughout; he denied the offences, claiming to have been in a bar on the evening in question, but could produce nobody to corroborate this. He admitted to having purchased a gun the previous autumn but said he had got rid of it because he was afraid his parole officer would have him sent back to jail. He was nonetheless convicted and sentenced to life imprisonment.

Two months afterwards a number of charges were brought against Woodfield in connection with the murders of the fireman's wife and stepdaughter. About the same time it was announced that the gun which had been used in the Beaverton murder case had been found in a river a few miles from the place where he had lived before his arrest.

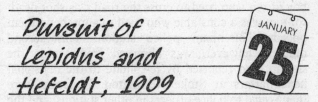

Pursuit of Lepidus and Hefeldt, 1909

JANUARY
25

On the afternoon of 25 January 1909, two young Russians, Jacob Lepidus and Paul Hefeldt, stood outside a rubber factory in Tottenham, north-east London. They had revolvers in their pockets and were awaiting the arrival of a youth carrying the firm's wages. At the same time Mr Schnurmann, the head of the firm, was standing at the factory door, also waiting for the wages to arrive — as he did every Saturday. The street was crowded, and it is unlikely that anyone took any notice of the Russians or they of Mr Schnurmann.

Suddenly a car drew up outside the factory, and the youth got out, carrying the money — about £80 — in a bag. He made his way towards the entrance, while the driver remained in the car and kept the engine running, but the Russians made a quick move, wrenched the bag from his hand, and ran off with it. Mr Schnurmann, who had witnessed the crime, tried to stop them, but was unable to catch either. He immediately got into the car, shouting, 'Stop thief!'

A police constable who had just appeared on the scene got in with him, and in a moment they were speeding along the road after the robbers, the driver keeping his fingers on the horn. The Russians started shooting at them, one bullet shattering the windscreen while another wounded the driver and put the engine out of action. When the policeman got out and went after them on foot, he was shot in the leg and seriously wounded. At this, Mr Schnurmann gave up the chase.

Lepidus and Hefeldt ran on, becoming desperate. A boy of ten who tried to cross the road was shot dead; so, too, was a constable who tried to apprehend them outside Tottenham police station. This second murder, however, was observed from inside the station, and reported by telephone to the divisional headquarters at Stoke Newington. Firearms were then issued to police officers in other stations, and the district was cordoned off. Those in Tottenham were ordered to pursue the murderers and drive them into an ambush.

The Russians ran on blindly and, turning a corner, saw a tramcar ahead of them. They raced towards it and jumped aboard with their guns still in their hands. The driver stopped the vehicle, ran up the stairs unnoticed, and hid on the upper deck, which was otherwise empty. The conductor was therefore forced to drive the tram at gunpoint.

The only other people on board were an elderly

man and a woman clutching her child.

Civilians armed with shotguns had joined in the pursuit, and they began firing at the tram as it gathered speed. Lepidus stood on the rear platform, shooting back at them, while Hefeldt kept his gun pointed at the conductor. When the elderly man tried to remonstrate with them, he was shot in the neck. The woman cried hysterically; the driver continued to crouch on the upper deck. Finally, the conductor tricked the gunmen into thinking that they were approaching another police station, and they jumped off the tram and ran along a side turning. The conductor drove on to the depot, to get help for the wounded man.

In the side turning the desperadoes stole a milk-cart after shooting the driver, but overturned it at the next corner. They then stole another cart and drove towards Chingford. The police behind them commandeered private cars in order to continue the pursuit. But, finding themselves in open country, the fugitives stopped the cart and made off across the fields. In doing so, they avoided a police ambush.

As the chase continued on foot, Lepidus and Hefeldt suddenly found a high fence in front of them. Lepidus, the taller man, climbed over it, but Hefeldt could not. He stood facing his pursuers for a moment, then called out to Lepidus that he was running out of ammunition. Suddenly he turned the gun on himself and fired.

Lepidus ran on alone, managing to stay ahead of the police for a little longer. But he, too, was running short of ammunition and, trying to hide in a nearby farm labourer's cottage, found himself trapped. He watched helplessly from a bedrooom window as the place was surrounded.

Two armed police officers entered the cottage and called on him to surrender. When he failed to do so shots were fired through the bedroom door, one of them hitting him above the left eye. With blood pouring down his face, he opened the door, then shot himself in the head as one of the police officers fired again. He died instantly.

Paul Hefeldt, in the meantime, had been taken off to hospital, where he remained until his own death almost three weeks later.

Execution of Harry Dobkin, 1943

On 27 January 1943, Harry Dobkin, aged forty-nine, was hanged at Wandsworth Prison for the murder of his wife Rachel. The couple had been separated for some years and Dobkin had been in trouble for failing to comply with a maintenance order which had been made against him. It seems that the murder was an act of desperation rather than callousness.

As far as the police were concerned, the case began in July 1942, when workmen clearing a bombed chapel in Lambeth, south London, discovered a skull and a number of bones. When these were examined by Dr Keith Simpson in his laboratory at Guy's Hospital they were found to be the remains of a woman who had died between twelve and eighteen months previously. The head and limbs had been severed from the rest of the body, and there were signs of strangulation.

The police searched lists of missing persons and discovered that Rachel Dobkin, whose husband had been a fire-watcher at the chapel, had been reported missing fifteen months earlier. By checking the teeth of the skull against her dental records, Dr Simpson was able to identify the remains with certainty. He then provided additional proof of identity by superimposing a photograph of the skull on a snapshot of the missing woman, showing that it matched her features exactly.

Dobkin was found to be living a few miles from Lambeth. He was a strong, heavily-built man, who made his living working in the building trade. It was discovered that the differences between his wife and himself over the payment of maintenance had continued after his release from prison, and that on one occasion he had failed to report a fire at the chapel where the remains had been buried.

On being brought to trial at the Old Bailey, Dobkin denied the offence. He gripped the spikes round the dock, sweating profusely as he heard the evidence being given against him, and collapsed when the verdict was delivered. After he had been hanged Dr Simpson carried out the routine autopsy on his body.

Death of Juliette Deitsh, 1889

On 30 January 1889, Juliette Deitsh, a girl of twelve, died from an overdose of chloroform at the home of Dr Etienne Deschamps in St Peter Street, New Orleans. She had gone there to take part in what Deschamps, aged fifty-eight, called 'an experiment', the chloroform being given to her on a handkerchief while she and the doctor were lying on a bed together, both of them naked. Her death was followed by an

apparent suicide attempt by the doctor.

Deschamps, who had been born in Rennes, was actually a skilled dentist. Since his arrival in New Orleans in 1884 he had set himself up as a doctor, giving 'magnetizing' treatment. He also claimed to have occult powers, and was not above trickery.

In 1888 he became friendly with Juliette's father, a gullible widower living with his two daughters in the Rue Chartres, and informed him that he needed a young virgin as a medium, to help him to find buried treasure in the swamps of Barataria by psychic means. Deitsh, a carpenter, was sufficiently impressed by this idea to allow Juliette to be used for the purpose, and for the next six months she made regular trips to the doctor's home, accompanied by her sister Laurence, who was three years younger than herself. It was Laurence who, on the day of the tragedy, ran to tell her father what had happened.

Jules Deitsh, on arrival at the house, found Deschamps lying on the bed, covered in blood, beside Juliette's body; he had stabbed himself in the chest several times with a dental instrument.

The doctor's wounds proved to be superficial, and after being questioned by the police he was held in custody. He apparently made a second suicide attempt in his cell a few days later, but, if so, it was also unsuccessful, and he was brought to trial for murder on 29 April.

The police investigation had revealed that Juliette had been the doctor's mistress, and that he had generally, if not invariably, given her chloroform before making love to her. He would make Juliette and her sister both promise to tell nobody what had occurred, saying that he had cast a spell which would not work if anyone else knew about it.

Though Deschamps claimed that the girl had given her consent to what had taken place between them, and that the chloroform had been used for her comfort, it was only to be expected that such an affair, if it became known, would cause a scandal.

There were also a number of other things which were hardly in the doctor's favour. Deschamps claimed falsely that Juliette had been seduced by a local jeweller, and letters found in his possession, ostensibly from the dead girl to himself, were shown to be forgeries. It was known, too, that after stabbing himself, Deschamps had sent Laurence to tell her father, not that Juliette was dead, but that he (the doctor) was dying.

The prosecution contended that Deschamps had killed the girl on purpose because he was afraid that she would reveal their affair to others, and after a short trial he was convicted and sentenced to death. While in jail, awaiting the outcome of an appeal, he became disorderly and violent; he tried repeatedly to escape by making a run for it when his cell door was opened, and threatened to cause a war between France and the United States.

His appeal was unsuccessful and, in spite of being declared insane by a self-appointed commission of doctors, he was hanged on 12 May 1892.

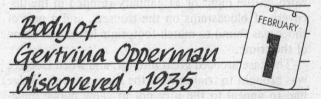

Body of Gertrina Opperman discovered, 1935

FEBRUARY 1

On 1 February 1935, the body of Gertrina Petrusina Opperman, an unmarried South African girl, was found near a railway line nineteen miles outside Pretoria. She had been savagely battered and shot through the head, but had given birth to a child shortly before her death. The child, though born alive, had died soon afterwards.

The girl was identified by M.J. Van der Bergh, a farmer of Northam, for whom she had worked as a nurse and general help. Mr Van der Bergh told a police officer that Miss Opperman had left Northam for Pretoria, 126 miles away, by train on the evening of 30 January, and produced a letter which had arrived for her from Pretoria, dated 29 January. The letter, which was signed 'J.H. Coetzee', read:

'I have just received your two letters. I was away from the second until yesterday. I will meet you on Thursday morning at about nine o'clock at the Pretoria Railway Station. Everything is still arranged. We will then talk.'

The letter had, in fact, been written by a young detective sergeant attached to the Railway Police — one of the first police officers to arrive at the scene of the crime.

Jacobus Hendrik Coetzee, who was engaged to the daughter of his chief officer, was found to have been on intimate terms with the dead girl, though he had at first pretended that he did not know her. He was arrested on the morning of 3 February, and bullets of the type recovered from the girl's body were found in his possession. An examination of the clothes he had worn on the night of 31 January resulted in the discovery of bloodstains on the trousers, and a pair of shoes was found to match footprints left at the scene of the crime.

The case aroused great interest, and when Coetzee was brought to trial in May the same year, the judge had to appeal to the jury not to allow public indignation to influence them in their consideration of the evidence.

It was contended by the prosecution that Coetzee had murdered Miss Opperman because he was afraid that she would ruin his career and marriage prospects. He had tried at first to kill her with his hands, and had left her for dead on the railway line, so that her body would be mutilated by the first train that came along. But later, on returning to the scene, he found that she was still alive, having managed to drag herself away from the line. He therefore shot her.

Coetzee denied having killed Gertrina Opperman. He admitted that he had been intimate with her and that he had offered to help her financially, but claimed that he was not the father of her child. He said that on the night in question he had gone to meet her at the railway station in Pretoria, but was unable to find her there.

The jury found the prisoner guilty, but added a recommendation of mercy because he had been 'wrongly saddled with the paternity of the unborn child of the deceased'. Coetzee was accordingly sentenced to life imprisonment with hard labour.

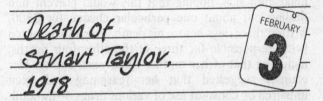

Death of Stuart Taylor, 1978

FEBRUARY 3

On 3 February 1978, Stuart Taylor, a fifty-three-year-old tobacco farmer of St Pauls, North Carolina, died in hospital in the nearby town of Lumberton. He had been admitted twice in two days, each time suffering from severe stomach pains, vomiting and diarrhoea, but on the first occasion had seemed well enough to go home after just a few hours. By the time he was re-admitted, however, his symptoms were so bad that he died while doctors were attending him. A

41

post-mortem examination then revealed that his death had been caused by arsenic poisoning.

The police investigation which followed led to the arrest of Taylor's fiancée, a twice-widowed woman of forty-five named Margie Velma Barfield, with whom he had been living at the time of his death. It also led to the discovery of lethal amounts of arsenic in the exhumed bodies of four other people who had been closely associated with the same woman — her second husband, Jennings L. Barfield, her mother, Lillie McMillan Bullard, and two people she had known as a result of working in a Lumberton nursing home or serving as a part-time home help for the elderly.

Velma Barfield was brought to trial in Elizabethtown, in the same state, towards the end of November 1978. The prosecution produced evidence of several cheques forged on Stuart Taylor's account, and also of the deaths of the other four people with whom the prisoner had been associated, though no charges had been brought against her in connection with these.

Mrs Barfield admitted forging cheques on Taylor's account and said that she had given him poison to make him sick, hoping that this would prevent him finding out about one particular cheque for $300, written three days before his death. She also admitted being responsible for three of the other four deaths, including that of her mother three years earlier. Her counsel suggested that her reasoning had been impaired by constant use of various drugs — tranquillisers, anti-depressants and sedatives — over a long period, but she was found guilty of first-degree murder and sentenced to death.

She remained on Death Row for the next six years, while one attempt after another was made to save her life. Towards the end of that time she was frequently in the news, and television viewers watched the 'killer grandmother' giving interviews, walking along prison corridors, knitting, and so on. During the last days of her life, she chose her coffin and funeral clothes and agreed to donate her organs for transplant operations. She was finally executed by lethal injection in the early hours of 2 November 1984, at the Central Prison in Raleigh, North Carolina.

Velma Barfield, then aged fifty-two, was the first woman to be executed in the United Stated for twenty-two years. She had chosen to die by lethal injection rather than in the gas chamber because she did not want to sit upright, facing a crowd of spectators, at the end. She nonetheless wore pink pyjamas for the occasion.

A prison official said afterwards that the execution had been carried out smoothly and painlessly.

Disappearance of Miss Chubb, 1958

FEBRUARY
6

On the evening of 6 February 1958, Miss Lilian Chubb, a middle-aged department-store employee, failed to arrive back at the home she shared with her brother, sister-in-law and mother-in-law in Broadstairs, Kent. This was unusual for her, for she was a creature of habit, but nothing was done about it until the following day, when she had still not returned. Her sister-in-law, Mrs Edith Daisy Chubb, then telephoned the store — which was some miles away, on the outskirts of Margate — and, on being told that Lily had not been to work for two days, reported her sister-in-law's disappearance to the police.

Shortly afterwards Lily was found dead in a hedge not far from the house. She had been strangled with a scarf about twenty-four hours previously, and her handbag was missing.

During a post-mortem carried out by Professor Francis Camps, marks were found indicating that she had been placed in a chair for some time after death. In view of this, the discovery of an invalid chair in the Chubbs' garden shed was regarded as significant. So, too, was the fact that nobody could remember seeing Lily go off to work on the morning of her death, for she was normally seen by several people at this time of the day.

Edith Chubb, aged forty-six, was a hard-working woman with five children to look after in addition to keeping house for the other members of her family. Being poor, she also worked three twelve-hour nights every week as a hospital cleaner — though she was actually a trained nurse — in the hope of making ends meet. Even then she had been unable to pay her rent prior to her sister-in-law's death, though she had afterwards had more money then usual, and had been able to pay outstanding bills.

When this was discovered by the police it was not long before she made a confession. 'You are quite right, I killed her,' she said to Chief Inspector Everitt. 'I cannot bear to think about it, but I shall feel better if I tell you.'

She then told him that on the morning of 6 February she had pulled Lily's scarf tightly round her neck and unintentionally killed her as she was going out through the front door. Then, when she realized what she had done, she brought the invalid chair from the shed, lifted the body into it, then pushed it back to the shed and left it there until she could move it from the house unobserved. It remained there until early the following morning, when, having seen her husband off to work, she covered it with a rug and pushed it to the place where it was found.

Mrs Chubb gave Everitt no real clue to her motive

44

for this crime, claiming that she and her sister-in-law had got on well together; she merely said that she had taken £12 from Lily's handbag before destroying it. But later, after she had been arrested, she told a woman police officer that her sister-in-law had been smug and self-centred, and that she (Mrs Chubb) had been the subject of rude letters which Lily had written to her sister in Canada. Other remarks suggested that her resentment of her sister-in-law's attitude had been partly due to her poverty and exhaustion.

Mrs Chubb was brought to trial at the Old Bailey on 30 April. She told the court that she had reached a stage at which the slightest thing her sister-in-law did upset her, and that that was why the crime had taken place. 'I felt irritated at the way she put her cup down,' said Mrs Chubb. 'I followed her downstairs and pulled her scarf. I didn't intend to hurt her, I intended to give her a shake-up. She fell backwards onto the floor and struck her head on the post of the stairs.'

The prisoner had many friends from her nursing days, and some of them appeared to give evidence on her behalf. The matron of Haine Hospital, near Broadstairs, said that Mrs Chubb, whom she had known since 1936, was a sick woman, in need of a holiday; and the family doctor said that the previous year she had been on the verge of a nervous breakdown. The jury was sympathetic towards her, and although the judge's summing-up was not in her favour, she was found guilty only of manslaughter.

She was sent to prison for four years.

Attempted execution of Will Purvis 1894

On 7 February 1894, Will Purvis, the twenty-one-year-old son of a Mississippi farmer, was due to be hanged in Columbia, Marion County, following his conviction for the murder of Will Buckley, one of his neighbours at nearby Devils Bend. The crime had been committed on 22 June the previous year, after Buckley, his brother Jim and a black farmhand named Sam Waller had made disclosures about the activities of the White Caps, a secret organization similar to the original Ku Klux Klan, which had been disbanded some years earlier. Purvis had admitted being a former member of the White Caps, but denied taking part in Buckley's murder. He claimed to have objected to the crime and left the organization because of it.

The imminence of his execution nonetheless caused much excitement. It was to be carried out in public, as was usual at this time, and crowds began to gather at the scaffold several hours beforehand. When Purvis ascended it towards noon they fell silent, waiting for him to speak, but instead of making the confession which everyone expected, he once again claimed that he was innocent, and went on to say that there were people present who could save him if they wished to. The sheriff and his three deputies then went to work, adjusting the noose round the prisoner's neck, pinioning his arms and legs and pulling a black cap down over his face. A local pastor prayed loudly.

When all was ready the sheriff took up a hatchet and severed a stay rope holding the trap in place;

the trap then opened and the condemned man fell through. But to the horror of all concerned, the knot of the halter came undone and Purvis dropped to the ground, temporarily insensible but not seriously hurt.

A second attempt to hang him was prevented by the pastor and other influential citizens, who felt that what had happened was an act of God and a sign that Purvis had been wrongly convicted. The prisoner was therefore taken back to jail, and the sheriff reported what had happened to the state governor, saying that he, too, now had serious doubts about Purvis's guilt.

Governor John M. Stone had no such doubts and refused to commute the sentence. But a fresh attempt to carry it out was delayed by three unsuccessful appeals to the State Supreme Court, the prisoner being transferred to the town of Purvis, in Lamar County, in the meantime. When the execution date was finally fixed for 12 December 1895, a party of friends broke into the jail and set him free.

Will Purvis remained at large for over a year, but gave himself up in February 1897, after a new state governor had offered to show leniency towards him. His sentence was accordingly commuted, and later, in December 1898, he was pardoned in response to public pressure.

On being released, he went back to working for his father, who now had a farm in Purvis. He later acquired a farm of his own and married the daughter of a Baptist minister. They had eleven children.

His case was resurrected in 1917, when a sixty-year-old man named Joe Beard made a death-bed confession which cleared Purvis of Buckley's murder, and on 15 March 1920, Purvis was voted $5000 compensation by the state legislature.

He later gave public lectures and radio talks, and in 1935 published his *True Life Story*. His death took place on 13 October 1938, when he was sixty-six years old.

FEBRUARY

8

Human remains found in manhole, 1983

On 8 February 1983, a drains maintenance engineer found decomposed human flesh in a manhole outside a house in north London. The discovery was reported to the police and led to the questioning of Dennis Nilsen, a thirty-seven-year-old civil servant working for the Manpower Services Commission. Nilsen confessed that he was the person responsible, and revealed the whereabouts of further remains. He said that he had killed sixteen people.

Nilsen, a tall, bespectacled Scotsman, was a bachelor and a homosexual. In his top-floor flat in Cranley Gardens, Muswell Hill, police found three human heads, each of which had been boiled, and the lower part of a body. At another house, in Melrose Avenue, Cricklewood — where he had lived previously — they discovered an assortment of human bones, weighing twenty-eight pounds.

There had, in fact, been fifteen murders — one fewer than Nilsen had originally claimed. The victims were all men — mainly homosexuals and drifters whom he had met while he was out drinking, and later strangled with ties while they were asleep or drunk. Those who had not died from strangulation had been drowned in his bath.

Nilsen was unperturbed by questions about his crimes, which had clearly given him pleasure. 'What I did seemed right at the time,' he told police officers. 'I felt that my sole reason for existence was to kill.'

The first of these murders took place on 30 December 1978, the victim being an unknown Irish youth of seventeen or eighteen. Nilsen explained that he had been lonely and miserable over Christmas and wanted company for the New Year, 'even if it was only a body'. He kept the corpse in plastic bags under the floorboards for months before finally disposing of it on a bonfire in the garden. A later victim provided him with a set of steel knives, which he used to dismember subsequent ones.

Each of the first twelve murders took place while Nilsen was living in Melrose Avenue, the bodies all being hidden under the floorboards until he was ready to dissect them, and disinfectant used to mask the smell. Having dissected them, he threw some parts over the back fence, to be eaten by prowling animals, and burnt others on large bonfires, on which car tyres were also burnt to prevent the smell arousing suspicion. The bones were buried in the garden, the skulls having first been crushed with a garden-roller.

The other three murders took place at the flat in Cranley Gardens, to which Nilsen had moved in 1981. Having no access to the garden at this address, he resorted to flushing some parts down the lavatory and boiling others. The large bones were put out for the dustmen to take away.

During the course of the investigation it became clear that Nilsen had been very lucky on a number of occasions, sometimes as a result of negligence on the part of the police.

On 31 October 1979, a Chinese cook reported that Nilsen had tried to kill him, and that he had escaped only by throwing a brass candlestick at his assailant, who was thus knocked unconscious. When the police went to see Nilsen about the incident he denied all knowledge of it, and the cook was unwilling to pursue it further.

In November 1980 a Scotsman aged twenty-nine reported a similar attack, but Nilsen convinced the police that it was the result of a quarrel between two homosexual lovers, and no further action was taken at the time.

Another case of attempted murder took place in November 1981, but this was not reported until later.

On yet another occasion a microbiologist named Robert Wilson reported that he had found three carrier-bags full of human flesh in the street near Melrose Avenue. The following day he checked with police to find out what had happened, and was told that no written report had been made about the discovery.

In October 1983 Nilsen appeared at the Old Bailey on six charges of murder and two of attempted murder. He pleaded not guilty by reason of diminished responsibility, but after a trial lasting nine days he was convicted on all charges. The judge sentenced him to six terms of life imprisonment, recommending that he should serve at least twenty-five years.

The following year, in Wormwood Scrubs Prison, Nilsen's face was slashed with a razor by another prisoner. The resulting wound needed eighty-nine stitches.

Discovery of Evelyn Hamilton's body, 1942

FEBRUARY 9

On the morning of 9 February 1942, an electrician found a woman's body in an air-raid shelter in Montagu Place, west London. Evelyn Hamilton, a forty-year-old chemist's assistant, had been in London on her way from Hornchurch, Essex, where she worked, to her home in Newcastle-upon-Tyne. She had been strangled and her clothes were disarranged, though she appeared not to have been sexually assaulted. Her handbag, containing £80, had been stolen.

The following day another body was found, this time in a flat in nearby Wardour Street. Evelyn Oatley, aged thirty-five, a prostitute and former show-girl, had also been strangled, but afterwards her throat had been cut and the lower part of her body mutilated with a tin-opener. The body was found on her bed, almost naked.

Three days after that two more murders were reported. Margaret Lowe, a prostitute aged forty-three, had been strangled with a silk stocking, then mutilated with a razor in her flat in Gosfield Street, London, W1. She had been living alone and the crime was discovered when her fourteen-year-old daughter, an evacuee, went to visit her. A half-empty bottle of stout was found in the kitchen.

Shortly after this discovery, news of the fourth murder was received, the body of Doris Jouannet, the thirty-two-year-old wife of a hotel manager, having been found in the couple's flat in Sussex Gardens, near Marble Arch. She, too, had been strangled and mutilated.

These crimes, committed during the blackout, terrified the inhabitants of London, and all of Scotland Yard's resources were mobilized in an attempt to find the person responsible. But the culprit was soon to fall into the hands of the police as a result of his own carelessness.

On the evening of 12 February, the day before these two latest crimes were discovered, a Mrs Greta Heywood had met a young airman in Piccadilly. They went for a drink together, then walked down the Haymarket, where he tried to kiss her. Although she got away from him and ran off, he caught up with and attempted to strangle her in a doorway in St Alban's Street. But, luckily for her, a delivery-boy heard the scuffle, and when he went to investigate the attacker took to his heels. He left behind an RAF gas-mask, which he had placed on the ground.

Later the same night Mrs Mulcahy, a prostitute, was attacked by the same man in her flat in Paddington, near the home of Mrs Jouannet. She fought back violently and screamed, and the man then gave her money and left the flat. This time he left his belt behind.

From his gas-mask and belt the airman was identified as Gordon Frederick Cummins, a twenty-eight-year-old cadet billeted in St John's Wood. A number of items stolen from the murdered women were found in his possession, and his fingerprints matched others found in the homes of Mrs Oatley and Mrs Lowe.

Cummins was a married man. He was well-educated but unreliable, and had lost a number of jobs through dishonesty. His air force colleagues found him pretentious.

Charged with all four of the murders, he was tried only for that of Evelyn Oatley, for which he was sentenced to death. He was hanged at Wandsworth Prison on 25 June 1942, an air-raid taking place as the execution was carried out. Two other murders have since been attributed to him.

Body of Georgina Hoffman discovered, 1939

FEBRUARY
12

On the night of 12 February 1939, a man walked into Vine Street police station in London's West End and reported the discovery of a woman's body in a top-floor flat in Dover Street, Piccadilly. Police officers went to the scene at once and found the dead woman lying on the floor near the door. She was naked except for an underskirt round her neck and had two stab wounds — one in her chest near the left breast and the other in her back near the top of the left shoulder. There were signs of a struggle having taken place.

The woman was Georgina Hoffman, an attractive twenty-six-year-old prostitute also known as Iris Heath; she was a married woman, separated from her husband, and had been renting the Dover Street flat for £6 a week. As she had taken off some of her clothes herself, while others had been torn from her body after being cut with a knife, it appeared that she had been murdered by one of her clients. The murder weapon had not been left at the scene.

John Roman, the man who reported the crime, had gone to the flat at the request of one of the victim's friends — another prostitute who worked in the same area. When this woman was seen by police, she informed them that she had called on Mrs Hoffman in the early hours of 10 February and found her in the company of a young man with a speech impediment, whom she then tricked into staying there on his own — after he had given her money — while she left and spent the night with the witness.

The woman went on to say that she had seen Mrs Hoffman entering the flat with the same man on the evening of 10 February, and that later — about midnight — her friend had shown her a watch that he had given her, saying that he had no money with him then but would return with some the following day and buy it back. Once again, the victim had left and spent the night with the witness.

On the 12th the witness had seen the man again — this time standing in Berkeley Street. She asked him where Mrs Hoffman was, but he replied that he had not seen her. At that moment, however, John Roman appeared, having discovered the body. The witness therefore insisted that the stranger should not be allowed to go until he'd given his name and address.

The police naturally regarded this man as the most obvious suspect and, although the name and address he had given soon proved to be false, he was identified from photographs in the Criminal Record Office as Arthur James Mahoney, a twenty-three-year-old ship's steward with a criminal record. On the morning of 13 February, he was seen by police officers at his mother's home in Brixton, and following the discovery of a bloodstained shirt in a kitchen cupboard and a bloodstained handkerchief in one of his trouser pockets, he admitted the crime and produced a sheath-knife which he said was the murder weapon. He was then taken into custody and made a full confession.

On the night of 9 February he had met the victim in the street and gone to the flat with her, he said. While they were there, she asked if he would like to stay the night with her and induced him to part with £5, saying that she needed the money badly. He afterwards gave her another £1 — almost all the money he had left — to go out and buy some cigarettes.

When she returned, another woman arrived at the flat and Mrs Hoffman went off with her, saying that she would be back in twenty minutes. But she then stayed out for the rest of the night, and by the time he left the following morning, Mahoney realized that he had been tricked.

He acquired the knife with the idea of frightening her, partly because he wanted his money back but also because he wanted to reform her, he said. But when he saw her again, he told her that he was in love with her, and gave her his wrist-watch as he had no money at the time.

Mrs Hoffman told him on this occasion that she

loved him, too, but could not give up being a prostitute.

But on the third night when he again turned up without any money, she flew into a rage and began abusing and attacking him. At this, he said, he was so incensed that he pulled out the knife and struck her with it. 'I lost my head,' he continued. 'I pushed her on the bed and we were still fighting. The bed was fully made, with the eiderdown on top. I then noticed blood coming from underneath her armpit. She was still fighting with me and screaming. I got alarmed and tried to quieten her with pillows over her face. Eventually we rolled off the bed and, as we did so, the knife fell on the floor. So I picked it up and struck her again.'

Afterwards, while she was still moaning, he tore off her clothes, wiped the knife on one of her undergarments, and took his wrist-watch from her dressing-table. Having no money, he had to walk back to Brixton.

Charged with Mrs Hoffman's murder, Arthur James Mahoney was sent for trial at the Old Bailey; he pleaded insanity but was convicted and sentenced to death, the jury, on 6 March 1939, having taken only twelve minutes to reach its verdict. He was later certified insane and committed to Broadmoor, where he died in July the following year.

Murder of P.C. Edgar, 1948

On the morning of 13 February 1948, PC Nathaniel Edgar, aged thirty-three, was found fatally wounded in the drive of a house in Southgate, north London; he had been shot three times. There had been a recent increase in the number of burglaries in the area, and Edgar, who was patrolling in plain clothes, had been questioning a suspect when the shooting took place. Before dying in hospital, he was able to tell colleagues that the man's name and address were in his notebook, in his inside pocket.

The suspect was found to be Donald George Thomas, a twenty-three-year-old man with a criminal record, who was wanted by the military police for desertion. His address was in Cambridge Road, Enfield, but police did not find him there and appealed for information, saying that Thomas might be able to help them in their enquiries. They then learnt that a Mrs Winkless, a mother of three children, had left her home in Camberwell, south London, after falling in love with him.

A photograph of Mrs Winkless, provided by her husband, was published in the newspapers on 17 February, and seen by a Mrs Smeed, whose house in Clapham had been converted into bedsitters. Mrs Smeed told the police that she thought she recognized Mrs Winkless as one of her lodgers, and that she was occupying a room on the top floor in the company of a young man. She agreed to help police by taking up the couple's breakfast and leaving it outside their door, as usual.

When Thomas, wearing just his underpants, unlocked the door, police officers rushed into the room. During the struggle which ensued, the wanted man tried to use a Luger pistol, which he had hidden under his pillow, but was quickly overpowered. Mrs Winkless was in bed when the arrest took place.

'You were lucky,' Thomas told the police officers. 'I might just as well be hanged for a sheep as a lamb.'

Seventeen rounds of ammunition, a jemmy and a rubber cosh were found in the bedroom, and bullets from the pistol matched those taken from PC Edgar's body. Mrs Winkless made a statement, saying that Thomas had admitted the murder to her.

Donald Thomas had come from a middle-class family in Edmonton and had been well educated. At sixteen he had been sent to an approved school, having previously been on probation. He had been called up for military service in January 1945, but deserted and spent the next two years on the run. Giving himself up, he had then been sentenced to 160 days' detention — only to desert again at the end of this term.

Brought to trial at the Old Bailey in April 1948, he was found guilty of PC Edgar's murder and sentenced to death. This sentence was commuted to life imprisonment, as the death penalty in Britain had been temporarily suspended. He remained in jail until April 1962, when he was released on licence.

Charles Walton found murdered, 1945

FEBRUARY
14

On 14 February 1945, Charles Walton, a seventy-four-year-old hedger, was found hideously murdered in a field at the foot of Meon Hill, near the Tudor village of Lower Quinton, in Warwickshire. His throat had been slashed with a trouncing hook, which had been left in one of the wounds, and a hay-fork had been driven through his body, pinning him to the ground. It was also observed that his face was contorted with fear and that his arms were cut where he had tried to defend himself.

Walton, whose cottage was just a couple of fields away, had been a gnarled old man, suffering from rheumatism. Although his watch was missing, the nature of his injuries suggested that robbery had not been the motive for his murder, and a Warwickshire police officer drew attention to a sentence in a book of local customs and superstitions which read: 'In 1875 ... a young man killed an old woman named Ann Turner with a hay-fork because he believed she had bewitched him.'

To reinforce the idea that superstition had been the cause of the crime, Superintendent Alec Spooner then produced another book, *Warwickshire*, by Clive Holland, which states that stabbing to death with a pitchfork 'was evidently a survival of the ancient Anglo-Saxon custom of dealing with witches by means of "stacung", or sticking spikes into them'.

Though reluctant to accept such an explanation for this terrible crime, Chief Inspector Robert Fabian, the Scotland Yard officer heading the investigation, found that belief in witchcraft was very strong indeed among the inhabitants of this part of the country, and he and his assistant, Sergeant Albert Webb, were greatly hindered in their inquiries as a result.

At first they were merely received with lowered eyes and mutterings about bad crops and other misfortunes. But then, after a dog had been run over by a police car and a heifer had died in a ditch, there was more hostility, with many villagers refusing to speak to them at all and shutting doors in their faces. Some people even became ill after Fabian had questioned them.

In spite of all this, 4000 statements were taken; footprints found at the scene of the crime were traced to those who had left them, and twenty-nine samples of hair, clothing, etc., were taken from suspects to be analyzed. But no charges resulted and after a few weeks Fabian admitted defeat and returned to London. He had no idea who had committed the crime, and did not believe that anyone who *did* know would admit it to a stranger.

The murder of Charles Walton was therefore never solved.

Attempted shooting of Franklin D. Roosevelt, 1933

FEBRUARY
15

On the night of 15 February 1933, an unsuccessful attempt was made to shoot Franklin D. Roosevelt, the President-elect of the United States, in the amphitheatre at Bayfront Park, Miami. Roosevelt was sitting in the back of a Buick touring car, after making a short speech to a gathering of over ten thousand people, when five shots were fired in his direction by an unemployed Italian bricklayer named Giuseppe Zangara. Although he was unhurt, five other people were wounded; these included Anton Cermak, the Mayor of Chicago, who was so badly injured that he died nineteen days later.

The culprit, who was thirty-two years old, was only five feet tall and suffered from a chronic stomach-ache. He bore a deep resentment towards capitalist society, seeing his illness as a consequence of having been forced to work as a child in his native land and, as a result, he was in favour of murdering all presidents, kings and prime ministers — the people he saw as protecting capitalists. Even so, he was not a communist or anarchist, for he had no real interest in organized politics at all.

Zangara had lived in America since 1923, mainly in New Jersey. He had worked for most of that time, but hated cold weather, which always seemed to make his stomach-ache worse. With the decline in the construction industry, he began to live off his savings, and spent several months in Miami prior to the shooting. But as his money dwindled, his hatred of capitalists, and his desire to kill a head of state, became more intense. At one point he made up his mind to go to Washington and shoot President Herbert Hoover, whom he blamed for the Depression. But then he heard that Roosevelt was expected in Miami and decided to kill him instead. 'He is elect — that is President,' he explained after his arrest.

On 20 February, Zangara was brought to trial; he pleaded guilty to four counts of assault on others in an attempt to murder the President-elect, and was sentenced to eighty years' imprisonment. Then, on 9 March, he appeared for trial again, this time charged with the murder of Anton Cermak, who had died three days earlier. He pleaded guilty once more, and on this occasion was sentenced to death. He made no appeal, and was electrocuted at the state prison in

Raiford, Florida, on the morning of 20 March 1933 — just thirty-three days after the crime had been committed.

Following his arrest, Zangara had been elated by the publicity which he had received, and had been especially pleased to learn that items concerning him had appeared in the newsreels. Because of all this, he made the mistake of expecting cameramen to be present at his execution, and was angry when he found that there were none. 'Lousy capitalists!' he complained. 'No picture! Capitalists! No one here to take my picture! All capitalists lousy bunch of crooks!'

After the execution had been carried out his body was buried in an unmarked grave in the prison grounds.

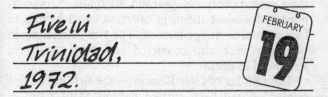

Five in Trinidad, 1972.
FEBRUARY 19

On 19 February 1972, a fire at Arima, about twenty miles from Port of Spain, destroyed the bungalow of Abdul Malik, a thirty-eight-year-old Black Power leader better known as Michael X. A racialist and a criminal with various celebrities among his friends, Malik had returned to his native Trinidad after jumping bail in Britain in 1969. The fire was later found to have been started by one of his associates after Malik had left for Guyana with his wife and four children.

On hearing what had happened, Malik sought an injunction preventing anyone visiting the scene. However, the police were already at work there, and during the next few days the bodies of two murder victims were found buried in his garden. Joseph Skerritt, a well-known local criminal, had been decapitated; Gale Benson, an attractive English girl known to have been living with one of Malik's followers, had been slashed and stabbed, then buried alive.

The dead girl's black American lover, Hakim Jamal, was located in Massachusetts, where he claimed to be looking for Gale, unaware of the fact that she was dead. Malik was later arrested in Guyana, while attempting to escape through the jungle to Brazil. He was returned to Trinidad, where, in August 1972, he was convicted of Skerritt's murder. He was sentenced to death, but not hanged until nearly three years later.

In July 1973 two of his other followers, Edward Chadee, aged twenty, and Stanley Abbott, thirty-four, were tried for the murder of Gale Benson. A third man, twenty-one-year-old Adolphus Parmasser, appeared against them, in order to avoid having to face a murder charge himself. The two defendants in this case were also convicted and they, too, were sentenced to death.

The murder of Gale Benson — the first of the two crimes — had been carried out on Malik's orders because he had begun to resent her presence in the commune in which he and his supporters lived. Joseph Skerritt had been killed because he had refused to take part in another crime — a raid on a country police post.

A fourth man involved in the murder of Gale Benson had disappeared while swimming in a nearby inlet shortly before Malik's departure for Guyana. And Hakim Jamal was murdered by gunmen in Boston in 1973, supposedly on instructions given by Malik from his death cell in Trinidad.

Malik, whose name had originally been Michael de Freitas, was well known in London, where he had spent some years living off prostitutes and harassing tenants of slum properties for the racketeer Peter Rachman before setting up an English Black Power movement. He changed his name to Malik on becoming a Muslim, and later — influenced by Malcolm X, the murdered American Black Power leader — had started calling himself Michael X.

In 1967 he was given a year's imprisonment for urging his supporters to kill any white man seen with a black woman — an offence under the new Race Relations Act — and in 1969 he was charged with robbery and demanding money with menaces. It was at this point that he jumped bail and left the country, to the relief of the British authorities, who made no attempt to get him extradited when they learnt that he was back in Trinidad.

Gale Benson was the daughter of Captain Leonard Plugge, an author, traveller and former MP for Chatham. Though Jamal's mistress, she had been dominated by Malik, who, having once described her as the prettiest woman he had ever seen, had eventually come to regard her as a 'white devil'. It seems that he suspected her of trying to make trouble of some sort between Jamal and himself.

Malik was hanged in Port of Spain on 16 May 1975, after appealing unsuccessfully several times, and Stanley Abbott remained on Death Row until his own execution on 27 April 1979. Edward Chadee's sentence was commuted.

Late at night on 20 February 1949, Marcel Hilaire, a French businessman aged forty-two, returned to his wife and three daughters in Mer, in the Loire Valley, having absconded with his twenty-year-old mistress two months earlier. His arrival prompted much gossip and speculation, for his affair with his former secretary, Christiane Page, was already common knowledge. But to Hilaire this was a matter of little or no importance.

As a rich mill-owner and a partner in a company selling American agricultural machinery, he did not see that he was answerable to anyone for his conduct — not even to Christiane's father, Jacques Page, who was also a partner in the same company — and he made no attempt to explain it. He merely took up his former way of life afresh, as though nothing out of the ordinary had happened.

Christiane Page did not return with him, and her parents and friends received no news from her. Nobody worried about this at first, for she was known to be an independent girl, well able to take care of herself: it was generally assumed that Hilaire, having grown tired of her, had given her money to go abroad. But after several months without hearing from her, Jacques Page finally asked his partner what had happened.

'We had a row over dinner at a little restaurant at Chamarande in February and she refused to get back in the car with me,' replied Hilaire. 'Roger Petit was with me. He can confirm what I'm saying. She was always talking of going to a convent, and that's probably what she did.'

Jacques Page did not doubt that Hilaire was telling him the truth. He had a high regard for his partner and, in any case, knew that Roger Petit, a former gendarme who had managed Hilaire's mill in his absence, was a man with an impeccable reputation. He therefore saw no need to make any further inquiries about his missing daughter. But by this time the matter had come to the attention of somebody else — somebody who was *not* satisfied with Hilaire's explanation.

Prior to returning home, Hilaire had been living with Christiane in a house in Sceaux, between Versailles and Paris; he had bought the house, with a sitting tenant, through an estate agent who was a friend of his. But the tenant, a schoolmaster, had heard many quarrels between them, and was aware that Hilaire had beaten Christiane unmercifully on some occasions. So when they suddenly disappeared he became suspicious and informed the estate agent, a man named Desdouets.

Desdouets, who had been to the house and heard some of the rows himself, wrote to Hilaire at his home in Mer and asked what had become of Christiane. He received no reply. Following a second letter, however, he had a personal visit from Hilaire's brother, who informed him that Christiane had left Hilaire after quarrelling with him in the restaurant in Chamarande. But when Desdouets went to the restaurant in question, he found that the proprietor remembered the couple, and learnt that they had left together in the company of Roger Petit. He informed the police, and an official investigation of the affair began.

Hilaire gave a number of different accounts of Christiane's disappearance, on one occasion claiming that she had been murdered by spies after becoming involved with a foreign secret service. But Roger Petit, on being questioned, told police that Hilaire had killed her. The following day Hilaire admitted that that was true; he had murdered Christiane because she had tried to blackmail him into divorcing his wife, he said. Her body had been dropped into a deep well on a piece of land near his mill, and the well had afterwards been filled with sand.

After their visit to the restaurant in Chamarande, he, Christiane and Roger Petit had gone to see Robert Bouguereau, a friend who owned a garage at Saint-Ay, to the south of Orléans, explained Hilaire. When they left, after drinking a bottle of wine, Bouguereau accompanied them, and they drove along the Route Nationale 20 towards the Messas crossroads. When they were almost there, Hilaire stopped the car, saying that there was something wrong with the wiring, and he and Christiane got out together. He then shot her twice in the back of the head, using Petit's pistol, while Petit and Bouguereau remained in the car. Hilaire's two companions then helped him to put Christiane's body on the back seat, and afterwards to dispose of it.

Hilaire, Petit and Bouguereau were all charged in connection with the crime, but it was not until 9 February 1953 — nearly four years after the murder had been committed — that they were brought to trial. The case was then heard at the Seine Assizes in Paris, and each of the accused admitted his own part in the affair, though with Hilaire's lawyer successfully contesting the charge that the crime had been premeditated.

At the end of the trial Marcel Hilaire was sentenced to hard labour for life, while Petit received two years' imprisonment for complicity in the crime and Bouguereau was given a two-year suspended sentence for receiving and disposing of a body unlawfully. Petit and Bouguereau, who had both spent two years in prison awaiting trial, were then released, while Hilaire was taken back to prison in a police van.

Four and a half years later it was reported that Marcel Hilaire had been made chief accountant of Melun penitentiary.

Bryn Masterman brought to trial, 1987

On 23 February 1987, Bryn Masterman, a forty-seven-year-old prison officer of Gertrude Road, Nottingham, was brought to trial at Nottingham Crown Court, charged with the murder of his first wife, Janet, twenty-two years previously. Janet Masterman, aged twenty-five, had died in May 1965, apparently as a result of falling down the stairs at the couple's home, and an inquest held at that time recorded a verdict of accidental death. Masterman's arrest followed disclosures made by his second wife, Selina, after he left her in May 1986.

Selina Masterman, aged fifty-one, of North Hykeham, near Lincoln, claimed that while she and her husband were still lovers he had told her that he intended to kill Janet, and that he had later admitted having pushed her down the stairs after hitting her with a stool. She kept this secret for twenty-one years, but finally told the police about it because she was bitter at being deserted. She then agreed to draw him into a conversation on the subject, with police officers recording it.

The tape recording was produced as evidence at Masterman's trial, with the judge, jurors, barristers and solicitors being issued with headphones, to enable them to listen to it. A Home Office pathologist,

Professor Stephen Jones, afterwards told the court that Janet Masterman had died from a single blow to the side of the head.

The prisoner denied having murdered her. He said that he and Janet had argued in bed over his infidelity, and that she threatened to leave him, taking their two young sons. At this he hit her on the head with a stool, then — seeking to reason with her — pursued her to the top of the stairs and grabbed her by her nightdress. When she turned and hit him on the nose, he instinctively pushed her — as a result of which she 'flew' down the stairs and cracked her head on the floor. She died without regaining consciousness.

The trial lasted five days, and the jury, after retiring for five and a half hours, found Masterman not guilty of murder but guilty of manslaughter. The judge, Mr Justice Boreham, described this as a 'merciful' verdict.

'I know it happened twenty-two years ago, but there is no doubt in my mind it was to fulfil your own selfish sexual desires, and a young woman died,' he told the prisoner. 'I accept it was not murder — it was manslaughter, but at your own hand.'

Masterman was sent to prison for six years.

Execution of Henri Landru, 1922

Henri Désiré Landru, the French 'Bluebeard' executed on 25 February 1922, was a cunning and heartless criminal who specialized in the seduction and murder of middle-aged widows and spinsters for the sake of their money. A small, bald-headed, bearded man with a wife and four children, he was actually a fugitive during the four-year period in which the murders were committed, having been convicted in his absence of a different type of offence — a business fraud — in July 1914. He made the acquaintance of several of his victims by means of 'lonely hearts' advertisements in Paris newspapers.

Landru had previously committed many frauds and thefts, and had served a number of prison terms since his first conviction in 1900. The sentence which he received in 1914 was one of four years' imprisonment, to be followed by banishment to the penal settlement in New Caledonia as an habitual criminal. It was allegedly to avoid being arrested that he decided to murder his later victims instead of merely defrauding them. None of the bodies of these victims was ever found and the means by which he had killed them was never discovered, either.

The first victims were Mme Jeanne Cuchet, a widow of thirty-nine who worked in a Paris store, and her eighteen-year-old son André. Landru made their acquaintance in February 1914, while he was calling himself M. Diard and claiming to be an engineer; the deception had caused André Cuchet to apply to him for a job, and his mother attended the interview with him. Landru and Mme Cuchet began to have an affair, and on 8 December of that year moved into a villa at Vernouillet, on the outskirts of Paris, together. Mme Cuchet and her son were last seen on 4 January 1915, in the garden of the villa, and nothing more was heard of them until Landru was arrested in April 1919.

Landru, having gained some 15,000 francs in money, jewels, furniture and securities as a result of this association, was soon on the look-out for another victim. In June 1915 he met Mme Thérèse Laborde-Line, aged forty-seven, a native of Buenos Aires and the widow of a hotel-keeper. She had little money, but her furniture and other possessions had some value, and Landru persuaded her to move into the villa with him. She was seen for the last time five days afterwards.

Shortly before meeting Mme Laborde-Line Landru had begun placing the advertisements which drew further women into his clutches. The first appeared in May 1915, stating: 'Widower with two children, aged forty-three, with comfortable income, affectionate, serious, and moving in good society, desires to meet widow with a view to matrimony.' There were to be six more advertisements of this type, and altogether nearly 300 replies were received. These replies were recorded in classified sections in a black loose-leaf notebook, the discovery of which was later to ensure his conviction.

Following the murder of his next victim, Mme Désirée Guillin, a fifty-one-year-old former governess with a legacy of 22,000 francs, Landru moved to the Villa Ermitage, near the village of Gambais. There he became known as M. Fremyet, though he used other names in his dealings with the women he met through his advertisements. Mme Heon, a fifty-five-year-old widow, went to live with 'M. Petit', and was last seen at the Villa Ermitage on 8 December 1915. Mme Anna Collomb, a widow of forty-four, believed Landru to be M. Cuchet until she learnt that he was otherwise called M. Fremyet.

Mme Collomb, arriving at the villa shortly after Mme Heon's disappearance, was last seen towards the end of the same month. Her sister later wrote to both Mme Collomb and 'M. Fremyet', and, receiving no reply from either of them, wrote to ask the local mayor if he knew 'M. Fremyet's' whereabouts. By this time Landru had claimed further victims, and the mayor had already received a similar letter about a 'M. Dupont', with whom a Mme Celestine Buisson, another forty-four-year-old widow, had been staying at the Villa Ermitage. The mayor put the two letter-writers — the second being Mme Buisson's sister — in touch with each other, and after meeting to discuss the disappearances they reported the matter to the police.

Landru was arrested after Mme Buisson's sister had seen him walking with a young woman in the Rue de Rivoli in April 1919. The black notebook was found in his possession, together with various papers and identity cards which had belonged to his victims, and a search of the Villa Ermitage led to the discovery of 295 fragments of bone in the ashes from Landru's stove. In 1921 he was brought to trial for the murder of ten women and one youth — Mme Cuchet's son — and convicted on all charges.

Maintaining a complete silence to the end, the fifty-two-year-old 'Bluebeard' went to the guillotine haughtily, refusing the ministrations of the priest and also declining the usual offer of a glass of rum and a cigarette.

Over forty years later various newspapers reported the discovery of a brief confession, in Landru's handwriting, on the back of a drawing which he had done while under sentence of death. The drawing had been framed and given to one of his lawyers.

Execution of Robert Morton, 1974

On 27 February 1974, Robert Victor Morton, aged twenty-three, was hanged in Pretoria for a horrifying

murder committed in a suburb of Cape Town just over a year earlier. The victim of the crime, fourteen-year-old Sharon Ashford, had been found dead at her home in Kensington Crescent, Oranjezicht, having been stabbed thirty-seven times — and after seeing her body one of the detectives working on the case said that he had never seen anything more gruesome. The motive for the murder was not known, but fingerprints and footprints found at the scene led to Morton's arrest soon afterwards.

Morton lived next door to his victim, at the home of a cardiac specialist who employed him to do general domestic work. He claimed that he had killed Sharon 'for the fun of it', because his whole life was a failure and he 'wanted to do something really big'. But his employer, for whom he had worked since the middle of 1971, said that he had found Morton to be pleasant and easy-going, 'with no wild fluctuations of mood or temper'. He did not seem restless or discontented — in fact, he appeared to be ambitionless. The reason he gave for the crime was therefore not the real one.

It was eventually learnt that on the day of the murder Morton had received a letter from a girl of fifteen with whom he had been in love for the previous two years; this had contained hurtful remarks and informed him that their relationship was at an end. That afternoon, having broken into the Ashfords' house and stolen various articles in the meantime, he telephoned the girl in question, but found her unwilling to speak to him. The murder was committed a short while after that, when Sharon arrived home from school.

Giving evidence at his trial, Morton's girlfriend, whose name was not published, intimated that she had not meant the things she said in her letter: she had seen Morton again the following afternoon and he had written to her from prison. But she was sure that he had believed them at the time and said he had since admitted to her that the letter was the cause of the crime. Even so, the court was convinced that there were no extenuating circumstances in the case, for there was evidence of premeditation but none of remorse.

Morton had given no evidence on his own behalf, and at first seemed indifferent to the prospect of being hanged. But while on Death Row he gradually sank into a state of despondency from which he never emerged.

His mother — from whom he had been parted for most of his childhood — appealed for a commutation of sentence on his behalf, arguing that he must have been insane at the time of the murder, but this was to no avail. Morton afterwards wrote to her, saying that she should not blame either herself or the girl who had pretended to reject him for the crime which he had committed.

Murder of June Cook, 1967

MARCH 2

On the night of 2 March 1967, two men driving along a country lane in Oxfordshire found Mrs June Cook, a forty-one-year-old school-teacher, lying beside a damaged red Mini in a stretch of woodland; she was suffering from serious head injuries which had evidently been sustained when the car hit a tree. Her husband, Raymond Sidney Cook, a draughtsman aged thirty-two, was found inside the car — in the passenger seat — with a small abrasion on his left knee but no other injuries. The two men called an ambulance to the scene, but Mrs Cook died at Battle Hospital, Reading, shortly afterwards.

Raymond Cook said that he and his wife had dined together at a riverside hotel in Pangbourne, Berkshire. They were returning to their home at Spencers Wood, Reading, when his wife — dazzled by the headlights of another car — suddenly drove off the road and hit the tree. The doctors found nothing suspicious in this account, for it seemed to them that Mrs Cook's injuries could have been caused as a result of her head hitting the tree when she was flung through the windscreen. But PC Stephen Sherlock, a village policeman of Nettlebed, near Henley-on-Thames, was not satisfied with this explanation.

Sherlock had already been to the scene of the tragedy, and had noticed that the damage to the car had only been slight; he had also noticed that the windscreen was still intact. He therefore returned to the scene in the early hours of the morning and examined it afresh with the aid of his flashlamp. This time he found blood on the road over fifty yards from the car.

His suspicion that Mrs Cook had been murdered was soon found to be justified, for an examination of the car by another police officer revealed that it had been travelling at no more than ten miles an hour when it hit the tree. A Home Office pathologist found seven separate injuries to Mrs Cook's head and said that he did not believe they had been caused by a collision. Moreover it was known that the men who called the ambulance had seen another motorist — the driver of a blue Cortina — leave the scene quickly when they stopped to help. In view of these suspicious circumstances, Raymond Cook was arrested as he left the coroner's court on 17 March and charged with his wife's murder.

The owner of the blue Cortina was eventually

found to be Eric Jones, a forty-six-year-old plant manager and undischarged bankrupt of Wrexham, Denbighshire, who was also suspected of being an abortionist. Jones denied having been near Reading on 2 March, but when police searched his car and found that the jack was missing, they suspected that it had been used for the murder. It was later found in a yachting pool not far from Wrexham and by this time it was known that Jones had been seen in the Reading area on the night in question. He had been driving his blue Cortina, accompanied by a local girl named Valerie Newell.

Valerie Newell, known as 'Kim', was an attractive blonde aged twenty-three. Raymond Cook had recently been having an affair with her, and Eric Jones had been her lover some years earlier. The police were later informed by Mrs Janet Adams, of Thatcham, Berkshire — Kim Newell's sister — that Kim and Eric Jones had both been concerned with Cook in his wife's death; Kim had confessed this to her after Cook was arrested, said Mrs Adams. Kim Newell and Eric Jones, both of whom had already been under suspicion, were then charged in connection with the crime.

The three prisoners were brought to trial together at the Oxfordshire Assizes in June 1967. They each pleaded not guilty at first but Jones later changed his plea to guilty. Having been sentenced to life imprisonment, he appeared as a witness against the other two, and told the court that Kim Newell — for whom he had performed several abortions — had blackmailed him into taking part in the murder. He had agreed to do so, believing that he would only have to help the others to simulate an accident, he said. But when the Mini stopped at the prearranged place, Cook got out and handed him the car jack, making it clear that he was expected to kill Mrs Cook with it.

Jones went on to describe the murder, saying that

he struck Mrs Cook with the jack, then ran the car into the tree while she and her husband were inside it. He afterwards struck Mrs Cook again as she lay on the ground.

Raymond Cook told the court that he had lived with Miss Newell for seven weeks towards the end of 1966, but later returned to his wife, fearing that she might otherwise commit suicide after ensuring that he would inherit nothing from her. He later gave Eric Jones — to whom he had been introduced by Kim Newell — £100 to concoct grounds for a divorce, and on the night in question expected that his wife would be drugged and abducted for this purpose. He also claimed that he had tried to stop Jones killing her, and that Jones had then struck him.

Kim Newell, who was pregnant, gave evidence for two days. She said that Cook had told her that Jones was going to kidnap his wife, and that she had spoken to Jones about it herself to try to prevent Mrs Cook being harmed in the process. On 2 March Jones showed her the place where the crime was to be committed, but she told him that she did not want to be involved in it. He later told her what had happened and warned her against going to the police. Cook, in the meantime, had declined to tell her about it himself.

It was stated during the course of the trial that although Cook had had little money of his own, his wife had had assets worth about £11,000, which he stood to gain in the event of her death. The prosecution contended that Kim Newell had known this and that she was the person who had instigated the murder. She had wanted Cook to return to his wife, to make sure that she left a will in his favour, it was alleged.

At the end of the thirteen-day trial Raymond Cook was convicted of murder and Kim Newell of being an accessory before the fact; they were both given sentences of life imprisonment. When Kim Newell gave birth to a child seven weeks later, her father said that it would be adopted, so that it would never know its background.

Body of Sarah Blake discovered, 1922

MARCH
4

On the morning of 4 March 1922, a fifty-five-year-old widow was found brutally murdered in the kitchen of an Oxfordshire public house. Sarah Blake, who managed the Crown and Anchor Inn on Gallows Tree Common — between Henley-on-Thames and Pang-bourne — had been so badly battered and hacked that more than sixty wounds and bruises were found on her head, face, neck, hands and arms, and blood was found on the ceiling and on her furniture. A thick iron bar used in the attack had been left beside the body, but a knife which her murderer had also used — leaving a stab-wound in her neck — had been taken away.

Mrs Blake had been seen alive at 6.30 the previous evening, but her murder had taken place not long afterwards. Police inquiries revealed that there had only been two customers in the pub that evening: a youth of fifteen named Jack Hewett, who had had some ginger beer, and a man who had left quickly after just one drink. Hewett told the police that he had returned later to get some beer for his mother but found the place closed and in darkness. Two other men had found the place closed about 7.40 p.m., and gone to drink elsewhere.

The missing knife was discovered in a hedge near the Crown and Anchor on 14 March, and three days later a man held in Reading for a minor offence made a statement confessing to the murder. Robert Alfred Shepperd was accordingly charged, but had to be released when his confession was found to be false. Then, on 4 April, Jack Hewett confessed that *he* was the murderer, saying that he had killed Mrs Blake with a flat-iron from the wall of the beer cellar. 'I'm very sorry it happened, and don't know what made me do it,' he said.

Hewett was brought to trial in Oxford in June 1922, denying the offence. He seemed to have no real motive for the crime, except possibly revenge — as Mrs Blake had rebuked him three days earlier — and after being arrested had blamed 'the pictures' for what had happened. Although he withdrew his confession, he was convicted and sentenced to be detained during His Majesty's pleasure, as he was too young to be hanged.

It was one of the earliest cases in which the influence of the cinema was blamed for a violent crime.

Murder of Gertrude Robinson, 1959

MARCH
7

On 7 March 1959, Gertrude Robinson, a seventy-two-year-old widow, was found murdered at her home in Bermuda; she had been raped and beaten to death by an unknown assailant. The crime followed a series of attacks on women during the previous twelve months, and it was suspected that the same person was responsible. But the police had no idea who he was, and when a second murder took place two months later, Scotland Yard was asked to provide assistance. Detective Superintendent William Baker and Detective Sergeant John O'Connell were sent to the island without delay.

The second murder victim was Dorothy Pearce, a fifty-nine-year-old divorcee. She was found raped and beaten to death in her bedroom on 9 May, with teeth-marks and scratches on her body, and money and jewellery left untouched in the same room. In this case fingerprints were found, but they did not corres-pond with those of any known criminal in Bermuda. The police therefore began fingerprinting every man in the locality aged between eighteen and fifty, but were still unable to identify the culprit. Six weeks after their arrival, the two Scotland Yard men abandoned the investigation and returned home.

Then, on 3 July, Rosaleen Kenny, aged forty-nine, was attacked by an intruder as she lay in bed. Her screams attracted the attention of neighbours, and the man — described as 'dark-skinned' — fled from the house. Another woman was murdered before he was finally apprehended.

Dorothy Rawlinson, a twenty-nine-year-old English office worker, was reported missing on 28 September, having left her lodgings to go swimming the previous afternoon. During a search of the beach, her blood-stained clothes were found buried in the sand; her body, partly eaten by sharks but still showing signs of a murderous attack, was later found at a coral reef two miles away.

It was learnt that Wendell Willis Lightbourne, a nineteen-year-old black youth who worked as a golf caddie, had been seen on the beach in an agitated state and wearing wet trousers on the day of Miss Rawlinson's disappearance.

Questioned about the murder, Lightbourne said that he had been fishing in the vicinity on 27 Septem-ber and admitted having seen the girl sun-bathing.

Eventually he broke down and confessed that he had killed her, saying, 'I want to get it off my mind. I can't go to Heaven now.' He then admitted the other two murders, remarking, 'I get nasty.' The crimes had been committed because he suffered from feelings of inferiority and envied the wealthier people attracted to the island.

Charged with the murder of Dorothy Rawlinson, Wendell Lightbourne was tried in December 1959 before the Bermuda Supreme Court, and on being convicted, he was sentenced to death. His sentence was afterwards commuted to one of life imprisonment, to be served in Britain.

Execution of Beck and Fernandez, 1951

Martha Beck and Raymond Fernandez, who were executed at New York's Sing Sing Prison on 8 March 1951, were heartless killers who preyed on lonely women; they had been charged with three murders and were suspected of seventeen others. The public had no sympathy for them when they were sentenced to death, and few people were horrified to learn that Martha's execution had been more protracted than usual.

The couple had met as a result of an advertisement in a 'lonely hearts' magazine towards the end of 1947. Martha, a fat, twenty-seven-year-old divorcee, was the superintendent of a home for crippled children in Pensacola, Florida: her bulky figure and craving for sex caused much amusement among those who knew her. Fernandez, already a swindler, accepted her as an accomplice when they became lovers, and she gave up her job and left her two children in order to be with him.

Fernandez was a Spaniard, six years her senior. He had been born in Hawaii, brought up in Connecticut and had then lived for some years in Spain, where he had a wife and four children who had long been abandoned. He had fought for Franco and later worked for British Intelligence in Gibraltar, but in 1945 had sustained a head injury while working his passage back to the United States. It was after this that he had begun to live by swindling.

Always a philanderer, Fernandez believed that he had a supernatural power over women which enabled him to pursue his criminal activities with ease. Having claimed over 100 victims on his own, he went on to find many others in partnership with Martha, who posed as his sister. But Martha's jealousy hampered him, for she accompanied him everywhere and did her best to prevent him sleeping with any of the women concerned. When she did not succeed in this a violent quarrel took place between them.

In December 1948 Fernandez became acquainted with Janet Fay, a sixty-six-year-old widow living in Albany, New York. He persuaded her to part with $6000 and join Martha and himself in an apartment in Long Island; she was then battered over the head with a hammer and strangled with a scarf. Having cleaned the place to prevent blood dripping through into the apartment below, Fernandez made love to Martha while the widow's corpse lay on the floor. The dead body was afterwards buried in the basement of a rented house.

Less than three weeks after Janet Fay's death, the murderous pair met Mrs Delphine Downing, a widow aged twenty-eight who lived with her twenty-one-month-old daughter Rainelle in Grand Rapids, Michigan. Before long they moved into her house, and Fernandez — having become her lover — persuaded her to sell some property which she owned and give the money to him. Then, just a few weeks after meeting her, he and Martha forced sleeping pills down her throat, shot her through the head and drowned her daughter in the bath.

They buried the two bodies in the cellar, covering them with cement, but suspicious neighbours reported the disappearances to the police and a search of the premises began. Upon being arrested, they both made confessions, admitting the murder of Janet Fay as well as those of Mrs Downing and her daughter. However, they denied having committed any of the other seventeen murders of which they were suspected, including that of Myrtle Young, a middle-aged widow whom Fernandez had bigamously married in August 1948.

The two 'lonely hearts' killers were sent back to New York, as that state still had the death penalty, whereas Michigan did not. Their trial began in July 1949 and lasted forty-four days, with Martha giving details of their sex life which made headline news. Afterwards, on Death Row, they went on declaring their love for each other to the very end. They were eventually executed in the electric chair.

Flora Gilligan found dead, 1953

MARCH
10

On 10 March 1953, Miss Flora Jane Gilligan, aged seventy-six, was found murdered outside her home in Diamond Street, York. She was naked and had died from skull injuries, having been raped, beaten and then pushed from her bedroom window in a clumsy attempt to give the impression that she had committed suicide. Nothing had been stolen during the course of the crime, even though there was money in the house. But the man responsible had tried unsuccessfully to break into the house next door before entering Miss Gilligan's home through an open window.

He had left his fingerprints at the scene of the crime, and also a footprint in a laundry basket; his shoe had recently been repaired and had a distinctive heel and sole. The police began fingerprinting soldiers at a nearby military camp and before long discovered the culprit: Philip Henry of the King's Own Yorkshire Light Infantry, a twenty-five-year-old coloured man who had been due for posting overseas on 19 March. There were other camps in the same area, and the police had been lucky to choose the right one first time.

It was found that Henry had not returned to camp on the night of the murder — though he pretended otherwise — and that he had afterwards cleaned his clothes thoroughly. Although he had disposed of the shoes which he had worn on the night in question, a cobbler was found who remembered repairing them for him. On being brought to trial at the York Assizes in June, the prisoner continued to claim that he was innocent but was found guilty and sentenced to death. He was hanged in Leeds on 30 July 1953.

On 11 March 1892, there was an explosion at a house in the Boulevard St Germain, in Paris, causing a lot of damage and slightly injuring one person. One of the inhabitants of the house was a judge who, the previous year, had presided at the trial of a group of anarchists, and when the remains of a bomb were found among the débris it was suspected that he had been the intended victim of the outrage. This was indeed the case, as was shortly to be proved.

The police learnt that the bomb had been planted by a man called Ravachol, who was also an anarchist and sometimes gave his name as Léger. He was described as being about five feet four inches tall, with a sallow complexion and dark hair. But attempts to trace him were unsuccessful at first, and on 27 March there was another explosion — this time in the Rue de Clichy — and on this occasion five people were gravely injured.

Three days later Ravachol was arrested by five policemen as he left a restaurant on the Boulevard Magenta. After a fierce struggle he was taken to the Sûreté, making several attempts to escape and calling out repeatedly to spectators, 'Follow me, brothers! Long live anarchy! Long live dynamite!' But by then it was known that Ravachol, whose real name was Claudius-François Koenigstein, was also wanted for several earlier crimes, including five murders.

Ravachol was the son of a Dutchman. Born in St Etienne, forty miles from Lyons, he was a dyer by trade, but had a reputation for brutality as a result of beating and threatening to kill his mother, whose maiden name he had adopted. His five known murders — all of which had taken place in the same region of France — were those of an eighty-six-year-old man and his housekeeper; a rich eccentric known as 'the hermit of Chambles', and two women (mother and daughter) who kept an ironmongery shop.

Ravachol had killed all of these people for personal gain and was also known to be guilty of smuggling, burglary, arson and stealing from a funeral vault. It was only after his second double murder that he went to Paris and became involved in revolutionary activities. But when he appeared for trial on 27 April the charges concerned only the recent bombings and Ravachol, having admitted that he was responsible for these, was allowed to read a statement declaring that anarchists were the champions of the oppressed and that it was wrong to treat them as ordinary criminals.

The casualties which had been caused by the second explosion had been serious enough to warrant the death penalty, but instead Ravachol was sentenced to life imprisonment. He was then taken to Montbrison, near St Etienne, to stand trial on other charges, and there, though he refused to answer questions about the women who kept the ironmongery shop, he admitted the murder of the 'the hermit of Chambles,' from whom he had stolen 35,000 francs. This time he was sentenced to death.

Ravachol, who was in his early forties, was executed in July 1892, singing as he went to the guillotine. Despite the unsavoury revelations which had been made about him, he was already regarded as a hero in revolutionary circles as a result of the defiant manner in which he had conducted himself at his trials. At his death he therefore became accepted as France's first great martyr of the anarchist cause.

Execution of Stephen Morin, 1985

On 13 March 1985, Stephen Peter Morin, the murderer of three women, was executed at the state prison in Huntsville, Texas, by means of a lethal injection. The thirty-seven-year-old prisoner had wanted the death sentence to be carried out, and had ordered his lawyers not to try to get him reprieved. But the execution proved to be a frightful ordeal for everyone concerned, for several attempts had to be made before a suitable vein was found, and these took no less than forty minutes. This delay, according to doctors and nurses at the prison, was due to Morin's long history of drug addiction.

'Drug abuse had made his veins brittle and almost impossible to find,' a spokesman explained.

Two years later, in the same town, the execution of Elliot Rod Johnson, another former drug addict, took almost as long. Johnson had committed a murder following a jewel robbery.

Death by lethal injection, America's newest method of execution, was first used in the case of Charlie Brooks, also in Huntsville, in 1982. On that occasion, there was no mishap: the condemned died quickly and painlessly (see vol 1, 7 December).

The following year, again in Huntsville, James David Autry, who had murdered a grocery shop assistant for three dollars' worth of beer, was injected with a saline solution in readiness for the administration of lethal drugs when a stay of execution was granted. Autry, aged twenty-nine, was eventually executed some months later, in March 1984.

Murder of Jacques Rumèbe, 1925

On 14 March 1925, Pierre Bougrat, a Marseilles doctor in serious financial difficulties, murdered Jacques Rumèbe, an old wartime friend with whom he had fought side-by-side at Verdun. Bougrat had a luxury flat and consulting-room in the Rue Senac, where he had once received many rich patients. But by this time he had few patients at all, and his practice no longer provided him with an adequate income. His crime was an act of desperation.

Rumèbe, who was the wages clerk of a local pottery, had contracted syphilis during the First World War and was being treated by Bougrat with weekly injections of mercuric cyanide. He visited the Rue Senac for this purpose on Saturday mornings, before going to collect his firm's wages money from the bank. On this particular Saturday, however, he arrived at the bank much later than usual and afterwards went to see Bougrat again, carrying the money — 25,000 francs — in a briefcase. It was then that the murder was committed.

Bougrat, the son of a schoolmaster, had been born in Annecy in 1887. On being discharged from the army in 1919, he had married the daughter of a professor at the Marseilles Medical School, to whom he owed both his flat and his practice. But his wife had since left him — taking their one little daughter — and had started divorce proceedings as a result of an affair which Bougrat had been having with an ex-prostitute named Andrea Audibert. It was the scandal caused by this which had ruined his practice.

Bougrat had met Andrea in 1924, and was so captivated that he arranged to buy her from the man for whom she was then working, paying part of the agreed sum by monthly instalments. Later, when his wife left him, Andrea had moved into the flat in her place, but stayed only a short while before disappearing with some of his valuables. He then did not see her again until she suddenly returned, begging him to forgive her and take her back. By that time he had Rumèbe's corpse hidden in his dispensary.

The corpse had been placed in a long narrow cupboard just below the ceiling, and the doors of this had been covered with wallpaper to prevent it looking like a cupboard. Bougrat had obviously only intended to keep it there until he found a safe way of disposing of it, but with Andrea living in the flat again this would be more difficult than he had anticipated. Even so, he wanted her back, and so she remained with him until his arrest two months later. But the body remained there, too, and soon began to smell.

Towards the end of May, Bougrat was taken into custody for issuing worthless cheques. His father, now in retirement, offered to settle his debts for the sake of the family honour. But the arrest led to a search of Bougrat's premises and Rumèbe's body was soon found.

Bougrat denied having killed him, saying that Rumèbe had committed suicide in the consulting-room after being beaten up and robbed of the wages money elsewhere. He explained the hiding of the body by saying that he was afraid that he would be accused of stealing the money himself. But this explanation was not good enough to prevent him being charged with murder and theft.

At his trial, which began at Aix-en-Provence on 23 March 1927, it was contended that Bougrat had given Rumèbe a second dose of mercuric cyanide when he returned from the bank and that, having thus caused him to lose consciousness, he had killed him by forcing him to inhale prussic acid fumes.

Andrea, who had known nothing of the murder — and believed the smell in the dispensary to have been caused by a dead rat which nobody could find — was one of the witnesses who appeared against him.

Bougrat's defence was that he had given Rumèbe a second injection at his own request because he felt that the first had not been strong enough, and that his friend had collapsed and died unexpectedly a few minutes later. Bougrat had then panicked, hidden the body and stolen the 25,000 francs, it was claimed on his behalf. It was also pointed out that the prisoner had once been decorated for saving Rumèbe's life on the battlefield. He was nonetheless found guilty of premeditated murder as well as theft.

Sentenced to hard labour for life on Devil's Island, Bougrat arrived in French Guiana shortly before Christmas 1927 and, as a doctor, was set to work in the hospital on the mainland. A few months later, with a number of other convicts, he escaped to Venezuela, where he spent the rest of his life. He died, at the age of seventy-five, in 1962.

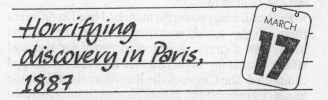

Horrifying discovery in Paris, 1887

MARCH 17

On the morning of 17 March 1887, police officers in Paris forced open the door of a third-floor luxury apartment at 17, Rue Montaigne, and found three bodies. The occupant — a courtesan named Marie Regnault — the chambermaid and the chambermaid's daughter had all been horribly murdered: Marie

Regnault had been decapitated and the other victims had had their throats cut. As valuable articles of jewellery were missing and an unsuccessful attempt had been made to open a safe in the apartment, it was obvious that robbery had been the motive for the crime.

Marie Regnault, known as 'Régine de Montille', had for a long time had three lovers, each of whom believed himself to be catering for all her needs. Since losing her favourite she had taken to drinking heavily and entertaining other men, and when a number of articles apparently belonging to a 'Gaston Geissler' were found at the scene, it seemed likely that he was the person responsible for the crime. But it was soon discovered that they had been left on purpose, in order to hinder the investigation.

On 20 March a brothel-keeper in Marseilles reported that a client had given one of her girls a watch set with diamonds and a pair of ear-rings. As these proved to be items stolen from Marie Regnault's apartment, the client, a Levantine named Pranzini, was traced and questioned. He refused to explain how the articles had come into his possession, and so was taken back to Paris. He then called on a woman who had been his mistress to give him an alibi for the night of the murder, but she refused to do so.

Pranzini, a big, powerful man, had lived in different parts of the world, including Turkey, Egypt and India, had a great variety of occupations and had affairs with many women. It was believed that he had committed 'the Crime of the Rue Montaigne' because he needed money to go back to his own country, where a rich young American woman was waiting to marry him. But, being unable to open Marie Regnault's safe, all he had gained was jewellery which he knew he could not sell without risking arrest (though he evidently thought that he could give it to other prostitutes without taking such a risk).

At his trial before the Assize Court, Pranzini claimed that he had spent the night of the murder with a married woman, whom he refused to name, and his counsel tried to convince the jury that he was a chivalrous man, putting his own life in jeopardy in order to avoid compromising the woman in question. But the jury found him guilty of murder without extenuating circumstances, and he was sentenced to death. He was executed by guillotine in the Place de la Roquette on 1 September 1887.

Death of Joan Hill, 1969

On 19 March 1969, Joan Hill, the wife of a wealthy plastic surgeon of Houston, Texas, died at the Sharpstown General Hospital after being admitted the previous day. Following a brief examination of the body, her death was put down to an infection of the liver; her funeral then took place without delay. But her adoptive father, an oil millionaire named Ash Robinson, was not satisfied that the cause of her death had been properly established and accused her husband, Dr John Hill, of withholding medical treatment which could have saved her. This allegation caused Hill to threaten his father-in-law with a lawsuit for defamation.

It was known that for some years Hill's relationship with his wife had been deteriorating and that he had been having affairs with other women. When he remarried only three months after Mrs Hill's death the allegations of foul play began afresh and in

August 1969 the body of his first wife was exhumed for a further examination. A brain which was said to have been preserved at the hospital after the first post-mortem showed signs of meningitis, but doubt was expressed about whether this was really the brain of Mrs Hill. The second post-mortem revealed that Joan Hill had died of an acute inflammatory disease of unknown origin.

The investigation continued and eventually Dr John Hill was charged with 'murder by omission', and brought to trial in 1971. By this time he had divorced his second wife, Ann Kurth, who was called to give evidence against him.

Ann Kurth claimed that on one occasion the accused had tried to kill her by crashing his car against a bridge and also that he had confessed to having murdered his first wife. He had killed Joan Hill, it was stated, by injecting her with a bacterial culture made from 'every form of human excretion', and not taking her to hospital until she was in a state of irreversible shock. The case ended suddenly with the declaration of a mistrial, and a second trial was ordered. But before this could be heard John Hill was murdered by a gunman at his home in Houston.

The murder, which took place in September 1972, was the work of a contract killer named Vandiver, who was arrested but later killed by a policeman after jumping bail. Two women convicted of complicity in the crime stated that Ash Robinson had put out a contract for Hill's death, but a lie-detector test produced no evidence against him and he was never indicted. The case thus remains officially unsolved.

James Baigrie discovered, 1985

On the morning of 20 March 1985, four police officers went to a flat in London's Earls Court to arrest James Baigrie, a thirty-three-year-old convicted murderer. Baigrie, who had been on the run since his escape from an Edinburgh prison in October 1983, had been traced to the flat in Philbeach Gardens, a quiet crescent near Earls Court station. But when they arrived at 6.30 a.m., the police found only his flatmate there. Baigrie, armed with a shotgun, was hiding in his van out in the street.

It was not long before his whereabouts were discovered, and the police surrounded the van, calling on Baigrie to surrender. When he refused, the police prepared themselves for a siege, cordoning off the road and evacuating the residents from nearby buildings. But while guns were levelled at the van from different directions, a field telephone was provided so that trained negotiators could keep in regular contact with him.

The fugitive accepted the telephone, but resisted further attempts to persuade him to give himself up, both that day and the next. Eventually, just before 1.45 a.m. on 22 March, two CS gas cartridges were fired through the rear windows of the van, and a final appeal was made to him through a loudspeaker. Seconds later the sound of a shot was heard, and Baigrie was found dead from a bullet wound which had left his face unrecognizable. The siege thus came to an abrupt end over forty-three hours after it had started.

At the inquest which followed the police were

criticized by the National Council for Civil Liberties for allegedly refusing to let Baigrie speak to friends who might have been able to influence him. But the police claimed that Baigrie had not wanted to speak to his friends, and that he had made up his mind to commit suicide a short while before they fired the gas cartridges. The jury, in recording a verdict of suicide, added a rider saying that they approved of the tactics which the police had used.

Baigrie had been given a life sentence in July 1982 for shooting an Edinburgh barman in the back, but had served only fifteen months before escaping from Saughton high-security prison. After his death two other men were charged with assisting him with intent to prevent his arrest. However, at the West London Magistrates' Court on 9 May the police offered no evidence against either of them, so the charge in each case was dismissed.

Murder of Francis Rattenbury, 1935

MARCH
24

On the night of 24 March 1935, a doctor was called to the home of Francis Rattenbury, a retired architect aged sixty-seven, of Manor Road, Bournemouth, who had been battered over the head, apparently as he sat sleeping in his armchair. He found the old man unconscious, with blood flowing from his wounds, and his thirty-eight-year-old wife Alma very drunk. 'Look at him!' cried Mrs Rattenbury. 'Look at the blood! Someone has finished him!'

The doctor telephoned for a surgeon, but by the

time he appeared Mrs Rattenbury was even more drunk and her presence made it impossible for him to carry out an examination. Rattenbury was therefore removed to a nursing home, where three wounds were found on his head and an operation was carried out.

The police were informed of what had happened, and several officers arrived at the injured man's home. They found lights switched on all over the house and the radiogram being played loudly. Mrs Rattenbury, who was incapable of answering questions coherently, laughed and cried, kissed some of them and made statements to the effect that she was responsible for the attack. She was given morphia and put into bed, but the following morning repeated her assertion that she was to blame for what had happened.

She was then taken into custody, her husband's chauffeur, eighteen-year-old George Percy Stoner, remarking as she was escorted from the house, 'You have got yourself into this mess by talking too much!'

Three days later Rattenbury died of his injuries, and on 29 March, Stoner — who by now had also been arrested — told the police that *he* was the person responsible for the crime. 'When I did the job I believe he was asleep,' he said. 'I hit him and then came upstairs and told Mrs Rattenbury.'

A bloodstained mallet which had been found was clearly the murder weapon, and Stoner, who lived in the house in Manor Road, had brought this from his grandfather's home the previous evening. Even so, the police did not altogether believe his confession, for Stoner had been Mrs Rattenbury's lover and it appeared that they were both guilty of the crime. They were therefore both charged with murder.

Stoner had entered Rattenbury's service as a handyman in September 1934, taking up residence in the house three months later, when the job of chauffeur was added to his other duties. Francis and Alma

Rattenbury, who had both been married before, had ceased to live as man and wife after the birth of their son John in 1929, and Alma later maintained that her husband knew of her affair with Stoner and did not object to it.

A few days before the murder she took Stoner to London and they stayed at the Royal Palace Hotel in Kensington, occupying separate rooms. She bought him expensive clothes and he was treated as her equal by the hotel staff. But on 24 March, on learning that she and her husband were to visit a friend in Bridport the following day, Stoner became angry and threatened her with an air-pistol. It was nonetheless contended at their trial that the murder had been the result of a conspiracy between them.

The trial opened at the Old Bailey on 27 May and lasted five days, with both defendants pleading not guilty. Alma Rattenbury now said that Stoner had been unnecessarily jealous of her husband and that on the night of the attack he had entered her bedroom and told her what had happened. 'He said that I should not go to Bridport next day, because he had hurt Rats,' she said. 'I did not understand at first. Then I heard Rats groan and my brain became alive. I ran downstairs.' She also said that she had no recollection of the statements which she had made afterwards.

Stoner, who claimed to have committed the crime under the influence of cocaine, did not give evidence.

The jury considered their verdict on 31 May, retiring for forty-seven minutes. Mrs Rattenbury was acquitted and Stoner convicted, though with a recommendation of mercy. Mrs Rattenbury was therefore released, while Stoner was sentenced to death.

But it was Mrs Rattenbury, not Stoner, who was to die, for she was ill from fear and grief over her lover's impending execution, and the constant demands of newspaper reporters made her recovery impossible.

On 4 June 1935 she took her own life, stabbing herself six times beside a stream near Christchurch, Hampshire. Stoner's sentence was later commuted to life imprisonment.

Death of Christiaan Buys, 1969

MARCH 28

On 28 March 1969, Christiaan Buys, a forty-four-year-old South African railway labourer of Harrismith, Orange Free State, died at the Voortrekker Hospital in Kroonstad after an illness lasting several weeks. It appeared at first that the cause of his death had been lobar pneumonia, but when his kidneys, liver and stomach were sent for analysis it was found that he had been poisoned with arsenic.

His wife Maria, who was eleven years his junior, had for some months been having an affair with Gerhard Groesbeek, a shunter aged twenty who had lodged at their home for a short while at the end of the previous year, and it was known that she had been seeking a divorce at the time of her husband's death. Her sudden marriage to Groesbeek on 11 June therefore gave rise to rumour, and the couple were both arrested thirteen days later.

Maria admitted that she had given the deceased ant poison containing arsenic, and said that she had suffered much hardship, including a number of assaults, at his hands. But she denied that she had intended to kill him. 'I just wanted to avenge myself on Chris,' she said. 'I wanted to make him thoroughly sick, so that he would give me permission to divorce him.'

Other confessions followed, and in November Maria stood trial on her own before a judge and two assessors at the Bloemfontein Criminal Sessions. The evidence against her was overwhelming, and the allegations which she made against the victim of the crime were not believed, for witnesses declared that Christiaan Buys had been a quiet man, fond of his wife and children, and always kind to them. It was also claimed that Maria had said that she was tired of Buys and had threatened to 'damned well poison him' if he would not agree to divorce her. She was convicted and sentenced to death.

Gerhard Groesbeek was tried separately, also before a judge and assessors, seven months after Maria's conviction, but the case against him was not conclusive. There was no evidence that he had administered any of the poison, and though he had allegedly admitted to fellow prisoners that he was Maria's accomplice, this was not thought to be sufficient to prove him guilty beyond reasonable doubt. He was therefore acquitted.

Maria Groesbeek remained in the death cell in Pretoria while the question of a commutation of her sentence was considered. She spent much of her time praying and reading the Bible, frequently expressed sorrow for what she had done, and implored relatives to look after her children. She was finally hanged on 13 November 1970.

Poisoning of Alfred Jones, 1924

On 29 March 1924, Alfred Poynter Jones, thirty-seven-year-old landlord of the Blue Anchor Hotel in Byfleet, Surrey, awoke with a hangover after a party at the hotel the previous night. He went to the bar parlour, found a bottle of bromo salts and drank part of the contents in a glass of water. But, far from feeling better, he died soon afterwards in agonizing convulsions. The bromo salts had been poisoned with strychnine.

Jean-Pierre Vaquier, a vain forty-five-year-old French inventor staying at the hotel, had been present at Mr Jones' death. Though he told police that he had loved the dead man 'like a brother', it soon became clear that his reason for staying at the hotel was his attachment to Mrs Mabel Jones, the landlord's widow, whom he had met in Biarritz a few months earlier. Later he was identified from a newspaper photograph as a man who had bought strychnine from a London chemist, signing the poison book 'J. Wanker'. He was then arrested and charged with murder.

At his trial at the Guildford Assizes in July it was revealed that Vaquier had been employed at the Victoria Hotel in Biarritz, operating a wireless set for the benefit of guests. Mabel Jones, spending a holiday there on her own, had been drawn into a passionate affair with him — an affair which involved considerable use of a French-English dictionary, as they did not speak each other's languages — with the result that when she returned to England he followed her, trying to persuade her to leave her husband. He explained his visit to England by saying that he was trying to sell the patent rights of a new type of sausage-mincer which he had invented.

The purchase of the strychnine had taken place on 1 March, 'Mr Wanker' telling the chemist that he needed it for wireless experiments. After Mr Jones' death, the bottle which had contained the bromo salts was found in the kitchen of the Blue Anchor, having been emptied and washed out, though not thoroughly enough to remove all traces of the poison. Vaquier claimed at his trial that he had bought the strychnine for Mrs Jones' solicitor, who had advised him to give a false name.

Though the prosecution's case was very strong, the prisoner was confident of being acquitted and displayed his vanity throughout the trial. But on being found guilty he shouted abuse at the judge and had to be dragged from the dock. He was hanged at Wandsworth Prison on 12 August 1924.

Child's body found in Thames, 1896

MARCH 30

On 30 March 1896, the body of a baby girl was found in the River Thames at Reading, Berkshire. She had been strangled with a piece of tape, which was still tied round her neck, and afterwards wrapped in a brown paper parcel and weighted with a brick. The brown paper bore the name Mrs Thomas and an address in Caversham, a village outside Reading, but 'Mrs Thomas' was found to be an alias of Mrs Amelia Elizabeth Dyer, a fifty-seven-year-old baby-farmer who had already moved to another address. On being identified, Mrs Dyer was arrested; the river was then dragged for further corpses.

Amelia Dyer, a native of Bristol, was separated from her husband and lived with an old woman known as Granny Smith, whom she had met in a workhouse the previous year. She took charge of unwanted children, her terms being £10 for each, and several of her charges were found at her house when she was taken into custody. Her daughter and son-in-law, who lived in rented rooms in Willesolen, Middlesex, were also arrested in connection with Mrs Dyer's activities.

The dragging of the Thames led to the recovery of six more strangled children, three of whom were never identified. Two bodies found in a weighted carpet-bag proved to be those of Doris Marmon, aged four months, who had been entrusted to Mrs Dyer's care in Cheltenham, Gloucestershire, on 31 March, and Harry Simmons, aged one year, who had been handed to Mrs Dyer and her daughter, Mrs Mary Ann Palmer, at Paddington Station, London, the following day.

At Reading police station Mrs Dyer made two attempts to take her own life: the first with a pair of scissors, the second with a boot-lace. Later, while in prison, she wrote to the Superintendent of Police, declaring that her daughter and son-in-law were innocent. 'I do know I shall have to answer before my Maker in Heaven for the awful crimes I have committed, but as God Almighty is my Judge in Heaven as on Earth, neither my daughter, Mary Ann Palmer, nor her husband, Arthur Ernest Palmer, I do most solemnly swear that neither of them had anything at all to do with it,' she said. Mary Ann Palmer, known as 'Polly', later became the prosecution's chief witness against her mother.

Though Mrs Dyer was believed to have been

responsible for all seven known murders — and it was suspected that she had committed others during her twenty years of baby-farming — she was tried only for that of Doris Marmon. Her trial on that charge took place at the Old Bailey in May 1896, when her daughter told the court that the victim had been taken to her rooms in Willesden on 31 March, and evidently strangled while she (the witness) was out fetching coal. Afterwards, she said, she found Mrs Dyer shoving the carpet-bag, which now contained the child's body, under her sofa. Mrs Palmer then went on to state that Harry Simmons must have been murdered in her rooms the following night, before she, her mother and her husband went out to a music-hall.

Mrs Dyer's counsel tried to save her life by introducing evidence of insanity, but two doctors appearing for the prosecution said that she was not insane; the symptoms had been feigned, they said. The jury took just five minutes to find the accused guilty, and she was sentenced to death. She was hanged at Newgate Prison on 10 June 1896.

Queensland mail train murders, 1936

APRIL **2**

Shortly after 6 a.m. on 2 April 1936, two railway officials in Brisbane entered a mail train which had just arrived from Bundaberg, 180 miles to the north, in search of the conductor, Thomas Boys. They found him lying in one of the sleeping compartments, with his face so badly battered that he was unrecognizable. Two male passengers in the same compartment had also been battered: one of them, a Postal Department engineer, was already dead, the other, a businessman, was dying. Their money had been stolen and their belongings ransacked.

The person responsible had also stolen the coat and trousers of a suit belonging to the engineer, together with his departmental bag, stamped with the initials P.M.G. in gold. It was clear, too, from an examination of the wash-basin in that compartment, that he had tried to cleanse himself of bloodstains before leaving the train. But as he had left behind the waistcoat of the stolen suit, the police were able to broadcast the colour and texture of the coat and trousers he was wearing immediately after the crime.

They were thus able to discover that he had left the train at the wayside station of Wooloowin and taken a taxi from there to South Brisbane, paying his fare with bloodstained coins. From South Brisbane he had taken another taxi to Southport, and the driver of this one was able to identify him from photographs as Herbert Kopit, an incorrigible twenty-three-year-old sneak-thief who specialized in pilfering from hotel rooms.

From Southport the trail led to Murwillumbah, in New South Wales, then to Casino and finally to Sydney, where it suddenly stopped. Herbert Kopit was captured soon afterwards at a hotel in Melbourne, where he had arrived dressed as a woman and been reported as a suspected pervert.

He admitted that he was responsible for the mail train murders, saying that he had become excited when Boys looked into the sleeping compartment just before dawn and caught him picking the pockets of the other two passengers. He struck the conductor with a tyre lever which happened to be in his possession; then, as the attack woke the other passengers, he struck both of them as well. He afterwards robbed them, then tried to wash the blood from his hands and put on the engineer's coat and trousers in place of his own bloodstained suit. He threw the murder weapon out of the window before leaving the train at Wooloowin.

Kopit was brought to trial in Brisbane in June 1936 for the murder of the Postal Department engineer, Harold Steering. There was sufficient evidence to ensure his conviction, even after he had repudiated his statement to the Melbourne police, and as the death penalty had been abolished in Queensland he was sentenced to life imprisonment. He was not tried for the second murder, but stayed in jail until his death in March 1951.

Thomas Boys had suffered brain injuries which left his memory and speech impaired, and was therefore unable to give evidence against his assailant. He remained an invalid for the rest of his life, and died in July 1950.

Murder of William Hall, 1924

On 3 April 1924, William Hall, a twenty-eight-year-old cashier, was shot dead at his bank's sub-branch in the village of Bordon, in Hampshire. He had been working there on his own, as usual, having been sent to the village from his bank's main branch, some miles away, and as the culprit took the precaution of locking the front door after the murder had taken place, the body was not discovered until over an hour

later. The murderer, in the meantime, had escaped with several hundred pounds in cash.

A bullet used in the shooting was recognized as Government ammunition, and a revolver belonging to an officer at the nearby army camp was found to be missing. A close watch was therefore kept on the camp, and for several days, during which all leave was cancelled, the place was in a state of tension. Then, on the afternoon of 8 April, Abraham Goldenberg, a young private in the East Lancashire Regiment, was seen behaving strangely. A search of one of the latrines after he had left it resulted in the discovery of a brown-paper parcel containing most of the stolen money.

Goldenberg was already known to the police officers investigating the murder. On the evening of 3 April he had volunteered information, saying that he had been to the bank to cash a cheque at 1.45 p.m. and that the cashier had been the only other person in the building at that time. Three days later he called in at the police station and said, 'No further developments have come to my knowledge. If anything does crop up, I will at once notify you.'

Two days after that, on being arrested, he confessed to being William Hall's murderer. 'I have been with my girl for some time, and I would not marry her unless I had money — and there was no chance of making any in the army,' he said. He went on to give details of the crime, and to reveal the whereabouts of the murder weapon and about a dozen bags of silver coins which he had stolen from the bank. However, he insisted that £37 which the police found in his pocket was his own money and had no connection with the crime.

At his trial, which took place in Winchester in June, an attempt was made to prove him insane, but he was found guilty and sentenced to death. As the judge finished pronouncing sentence, the silent spectators were astonished to hear the prisoner ask, 'Can I be assured that the thirty-seven pounds found upon me will be declared to be my property?'

A further plea of insanity was made at his appeal, but again without success. On 30 July 1924, Goldenberg was hanged at Winchester Prison.

Execution of Patrick Carraher, 1946

APRIL
6

Patrick Carraher, who was hanged on 6 April 1946, was a forty-year-old criminal from the slums of Glasgow who had been regularly in trouble since his youth. He lived by theft and housebreaking, and had several convictions for crimes of violence. During his last eight years, following a prison sentence for culpable homicide, he had the reputation of being a killer — a reputation which he did his best to enhance by boasting.

The crime which led to this conviction had taken place in August 1938, when he stabbed a soldier in the neck in a Glasgow street. The soldier died on his way to hospital and Carraher, who admitted the offence, was charged with murder. It was because he had been drinking on the night in question that the jury found him guilty only on the lesser charge, and he was jailed for just three years. He received a similar sentence in 1943, after a razor-slashing incident in which the victim's jacket was ruined but no injury was caused to him.

The offence for which he was hanged took place in November 1945, when his brother-in-law, a thug named Daniel Bonnar, became involved in a fight with three brothers named Gordon. Always ready for trouble, Carraher attacked one of the brothers with a wood-carver's knife, inflicting a deep wound in his neck, and the victim, a former prisoner-of-war, died on arrival in hospital. Carraher was arrested shortly afterwards and charged with murder for the second time.

At his trial in February 1946 the prosecution's case was overwhelming and included the evidence of some of Carraher's former friends. The jury had little difficulty reaching a verdict, and the prisoner remained motionless as sentence of death was passed. Following the dismissal of his appeal, Carraher was hanged at Glasgow's Barlinnie Prison.

Execution in Beirut, 1983

APRIL
7

On 7 April 1983, Ibrahim Tarraf Tarraf, a thirty-six-year-old Shia Muslim and former law student from south Lebanon, was hanged in central Beirut for the murder of his landlady, Mrs Mathilde Bahout, and her son Marcel. The execution was carried out at dawn on a public gallows among the palm trees of the Sanayeh Park, where Tarraf, in 1979, had dumped the remains of his victims in rubbish bags, after murdering them and dismembering their bodies with a saw.

Following his conviction, Tarraf had been sentenced to death in March 1983, and this sentence was ratified by President Amin Gemayel and counter-signed by the

Prime Minister, Mr Chaffik el-Wazzam, the day before it was carried out. Struggling and pleading for mercy, the prisoner was dragged by policemen to the gallows, where he was handed over to two executioners, both wearing white hoods. A small group of spectators watched the proceedings in silence.

It was Lebanon's first use of the death penalty since 1972, when a blacksmith named Tewfik Itani was hanged in a Beirut prison for the murder of his brother-in-law, and the gallows stood opposite the building in which the murders had taken place. Tarraf's counsel, Mr Nimeh Nanieh, had tried unsuccessfully to obtain a stay of execution on a plea of temporary insanity.

Death of 100-year-old Murderess, 1944

APRIL
10

On 10 April 1944, a well-known and much-respected figure died in a hospital in Strathfield, near Maitland, New South Wales, two months after celebrating her 100th birthday. Ruth Emilie Kaye, an unmarried Englishwoman, had lived in Australia for many years. She was a trained nurse and had been the matron of a nurses' home in Maitland from 1910 to 1936, when she finally retired. It was not realized at the time that 'Miss Kaye' was an assumed name and that this frail old lady had once committed a horrifying murder. She had, in fact, served a life sentence before setting foot in Australia.

Ruth Emilie Kaye's real name was Constance

Kent. She was one of the daughters of Samuel Savill Kent, an inspector of factories in the west of England, and had been born in Sidmouth, Devonshire, on 6 February 1844. Samuel Kent was married twice and had fifteen children, several of whom did not survive infancy. His second marriage — only a year after his first wife's death — was to his children's governess, who, having become his mistress, had gradually taken over the running of the household while the first Mrs Kent was still alive.

Constance was the last but one child of the first marriage. Her crime was committed on the night of 29 June 1860, at a mansion in the village of Rode, in Wiltshire, where the family was then living, and the body of the victim — her stepbrother Savill, aged three years and ten months — was found in the privy the following morning. His throat had been cut so deeply that he had almost been decapitated, and there was a four-inch stab wound in his chest. There was also a blackened area round his mouth.

An unsuccessful attempt was made to prosecute Constance — then a sullen and troublesome girl of sixteen — and this was followed by an equally unsuccessful attempt to prosecute Elizabeth Gough, the children's nursemaid. During the hearing against the latter it was revealed that Samuel Kent had done his best to obstruct the investigation of the crime, and this caused the villagers of Rode to suspect that he was the murderer. As a result, his life was made unbearable, and it remained so until the family moved in 1861.

The crime remained unsolved for five years, until Constance, after entering a religious home in Brighton as a paying guest, suddenly travelled to London and handed a written confession to the chief magistrate at Bow Street, stating that she was the culprit and that she had committed the murder 'alone and unaided'. Three months later, on 21 July 1865, she appeared for trial at the Wiltshire Assizes, pleaded guilty and was sentenced to death. The sentence was commuted to life imprisonment four days afterwards.

She spent the next twenty years in prison, part of the time in Millbank, where she worked in the infirmary. In one of a number of petitions for release, she explained her hatred of her stepmother who, she said, 'had taught her to despise and dislike her own mother' and 'robbed that mother of the affection both of a husband and of a daughter'. She then went on to state that it was in order to cause her stepmother 'the mental agony her own mother had endured' that she had committed her terrible crime.

Constance was forty-one years old at the time of her release — by which time her father and stepmother were both dead — and she was determined to make a new life for herself. Her brother William, a naturalist, was living in Tasmania, where he was known as William Saville-Kent; and when, the following year, he returned there after a visit to England, she accompanied him, using the name which she was to keep for the rest of her life.

She began training as a nurse in Melbourne in 1890, after responding to a call for volunteers to help deal with a typhoid crisis, and within a few months of completing the two-year course was appointed matron of a private hospital in Perth. She went on to hold posts in Sydney, Parramatta and Mittagong before settling in Maitland.

Though Constance maintained that she had acted alone on the night of the murder, she never explained how she was able to take the child from its cot without disturbing Elizabeth Gough, who slept in the same room. She likewise never explained why there was much less blood than might have been expected in the privy, where she claimed that the crime had been committed, or what had become of the weapon: a razor belonging to her father. Nor, for that matter,

110

was any reason given for Samuel Kent's seemingly inexplicable behaviour in hindering the police investigation.

The case has therefore been the subject of much speculation, the most recent book on the subject being *Cruelly Murdered* (1979) by Bernard Taylor, in which the details of Constance's later life are to be found.

Taylor advances the theory that Samuel Kent was having an affair with Elizabeth Gough, and that they were in another room together when the murder took place. The crime, according to this theory, was committed by means of suffocation, and Samuel Kent, after the discovery of the body, inflicted the razor injuries himself and then disposed of the weapon in an attempt to divert suspicion away from the household.

It was only by doing this that he was able to avoid confessing his infidelity.

Murder of Ruby Keen, 1937

APRIL
11

On the evening of 11 April 1937, Leslie Stone, a quarry labourer aged twenty-four, met his former girl-friend, twenty-three-year-old Ruby Keen, in the saloon bar of the Golden Bell Hotel in Leighton Buzzard, Bedfordshire. He had known her since 1931, when he had courted her for some months prior to joining the Army, and on meeting her by chance the previous weekend had persuaded her to spend an evening with him 'for old times' sake'. He was hoping to resume the courtship, which had only ended when he was posted to Hong Kong in 1932.

Ruby Keen, an attractive young woman who worked in a factory, had had other admirers besides Stone and was now engaged to a policeman. During the course of the evening, in two different public houses, Stone was overheard pleading with her to break off the engagement and marry him instead. Though Ruby was unwilling to do this, their exchanges were such that when they left the second pub, a few minutes before closing time, a couple of the regulars followed them at a discreet distance. They were then seen entering a coppice on the outskirts of the town, having walked past Ruby's home in Plantation Road.

The following morning Ruby's body was found in the coppice, beneath a tall fir tree. She had been raped and then strangled, her attacker kneeling beside her on the ground as he pulled her scarf tight round her neck. Her dress had been torn right down the front.

Stone was an obvious suspect. On being interviewed by police officers, he admitted having spent the evening with Ruby but claimed to have left her near her home about 10.15 p.m. The suit and shoes which he had been wearing at the time were taken for examination, and it was found that although the suit was new the surface of the cloth had been worn thin by brushing at the knees. Even so, a few grains of soil remained embedded in the trousers, and these were found to match samples taken from the ground where the murder had been committed. A small thread of artificial silk which had been brushed into the jacket was found to be identical to fibres from the slip which Ruby had been wearing on the evening in question.

Leslie Stone was charged with her murder and brought to trial at the Old Bailey in June 1937. After hearing the scientific evidence produced by the prosecution, he changed his account of what had taken

112

place, saying that he and Ruby had quarrelled and struck each other at the scene of the crime, and that her dress had been torn as she fell to the ground. He added that he thought he had only stunned her and that he had not tried to interfere with her. He had walked away, expecting her to revive, and had brushed his clothes when he arrived back at his home.

After retiring to consider their verdict the jury sent a message to the judge, asking for his guidance on a point of law. 'If, as the result of an intention to commit rape, a girl is killed — although there is no intention to kill her — is a man guilty of murder?' they asked. The judge replied: 'Yes, undoubtedly.' A verdict of guilty was then returned and the prisoner was sentenced to death.

Following the dismissal of his appeal, Leslie Stone was hanged at Pentonville Prison on 13 August 1937.

Execution of Frederick Holt, 1920

APRIL
13

Frederick Rothwell Holt, who was hanged on 13 April 1920, was a Lancashire man from the upper middle class who had been invalided out of the army during the First World War, suffering from amnesia and depression. The victim of his crime was his mistress, Kitty Breaks, a young married woman who was separated from her husband. They had met in 1918, when Holt was thirty-one and Kitty twenty-five, and lived together for eighteen months before Kitty's body was found on sandhills at St Annes, near Blackpool, on the morning of 24 December 1919. She had insured her life for £5000 and made a will in Holt's favour just before her death.

That Holt had murdered her was never in doubt. She had been killed with shots from his service revolver, which had been left at the scene; a pair of his gloves and a set of footprints which matched the impressions of his shoes were also found there. Holt, though he had an income of £500 a year — which he had inherited — had been living beyond his means, and the prosecution contended that he had regarded the murder as a way of dealing with his financial difficulties after becoming tired of the victim.

But Sir Edward Marshall Hall, appearing for the defence, argued that his client was insane. Holt, he said, was mentally unbalanced as a result of his war experiences: the sort of man 'who might go mad at any moment'. He had been passionately devoted to Kitty and jealous of other men in her life, fearing that he might lose her. The murder had taken place as a result of an uncontrollable impulse, the perpetrator having been deprived of the will to resist it by reason of mental illness.

The fact that Holt had made no real attempt to conceal his guilt was cited as evidence of his insanity, and his love-letters to his victim were read aloud to great effect. But the prisoner's apparent indifference to the proceedings served to reinforce the prosecution's claim that he had committed a callous murder for the sake of money, and the jury found him guilty.

Holt, upon being sentenced to death, was characteristically unperturbed. 'Well, that's over,' he remarked. 'I hope my tea won't be late.'

During the following weeks he continued to show no emotion, and was pleasant to all concerned. On the morning of his execution he greeted the hangman with a friendly nod.

On the night of 15 April 1942, Edward Thomas Lee, a twenty-six-year-old able seaman in the Royal Navy, telephoned the police from a public house in Hill Lane, Southampton, and told them that there was a woman's body on the nearby common. A car was sent and he went out to meet it, but before leading police officers to the place where the dead woman lay he told them that he had killed her. He was immediately cautioned, but later repeated the statement.

The dead woman was Vera Margaret Bicknell, a clerk aged twenty-two with whom Lee had been having an affair for some time, and for whom he had left his wife and child. She had been strangled during a quarrel after telling him that she wanted to end their association, as Lee's wife had refused him a divorce. Lee was charged with her murder and brought to trial at the Hampshire Assizes in July.

He denied having killed her intentionally and, as the victim had suffered from tuberculosis, it was suggested that she had collapsed and died more quickly than a person in better health would have done; it was also stated that Lee had been suffering from a nervous condition as a result of his experiences at sea. The jury was evidently in sympathy with him, for, although the judge had told them that there were no grounds for such a verdict, they found him guilty only of manslaughter.

The judge was taken aback at this, and said that he did not know quite what to say. 'I directed the jury that it was not open to them to find manslaughter,' he continued. 'They have, in defiance of that direction and in falsity to their oaths, found that verdict. It is a verdict that I must accept, although there was no evidence, as I directed them, upon which they could act. They have chosen to do so, and that is all that I can say.'

Then, as a police officer was about to give evidence of Lee's character, Mr Justice Charles turned to the jury, which included three women, and said, 'You can leave the box now. You are not fit to be there!'

He afterwards sentenced the prisoner to fourteen years' penal servitude.

Murder of Helen Priestly, 1934

On the afternoon of 20 April 1934, Helen Priestly, aged eight, who lived on the first floor of a three-storey tenement house in Urquhart Road, Aberdeen, was reported missing. She had arrived home from school for lunch at 12.15 p.m., and was sent out at half-past one to buy a loaf of bread from a co-operative bakery just along the road. But she did not return after being served, and it was quickly discovered that she had not gone back to school, either. Her mother reported her disappearance without delay.

John Priestly, a house painter, and his wife Agnes took turns to drive through the streets in a police car, looking for her, and at the same time a search was carried out in the washhouse and coal sheds of the building in which they lived. But there was no sign of the missing child, and the search continued through the cold, rainy night which followed, with neighbours taking the place of the anxious parents when they became exhausted. Suddenly, at 5 a.m., a sack containing the little girl's body was found behind the stairs on the ground floor of the tenement house. She had apparently been raped and strangled.

The bay in which the body was found contained a lavatory, which had been used regularly during the night,. and it was established that the sack had been placed there after 4.30 a.m. As the sack was completely dry and rain was still falling outside, it seemed likely that one of the other tenants was responsible for the crime. Coal-ash and vomit were found round the child's mouth and cinders were found in her hair; part of the receipt which had been given to her at the bakery was still clutched in her hand. Some hours later a roofer who had been working next door told police that he had heard a child's scream coming from inside the building about 2 p.m. the previous day.

By questioning the inhabitants of the house, the police found one particular couple whose conduct struck them as being odd. Alexander Donald, a barber, and his wife Jeannie lived in a ground-floor apartment with their nine-year-old daughter. Neither of them had taken part in the search for Helen Priestly, and neither appeared to have taken any interest in what was happening in the building — except on the morning on which the body was discovered, when Donald had appeared in his doorway at 6.30, to ask whether there had been any new developments. Even then, on being told that the missing child had been found in a sack, he had gone back into his apartment without another word. Between 4 and 5 o'clock that morning a light had been seen in the Donalds' kitchen.

The Donalds kept themselves to themselves, speaking to their neighbours as little as possible. Jeannie Donald, aged thirty-eight, was a woman with a violent temper, who was known to have struck Helen Priestly on one occasion. Helen had given her a nickname, 'Coconut', which she would call out tauntingly as she went past their door.

When Alexander Donald was asked whether he had heard the commotion which followed the discovery of the body, he replied that he and his wife had heard it while they were lying in bed. Afterwards, he said, his wife had said to him, 'Do you hear? That's Mrs Joss' voice. She's screaming that the child was raped.' This surprised the police officer questioning him, because *he* had been in the hallway at the time and knew that no such thing had been said loudly enough for any of the tenants to hear. The condition of the body was known only to the police doctor, the officer in charge of the case, and himself. He did not comment on this at the time, but bore it in mind.

The autopsy revealed that the child's death had taken place at about 2 p.m., that the injuries which suggested rape had actually been inflicted with a sharp object of some sort while the child was still alive, and that the victim had had an enlarged thymus gland, which would have made her susceptible to fainting.

While Alexander Donald could prove that he had been at work at the time of the murder, his wife was unable to give a satisfactory account of her movements at the same time. Various statements of hers were found to be lies — for example, a claim that the family had no ash-can was contradicted by her daughter — and she was arrested. Forensic tests later showed that Helen Priestly's body had been in the Donalds' apartment.

It was believed that Jeannie Donald, annoyed at being taunted, had rushed out and grabbed her while she was passing the door and that the shock had caused the child to faint. Jeannie Donald, thinking that she had killed her, had then dragged her into the apartment and inflicted the injuries which suggested rape. Finally, she had panicked and strangled the child when she revived and began to scream.

Jeannie Donald was brought to trial in Edinburgh on 16 July 1934, the feeling in Aberdeen being such that she was unlikely to have a fair trial there. She did not give evidence in her own defence, and was convicted of the crime. Her death sentence was afterwards commuted to penal servitude for life, and she was released in 1944.

Body of Mary Moonen discovered, 1955

APRIL
23

On 23 April 1955, Mrs Mary Moonen, twenty-one-year-old wife of a soldier serving in Korea, was found dead in a fashionable district of Minneapolis; she had been left lying on a road after being strangled, though not robbed or sexually assaulted. A post-mortem revealed that she was three months pregnant — for which her husband could not have been responsible — and also that she had had sexual intercourse shortly before her death. However, her relatives and friends all claimed that Mrs Moonen, a Roman Catholic with a nine-month-old daughter, had been a respectable young woman with no interest in extra-marital affairs. They could not believe that she had had a lover in her husband's absence.

The police learnt that on the evening of 22 April, Mrs Moonen had had an appointment with her dentist, Dr Arnold Axilrod — and her sister, who gave them this information, went on to say that she, too, had been one of Dr Axilrod's patients but had found

119

his conduct objectionable. On one occasion, she said, he had given her a pill which left her unconscious for several hours, and had afterwards spoken to her suggestively; on another, he had made advances towards her in his office. It was as a result of this second incident that she had stopped going to see him.

Further information about Dr Axilrod came to light as the investigation continued, the police discovering that many other female patients had lost consciousness for several hours at a time as a result of taking pills which he had given them, and that no nurse was ever present when this happened. One of the women concerned was Mrs Moonen, who had told her doctor that the dentist had raped her while she was unconscious in his surgery, and that he was the father of her unborn child.

Dr Axilrod, a former mayor, was arrested. He said that the pills which he had given to his patients were only used to deaden their reflexes and rarely caused unconsciousness. While admitting that Mrs Moonen had been to see him on the evening of 22 April and that they had quarrelled about her pregnancy, he said that he could not remember whether he had had sexual intercourse with her or not, because he had suffered a blackout. He refused to sign a statement which he was afterwards alleged to have made, confessing that he had murdered her.

He was brought to trial in September 1955, but it was not until 10 October that the court was ready to hear evidence. The newspapers then had a field-day, the dentist being accused of being a philanderer who drugged his victims so that they could not resist him. He denied having killed Mrs Moonen, and said that he had not even been intimate with her; but this was not believed and he was convicted of manslaughter. On 3 November 1955, he was sentenced to five-to-twenty years' imprisonment.

Execution of Colin Ross, 1922

On 24 April 1922, Colin Campbell Ross, a former wine-bar licensee, was hanged at Melbourne Jail for the murder of a twelve-year-old girl found raped and strangled four months previously. He denied to the end that he had had anything to do with the crime, claiming that his conviction was a miscarriage of justice — and many people believed him, including the barrister T.C. Brennan, who published a book about the case later the same year.

The crime had been discovered on the morning of 31 December 1921, when a collector of empty bottles found the body of Alma Tirtschke lying on a drain-grating in Gun Alley, a cul-de-sac 115 yards from the condemned man's premises. The body was naked and had been washed and dried after death, presumably in order to remove clues to the murderer's identity. Detectives concluded that the person responsible had intended pushing it into the drain but failed to do so, perhaps because he had been disturbed.

Ross was among the first people to be interviewed in connection with the crime, but did not seem unduly worried about it, even when it was noticed that his floor had recently been scrubbed. He gave an account of his movements the previous day, saying that at one point he had seen Alma hanging about outside the home of a fortune-teller known as Madame Ghurka but had not spoken to her. He also invited the police officers questioning him to have a look round the bar, which, being unable to get his licence renewed, he was about to close for the last time.

Ross was not suspected at this stage, and the police

made no headway with the case for several days. During that time public feeling became so intense that the Victorian Government offered a reward of £1000 for information leading to the arrest and conviction of the murderer, and a further £250 was offered by a newspaper, the Melbourne *Herald.* But the people who were eventually given shares of these rewards were hardly the most reliable of witnesses.

On 9 January a woman named Ivy Matthews told police that on the afternoon of 30 December she had seen a girl she believed to be Alma — 'a little girl with auburn hair' — looking out of a curtained cubicle inside the wine-bar: a cubicle from which Ross himself had just emerged. She had afterwards challenged him and he had admitted the murder to her, vilifying the child in the process, she claimed.

This Ivy Matthews had worked for Ross as a barmaid until he sacked her a few weeks before the murder, and on 5 January had said that she knew nothing about the crime. In spite of this, she was to become the prosecution's most important witness when Ross appeared for trial.

Another prosecution witness was Sidney John Harding, a criminal with a record which included convictions for wounding, larceny, housebreaking, assault and escaping from custody. Harding was already in jail on remand when Ross was arrested on 12 January, and claimed that eleven days later Ross had told him that he was guilty of the child's murder. Harding also told police that part of this confession had been overheard by a third prisoner named Joseph Dunstan — a claim which Dunstan obligingly corroborated.

A further witness, a young prostitute named Olive Maddox, said that she, too, had seen Alma at the wine-bar on the afternoon in question, and that Ivy Matthews — to whom she had spoken about this — had told her to inform the police.

There were several discrepancies between the two confessions Ross was said to have made — for example, he had given Alma a glass of lemonade according to one of them, and three glasses of wine according to the other. The forensic evidence was also not very impressive, for blankets found in the prisoner's possession — said to have had hairs similar to those of the dead girl attached to them — apparently bore no bloodstains, even though the victim of the crime was known to have bled a good deal. No evidence of bloodstains was found during an examination of the floor of the wine-bar, either.

The trial of Colin Ross began on 20 February and lasted five days, the jury taking twenty-four hours to reach a verdict of guilty. On the morning of his execution, two months later, Ross declared, 'My life has been sworn away by desperate people. If I am hanged, I will be hanged as an innocent man.' Brennan, who was personally involved in the case, afterwards referred scathingly to the character of the chief prosecution witnesses, and claimed that Ross had been made a scapegoat in order to placate a furious public.

Edmund Duff taken ill, 1928

APRIL **26**

On the evening of 26 April 1928, Edmund Creighton Duff, a fifty-nine-year-old retired colonial civil servant living in Croydon, Surrey, went to bed suffering from cramp in his calf muscles and nausea after eating a meal prepared by his wife. When he died the following day food poisoning was suspected, so an inquest was held and parts of his organs were removed for analysis. However, no poison was discovered, and his death was attributed to natural causes.

On 14 February the following year Duff's sister-in-law Vera Sidney, a woman of forty who lived nearby with her widowed mother, suddenly became very ill after having lunch with her mother and an aunt. She appeared to recover — as did her aunt, the cook and the cat, who were also ill — but died in pain two days later. Her death, too, was put down to natural causes.

Then, on 5 March, sixty-nine-year-old Mrs Violet Sidney — Vera's mother — complained about the taste of some medicine prescribed by her doctor. After lunch she was sick, and declared that the medicine had poisoned her. She died a few hours afterwards, and this time food poisoning was accepted as the cause of death.

Mrs Sidney's son Thomas, a married man with children of his own, was not satisfied with this, and an examination of some of his mother's organs was carried out. Although nothing abnormal was discovered, somebody drew the attention of the Home Office to these two latest deaths, and on 22 March the bodies of both Mrs Sidney and her daughter were exhumed.

Post-mortems were carried out by Sir Bernard Spilsbury, and the women's organs were sent to one of the Home Office analysts. The result was that both women were found to have been poisoned with arsenic, a strong solution of which was also found in Mrs Sidney's medicine. Moreover, when Edmund Duff's body was exhumed on 18 May, this, too, was found to contain traces of arsenic. It seems that this was not discovered earlier because organs from another body had been examined by mistake.

Inquests on the three bodies took place over a period of five months. In the case of Mrs Sidney, the coroner's jury decided that there was insufficient evidence to show whether she had committed suicide or been murdered; in those of Vera Sidney and Edmund Duff, verdicts of murder against some person or persons unknown were returned.

Suspicion centred on Grace Duff, Edmund's widow, but there was insufficient evidence to bring a charge against her — or, for that matter, against anyone else — so the case was never officially solved. However, Richard Whittington-Egan, in *The Riddle of Birdhurst Rise* (1975), claims that Grace was indeed the culprit: that she killed her husband because she was in love with a local doctor, and her mother and sister because she stood to gain from their deaths.

Grace Duff died at the age of eighty-seven in 1973.

Discovery of Mary Phagan's body, 1913

APRIL 27

On 27 April 1913, a black nightwatchman employed by the National Pencil Company at its factory in Atlanta, Georgia, found the body of a fourteen-year-old white girl, Mary Phagan, in the basement of the premises: she had been beaten about the head and strangled. Having raised the alarm, the watchman, Newt Lee, was arrested, as notes found by the body — presumed to have been written by the dead girl — suggested that he had killed her himself.

But at the inquest James Conley, another black employee, made statements which amounted to an accusation of murder against Leo Frank, the factory superintendent. He said that Frank had asked him to help carry the body into the basement, and also to write the notes found beside it. Frank, a twenty-nine-year-old American Jew from Brooklyn, was then charged with first-degree murder.

He was brought to trial on 28 July 1913, the case receiving widespread publicity. Conley, the most important of almost 200 prosecution witnesses, repeated his allegations, adding that he had also seen the accused engaged in deviant sexual acts with girls on the factory premises.

It was expected that Frank, who claimed that Conley's allegations were lies, would be acquitted, for no white man had ever been convicted on the testimony of a black. But, to the delight of the noisy crowds outside, he was convicted and sentence of death was passed on him.

Applications for a new trial were made to various courts, including the United States Supreme Court, but all were dismissed. However, in August 1915 the State Governor, with the approval of the trial judge, commuted the sentence to life imprisonment.

This led to bitter press comment and public demonstrations, and before long an armed mob calling themselves the 'Knights of Mary Phagan' broke into the prison where he was being held and abducted him.

They drove him 175 miles to Marietta, where the dead girl had been buried, and hanged him from a tree near the grave. When he was dead the crowds which had gathered began to tear off pieces of his shirt to keep as souvenirs, and photographs of his body were displayed in shops.

Leo Frank, a shy, nervous man, had been convalescing from a knife wound at the time of his abduction. One member of the lynch mob said that the hanging was 'a duty of the state'.

On 29 April 1947, three masked gunmen raided a jeweller's shop in London's West End, leaving a stolen car parked in the crowded street outside. The firm's sixty-year-old director was beaten over the head with a revolver and a bullet was fired into the shop wall when the manager — who was seventy — threw a wooden stool at them instead of handing over the safe keys. But by this time a burglar alarm had been set off, and the three men suddenly fled from the shop empty-handed.

On reaching the stolen car, they found a lorry blocking their way; they therefore had to get out and run for it. As they did so, other people ran for cover or threw themselves onto the ground — some of them screaming — but a passing motor-cyclist, Alec de Antiquis, tried to obstruct the robbers by driving his machine across their path. He was shot in the head and fatally injured.

A moment later a further attempt was made, this time by a Mr Grimshaw, a surveyor. Mr Grimshaw tripped one of the villains up and jumped on him — but then had to let him go when he was kicked in the head and threatened with a gun. The three armed men then disappeared among the crowds.

Alec de Antiquis, the owner of a motor-cycle repair shop, was in his early thirties; he was a married man with six children. As he was lifted into an ambulance he uttered his last words: 'I'm all right. Stop them. I did my best.' He died in hospital not long afterwards.

The police officers investigating the crime made no headway for some days, for no fingerprints were found in the stolen car and widely differing descriptions of the gunmen were given by the many witnesses. But then a taxi-driver reported that on the afternoon in question he had seen two masked men enter an office block near the scene of the crime. The building was searched and a number of discarded items found. These included a raincoat from which the maker's name had been removed and a scarf which had been folded and knotted to make a mask.

A stock ticket under the lining of the raincoat enabled the police to trace it to a shop in Deptford, south-east London, and from the shop's records it was learnt that the raincoat had been sold to a man living in nearby Bermondsey on 30 December previously. The man was seen and, after some prevarication, revealed that the raincoat had been lent to his wife's brother, a twenty-three-year-old former Borstal boy named Charles Henry Jenkins, some weeks before the murder.

Jenkins, who had twice been convicted of assaulting policemen — and whose brother was in jail for manslaughter — was arrested. He refused to answer questions and had to be released when none of the twenty-seven witnesses identified him. But later he and his sister made statements claiming that the raincoat had been lent to a convict on licence named Bill Walsh. In the meantime Jenkins and two associates, Christopher James Geraghty, aged twenty-one, and Terence Peter Rolt, a youth of seventeen, had been placed under observation.

Bill Walsh, aged thirty-seven, was arrested in Plumstead, Kent, a few days later. He denied having borrowed the raincoat or taken part in the crime, but confessed that he had been involved with Geraghty and Jenkins in robbing a different jeweller's, and went on to state that he had personally absconded with all the jewellery stolen on that occasion! This proved to be true, and Walsh was charged accordingly. He was sent to jail for five years.

The murder weapon had already been found in the Thames at Wapping, in east London, and another gun — the one which had been fired in the shop the same afternoon — was discovered in the same area shortly afterwards. But no charges could be made in connection with this crime until Geraghty made a confession which implicated Rolt, and Rolt made another which implicated Jenkins. All three were then formally charged with murder and brought to trial at the Old Bailey on 21 July.

The trial lasted a week and resulted in Jenkins, Geraghty and Rolt all being convicted. Jenkins and Geraghty were both sentenced to death, their executions being carried out at Pentonville Prison on 19 September 1947. Rolt, on account of his youth, was ordered to be detained at His Majesty's pleasure for at least five years, and was not released until June 1956.

The executions caused an outcry, but, according to Sir Harold Scott, the former Metropolitan Police Commissioner, led to the disbanding of the criminal gang to which Jenkins and Geraghty had belonged. Ex-Superintendent Robert Fabian, who headed the investigation, tells us in his memoirs that they also prompted many other criminals to abandon their own guns.

Leonard Moules attacked, 1942

APRIL
30

On 30 April 1942, Leonard Moules, a seventy-one-year-old pawnbroker, was found unconscious in his shop in London's East End after being attacked during the course of a robbery. He was taken to Bethnal Green Hospital, where police officers waited at his bedside in the hope that he would be able to give them information about his assailants. But he died several days later, without regaining consciousness.

The old man had been beaten over the head with a blunt instrument, a single blow being struck from one angle and four more from another. It appeared from the bruising of his neck muscles that he had been held by one of his attackers while the battering took place. There was no sign of the weapon which had been used, and although a palm-print was found on the inside of the victim's safe, it could not be identified, as Scotland Yard had no index of palm-prints at this time.

The police officers concerned had therefore to resort to questioning known criminals in the area, and during the next two weeks over three hundred were seen without any further clue to the identity of the murderers being discovered. Then, on 15 May, a soldier in a Bethnal Green café was overhead remarking that he had seen two men examining a revolver in another café in the same district about the time of the murder.

One of the men was found to be George Silverosa, a twenty-three-year-old machinist, who lived at Pitsea in Essex. Upon being questioned, Silverosa, a former Borstal boy, admitted that he had taken part in the robbery at the pawnbroker's and blamed his accomplice, Sam Dashwood, for the old man's death.

Dashwood had suggested the robbery as they passed the shop on the day in question, and he (Silverosa) had agreed to take part in it on the understanding that no violence would be used, he said. As it was early closing day, the pawnbroker was putting up the shutters, and they waited until he had finished, then followed him into the shop.

'I closed the shop door, and as I turned round I saw the old man falling down,' said Silverosa. 'I didn't see Sam strike him, but I surmised what he had done. I said, "You silly sod, what did you do that for?" He said, "I had to. He was going to blow a whistle." I wiped some blood off the old man's head with my overcoat. I said to Sammy, "Well, we've done the damage, we had better do what we came here to do." We took some rings from the safe and off the table ...'

Sam Dashwood, aged twenty-two, also had a criminal record, and he, too, had been to Borstal. His version of what had happened was different from Silverosa's. 'George went in first,' he said. 'There was a man and a dog there. There was a scuffle, and the dog started barking. I hit the dog between the eyes. George and the old man were scuffling, and the old man went down. The old man then got up again and we both jumped on him to hold him down and he started shouting.'

He explained the violence which had been used by saying, 'I bent over the old boy to shut him up and he put his arms round my neck. I bent over him and hit him on the top of the head with the revolver ...' However, he omitted to mention the number of blows which had been struck.

When Silverosa and Dashwood were brought to trial for murder, they both avoided cross-examination by declining to give evidence. It was argued on Silverosa's behalf that there had been no common design to commit murder and that he had not used violence. But the judge dismissed this point in his summing-up, and the jury accordingly found both prisoners guilty. They were subsequently hanged.

In Pentonville Prison, a few days before the execution, Silverosa obtained permission to burn two letters in the incinerator. While they were burning, he snatched up a poker and attacked the two warders in charge of him, injuring them both. He was eventually overpowered and taken back to the condemned cell.

Disappearance of Louisa Luetgert, 1897

On 1 May 1897, Louisa Luetgert, the wife of a German immigrant, disappeared from her home in Chicago. Nothing was done about if for several days and when the police were finally informed Adolph Luetgert, a forty-nine-year-old sausage-maker with his own factory, was questioned at length. Later, following a search of the factory, he was charged with his wife's murder.

Luetgert, who weighed over seventeen stone, had lived in the United States since the 1870s. He had many mistresses, some of whom would visit him in his office — and for this reason he had had a bed installed there. Moreover, when the police emptied his steam vats they found that the sludge left in one of them contained pieces of human bone, some teeth and two gold rings. The rings were identified by relatives as having belonged to the missing woman.

The police believed that Luetgert had killed his wife, probably with one of the sharp knives used in the factory, and disposed of her body by turning it into sausages. Luetgert denied this, claiming that the rings had *not* belonged to his wife — even though her initials were engraved on one of them — and that the bone fragments were pieces of pig-bone. He maintained that he did not know his wife's whereabouts.

At his trial, which was understandably sensational,

some of Luetgert's mistresses gave evidence against him. The court heard that he had long been tired of his wife — and she of his infidelity — and that on one occasion he had said that he could take her and crush her. Though no weapon could be produced against him, and Luetgert persisted in his denials, he was found guilty of first-degree murder and sentenced to life imprisonment.

He died in the Joliet State Penitentiary in 1911, still claiming to be innocent.

Murder of Shirley Allen, 1957

MAY
4

At 8 a.m. on 4 May 1957, Mrs Doreen Dally, who lived in one of the basement flats of her own house in Bayswater, west London, was awakened by the sound of banging from the flat opposite. This noise was immediately followed by a woman crying out, 'No, Peter! No! Oh, Peter, please!' And this, in turn, was followed by a terrible scream.

Mrs Dally, aged fifty-five, went to the door in her nightdress and looked out into the passage. She saw, to her horror, that twenty-four-year-old Shirley Allen, one of the tenants who lived opposite, was at the door of her flat, with a wound in her head from which blood was streaming. She was evidently trying to leave the flat but being restrained by somebody inside. 'Oh, Mrs Dally, help me, please!' she said softly. 'Peter's gone mad!'

Mrs Dally caught hold of the woman's arm and managed to pull her into the passage. Pushing her into her own flat, she told her to lock the door and went off to telephone for help. As she reached the stairs, however, she heard a sound behind her and looked round.

Ginter Wiora, the thirty-four-year-old Polish art student known as 'Peter', with whom Shirley Allen cohabited, had come out into the passage, holding a Japanese samurai sword. He stared for a moment at the door of Mrs Dally's flat, his hands crossed against his chest, then turned and looked at her. Suddenly he moved towards her, lunging with the sword, and pierced one of her breasts.

The middle-aged landlady ran up the stairs, roused another tenant and telephoned the police. As she did so, she heard more screams from the basement. She then sat down in the other tenant's flat, her night-dress stained with blood. The police arrived shortly afterwards and, on learning what had happened, went down to the basement to investigate.

The door of Mrs Dally's flat stood open, and the dead body of Shirley Allen lay behind it. She had been stabbed in the chest with the sword, and also battered over the head with a standard lamp. Both weapons lay on the floor, the blade of the sword bent and the standard lamp broken. It was the chest-wound which had caused her death.

Wiora, in the meantime, had returned to his own flat, locked the door and attempted to take his own life. When the police broke in, they found him lying on the bed, moaning. He had stabbed himself with another sword, cut his wrists with a bread-knife, and tried to gas himself. It was later discovered that he had been jealous of Shirley Allen's association with other men and had suspected her of posing for pornographic photographs.

On 25 July 1957, Ginter Wiora was brought to trial at the Old Bailey, charged with murder. Pleading diminished responsibility, he was convicted of manslaughter and sentenced to twelve years' imprisonment. The following year he was committed to Broadmoor.

Mummified corpse found in Rhyl, 1960

MAY 5

On 5 May 1960, the mummified corpse of a middle-aged woman wearing a nightdress and dressing-gown was found in a landing cupboard at the home of sixty-five-year-old Mrs Sarah Harvey, a widow living in Rhyl, north Wales. The discovery was made by Mrs Harvey's son Leslie, a taxi-driver, who was redecorating the house while his mother was in hospital. The cupboard was a large fixed one that had been locked for many years, and Mr Harvey had to force it open with a screwdriver. The corpse, which was covered in dust and cobwebs, was rigid and stuck to a piece of linoleum on the cupboard floor.

On being questioned, Mrs Harvey told police that the dead woman was Mrs Frances Knight, a semi-invalid who had died while boarding with her in 1939, and explained the hiding of the body by saying that she had not known what else to do with it. This identification was corroborated by medical evidence, and it was accepted that the body had been mummified naturally as a result of a free circulation of air currents inside the cupboard. But a groove on the left side of the neck, from which a piece of knotted stocking was taken, suggested that the dead woman had been strangled.

Mrs Harvey was therefore charged with murder. But when she appeared for trial at the next assizes in Ruthin, Denbighshire, it was admitted that the cause of death was by no means certain, and the defence claimed that the position in which the body had been found was consistent with death from disseminated sclerosis, from which Mrs Knight was known to have suffered. It was also pointed out that there could have been an innocent explanation of the piece of stocking, as there was an old custom in some parts of the country of tying a stocking or sock round one's neck when one was ill.

The trial was brought to an end on its fifth day, when the Solicitor-General made a submission to the judge that he thought it would be wrong to invite the jury to find the prisoner guilty of murder. The judge concurred and a formal verdict of not guilty was returned. Mrs Harvey was, however, sent to prison for fifteen months for falsely obtaining £2 a week, due to Mrs Knight under a court order, by pretending — for twenty years — that she was still alive.

First of the 'Co-ed' murders, 1972

MAY 7

On 7 May 1972, Edmund Emil Kemper, a twenty-three-year-old labourer of Santa Cruz, California, committed the first of a series of shocking crimes which were later to be called the 'Co-ed Murders'. The victims were Anita Luchese and Mary Ann Pesce, two students at the Fresno State College, Berkeley, who had the misfortune to be out hitchhiking while he was roaming the highways in his car. Kemper stopped to give them a lift, then held them at gunpoint while he drove to a wooded canyon. There he stabbed both girls to death in frenzied attacks, and afterwards violated their bodies before taking them home in the trunk of the car.

Kemper, who was 6 feet 9 inches tall and weighed twenty stone, lived with his mother, whom he hated. She was not at home when he arrived and, putting the corpses into rubbish bags, he carried them up to his room, where he again had intercourse with each of them after cutting off their heads. He then dismembered them and took the pieces out to his car in plastic sacks, his mother — who had returned in the meantime — noticing nothing unusual about his behaviour. Finally, he drove into the nearby mountains, buried the sacks and washed his car with water from a stream.

It was by no means his first offence, for Kemper, whose parents had separated when he was seven, had murdered both of his grandparents on his father's side when he was fifteen. As a result, he had spent the next five years in a hospital for the criminally insane, and had then been sent to live with his mother by the California Youth Authority, into whose care he had been released. Since then he had picked up many female hitch-hikers, mostly college students, and a number of rapes, assaults and disappearances had been reported but not solved. The disappearance of Anita Luchese and Mary Ann Pesce also remained unsolved until Kemper, a year later, revealed what had happened to them.

Four months after their murder, on 14 September 1972, Kemper picked up Aiko Koo, a fifteen-year-old Japanese high school student, and drove her, also at gunpoint, into the mountains. Stopping the car, he put tape over her mouth and, in spite of her fierce resistance, suffocated her by holding two of his fingers up her nostrils. When she was dead he had intercourse with her, then took her body home and cut off her head. He once again had intercourse with the decapitated corpse before dismembering it and burying the pieces in the mountains. Once again, the crime remained undiscovered until he confessed to it.

The next murder was that of Cynthia Schall, who was abducted and shot dead on 8 January 1973. In this case Kemper kept the body overnight in his room, waiting until his mother — a college administrative assistant — had gone to work the following morning before engaging in sexual acts with it and then dissecting it in the shower. This time parts of the body were found and identified, Kemper having thrown them over cliffs in the Carmel area, but police were unable to find the person responsible. His next crime — another double murder — took place only a month later.

Rosalind Thorpe and Alice Lui were both picked up at the local campus on the evening of 5 February 1973, Kemper offering to drive them to a nearby small town where they both lived. While he was driving he suddenly took out a gun and shot them both in the head. He then stopped the car, put both bodies into the trunk and drove to his own home. He was unable to take them up to his room, as his mother was indoors, so he cut off their heads in the trunk and left them there till the morning — when he violated at least one of them in the usual way, and afterwards cut off Alice Lui's hands. The headless corpses were found by hunters in Eden Canyon, Alameda, nine days later, but still nobody suspected Kemper of being the murderer.

On the morning of Easter Sunday, 1973, he killed his mother by hitting her on the head with a hammer, then cut off her head and hid the body. Later the same day he invited a friend of hers named Sarah Hallett to dinner, knocked her unconscious with a

138

brick, then strangled her, cut off her head and had intercourse with the body. The next day he left the house for good, driving off in Mrs Hallett's car and later renting another with money from her handbag.

He now expected to be the subject of a manhunt and when, after a few days, there was no news of one, he telephoned the police in Pueblo, Colorado, and said that he was the 'Co-ed Killer'. To his surprise, they did not believe him, and he had to make several more such calls before he was finally taken into custody. He then made a detailed confession, claiming that he had not given himself up to the police in Santa Cruz for fear that they would 'shoot first and ask questions later'. This confession, which was so revolting that detectives interviewing him were visibly shaken by it, led to Kemper being charged with all eight murders.

Kemper was a sadist who had begun to torture animals when he was ten years old; he was also abnormally shy where women were concerned and could only satisfy himself with one who was either helpless with terror or dead. At his trial in Santa Cruz he was found to be legally sane, but his request to be executed was refused. He was sentenced to life imprisonment, without the possibility of being released on parole.

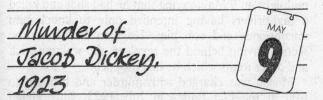

Murder of Jacob Dickey, 1923

On the night of 9 May 1923, Jacob Dickey, a taxi-driver, was shot dead outside his cab in a street in

Brixton, south London. The gunman escaped with a small sum of money from his victim's pocket, but left a number of articles at the scene of the crime, including his revolver and a gold-headed walking-stick. Though these offered no clue to the murderer's identity, the walking-stick was recognized from a published photograph as the property of Edward Vivian, a petty criminal who lived with a prostitute in Pimlico.

On being questioned, Vivian admitted owning the walking-stick, but denied having been involved in the murder. He said that an acquaintance named 'Scottie' Mason had been staying at his flat, and had purchased a revolver, intending to rob a taxi-driver. Vivian then went on to say that he had been suffering from food-poisoning on the evening in question, and that Mason had gone out alone, taking the walking-stick with him.

'Scottie' Mason was found to be a twenty-two-year-old deserter from the Canadian armed forces, whose real name was Alexander Campbell Mason. He was soon arrested, but denied all knowledge of the murder until confronted with evidence of his guilt. He then accused Vivian of it, saying that they had taken the taxi to Brixton together and that Vivian had shot the driver during the course of a struggle.

By this time Vivian had been questioned again and had given further information. He told police officers that Mason had arrived back at his flat about midnight on 9 May, saying that he had shot and killed a taxi-driver, having intended only to knock him unconscious and rob him. He then fled from the scene, leaving behind the revolver, the walking-stick and other items which he had dropped.

Mason was charged with murder and brought to trial at the Old Bailey in July 1923, with Vivian appearing as a prosecution witness. The prisoner was convicted and sentenced to death, but the sentence was afterwards commuted to life imprisonment. He served fourteen years, and died while serving in the Merchant Navy during the Second World War.

Double murder at Aldershot, 1982

MAY
10

On the afternoon of 10 May 1982, two women walking their dogs were savagely murdered by an unknown assailant on a common at Aldershot, in Hampshire. Mrs Margaret Johnson, aged sixty-six, and Mrs Ann Lee, forty-four — both local residents who regularly went out dog-walking together — died within minutes of each other, Mrs Johnson having been stabbed five times and her friend eleven times. Their dogs, a Red Setter and a Labrador, remained with their bodies until they were found by other walkers.

There was no apparent reason for the crime, and the murder weapon was not found during a search of the common. Two anonymous telephone calls were received, the caller on each occasion saying that the murderer was a young man named Peter Fell, who lived in a nearby bedsitter. But Fell was not at home when police went to see him and, on checking with his employers, they were told that he had been at work at the time of the murders. They therefore did not regard him as a suspect.

Even so, when they released a photo-fit picture of a man who had been seen on the common on the afternoon in question, it bore such a strong resemblance to Fell that several of his acquaintances remarked upon it — and Fell went to Aldershot police station to complain that publication of the picture was an act of 'harassment'. But no further notice was taken of him, and in August 1982 he moved to Bournemouth. The crime remained unsolved for almost another year.

Then, one night, the Bournemouth police received eleven anonymous calls, all accusing Peter Fell of being the Aldershot murderer. Now married and about to become a father, Fell was immediately arrested, and the police in Aldershot approached his former employers, asking them to re-check their records. They did so, and said that the information given earlier had not been correct. They could not give Peter Fell an alibi after all.

Moreover, on questioning others who worked for the same firm, the police were told that Fell had arrived late on the afternoon of the crime, and that he had been wearing a suit — which was out of character with him, as he was normally scruffy.

At Farnborough police station, near Aldershot, Fell admitted that he had killed the two women; he said that he had done so because they laughed at him, and because one of them looked like his mother, whom he had hated. He later retracted his confession, but was charged with the two murders just the same.

Peter Fell, a twenty-three-year-old ex-soldier, was brought to trial at Winchester Crown Court in July 1984, the case lasting nineteen days. There was no forensic evidence linking him with the murders, and the prosecution depended a great deal on his tape-recorded confession, which was played in court. It took the jury over twenty-five hours to return a majority verdict of guilty on each count.

The judge, after sentencing the prisoner to life imprisonment for each murder, praised the police officer in charge of the investigation for his zeal and thoroughness. But Fell, who had made all of the thirteen anonymous telephone calls himself, could hardly have been quite as impressed.

Born in Lancashire, Peter Fell had been put into a home at the age of four, when his parents were divorced, and had not seen his mother for the next twelve years. Having joined the army as a boy soldier, he had been medically discharged from the Royal Corps of Transport just two months prior to the murders. At the time of his arrest he was working as a porter in a Brighton hotel.

Death of James Maybrick, 1889

On 11 May 1889, James Maybrick, an English cotton-broker aged fifty, died at his home in the Liverpool suburb of Aigburth, after an illness lasting a fortnight. The circumstances surrounding his death were suspicious and when a post-mortem revealed traces of poison his twenty-six-year-old wife Florence, an American woman, was charged with murder. It was claimed at her trial that her husband had died of natural causes, having frequently taken poisons as medicine. However, she was convicted and sentenced to death.

Besides being over twenty years older than his wife, Maybrick had been a hypochondriac, constantly taking medicines of one sort or another; he had also kept a mistress, as Florence discovered by chance in 1887. For her own part, Florence had entered into a liaison with a young bachelor named Alfred Brierley, with whom she had spent a weekend at a London hotel in March 1889. Shortly afterwards, following a scene at the Grand National, Maybrick had beaten Florence and given her a black eye. He had then made a new will, leaving her nothing.

Maybrick was sick on 27 April, and stayed in bed the next day, complaining of pains in his chest. Having received medical treatment, he was well enough to go to work on 1 May, but two days afterwards took to his bed again, suffering from pains in his legs and vomiting. During the next few days he suffered continually from vomiting and also complained of other symptoms, and though he seemed much better on 7 May, the improvement lasted only a day. Thereafter his condition worsened, and continued to do so until his death.

Living in a mansion, the Maybricks had four servants, including Alice Yapp, a nanny who looked after their two children. On or about 23 April the nanny and a maid saw arsenic-based fly-papers soaking in a basin in the couple's bedroom, and Alice Yapp mentioned this and other suspicious matters to two women who called to see Maybrick on 8 May. The same day, when Florence asked her to post a letter addressed to Alfred Brierley, the nanny found an excuse to open it instead. The letter said that Maybrick was 'sick unto death', and urged Brierley to relieve his mind of 'all fear of discovery', as the invalid was 'perfectly ignorant of everything'.

These matters were reported to Maybrick's two brothers, Edwin and Michael, who were both staying at the house at the time of his death, and because of this Florence was kept in confinement while the place was searched. The search resulted in the discovery of a sealed packet with a label which said, 'Arsenic — Poison' (to which had been added, 'for cats'), together with a number of bottles which all contained traces of arsenic.

Although the body, at a second examination, was found to contain far less than a fatal dose of this poison — and traces of strychnine, hyoscine, prussic acid and morphia were also found — much was made at Florence's trial of her buying and soaking of fly-papers, which she had explained by saying that she used arsenic for cosmetic purposes. This, together with her admission that she had committed adultery, served to convince the jury that she was guilty, especially after the judge had summed up against her.

Florence Maybrick's death sentence was commuted to life imprisonment, and she was released in 1904, afterwards publishing a book about her experiences, entitled *My Fifteen Lost Years*. She died in Connecticut, at the age of seventy-eight, on 23 October 1941.

Body of John Whyte discovered, 1966

MAY 16

On 16 May 1966, the body of John Whyte, a forty-two-year-old former seaman with a record of house-breaking and theft, was found in a ditch near Nantwich, in Cheshire. He had been shot in the head and chest — though apparently not at the place where the body was discovered — and had been dead for at least three days. The Cheshire police, suspecting that he had been the victim of a gang-killing, asked Scotland Yard's help in tracing his movements during the previous few weeks.

John Whyte, a divorcee, was found to have been living for some time in hostels and lodging-houses. He had been in London at the end of March, and had hired a Morris 1100 car from a firm in Shepherd's

Bush. It was also learnt from a woman friend of his in Birkenhead — his home town — that he had said he was 'in trouble', but without explaining what he meant by this. The woman thought he had probably done something underhand.

As the investigation continued the police began to receive reports about the Morris 1100. On the evening of 3 May it had been seen parked without lights in Charing Cross, and during the following week it was seen at a caravan site in Skegness, where a man and a woman spent two hours cleaning its interior. Then, on 6 June, a woman was seen driving it near Doncaster — and finally, on 8 June, it was found burning on a piece of waste ground in south London. When bloodstains were discovered inside it the police were certain that it had been set on fire deliberately.

The couple who had been seen at the caravan site were identified as William John Clarke, aged forty-seven, and Nancy Patricia Hughes, forty, both of whom had recently finished serving eighteen-month prison sentences imposed for post office frauds. Clarke had a long record and had once been sent to Broadmoor after slashing a fellow prisoner with a broken bottle. He had spent only two of his last twenty-four years as a free man.

Clarke and Hughes, who lived together as man and wife, were traced to a hotel in Paddington, where evidence of further frauds was discovered. It was found that they had been involved with John Whyte in drawing money from post offices in various parts of the country by forging signatures on forms relating to stolen savings books. They were therefore taken into custody.

The police obtained no information from them about the death of John Whyte, Clarke suggesting that he could not tell them anything without putting his own life at risk. They were afterwards brought to trial in connection with the recent frauds and once again sent to prison. Clarke, on this occasion, was given ten years — reduced to seven on appeal — and Hughes two years.

But in the meantime the inquiries into Whyte's death went on, and the police learnt of a visit which Clarke and Hughes had made to a house in Morley, near Leeds, about a month before the crime had taken place. Clarke, during the course of this visit, had produced a gun and fired a bullet into the ceiling, from which it was now recovered by detectives. The bullet was found to have been fired from the same gun as those taken from John Whyte's body, and its discovery led to Clarke being charged with murder. It was believed that he had killed Whyte following a quarrel over the proceeds of their other crimes.

Clarke and Hughes were tried together at the Chester Assizes in November 1967. Clarke was convicted of murder and sentenced to life imprisonment; Hughes was sent to jail for three years for being an accessory after the fact. The jury's verdict in Clarke's case had been reached by a majority of ten to two.

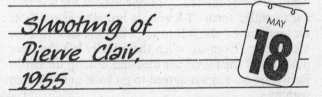

Shooting of Pierre Clair, 1955

At 8 o'clock in the morning on 18 May 1955, Pierre Clair, an accountant aged thirty-five, was approached by his former mistress as he left his hotel in the Latin Quarter of Paris to go to work. Simone Soursas, who was forty-two years old and seven months pregnant, had been waiting in the street to see him. But when

147

she tried to speak to him he said brusquely, 'It's all over. Leave me alone!' Simone then drew an automatic pistol from under her coat and shot him four times, as a result of which Pierre Clair fell to the ground and died, begging her forgiveness.

The couple had known each other for three years, having met in a cinema one night while Simone, the wife of a radio mechanic working in the Sudan, was waiting to join her husband. Both were ugly, he having the additional misfortune of being timid and helpless while she had that of believing herself to be stupid. As soon as they became lovers she changed her mind about joining her husband and wrote to tell him that their marriage was at an end.

Richard Soursas returned to Paris as soon as he received the letter, his calmness and consideration convincing Simone that she had behaved ridiculously; she therefore went to the Sudan after all. But Pierre wrote to her frequently, flattering and cajoling her, and she, finding her new life dull, soon left her husband and rejoined Pierre in Paris. This time they went to the Côte d'Azur, where they lived together as cheaply as possible for the next two months.

Their affair had been a violent one from the beginning, for Pierre often beat her. But while the beatings were followed by reconciliations she was willing to suffer them. 'I loved his brutality as much as his tenderness,' she was to say when she was tried for his murder. Even so, when they finally left the Côte d'Azur and she found her husband waiting for her in Paris, she once again agreed to go back to the Sudan with him.

Pierre's perversity then took a new turn. Finding himself a younger and prettier mistress, he wrote to Simone, saying that he intended to commit suicide. 'I am completely possessed by a burning passion for you and I have reached the point of total despair for which there is no remedy but you,' he said. Within

148

hours of receiving it she boarded a plane to Paris. But this time, though he agreed to resume the affair, he was less eager to be with her than before; the beatings became more frequent, the reconciliations less so. And, as luck would have it, she now found that she was pregnant.

Thereafter he behaved insufferably towards her. He taunted her over her ugliness, calling her his 'poor old woman', and made it clear that he no longer wanted her at all. During her seventh month of pregnancy, when she was suffering from low blood pressure, he gave her his jacket to repair, leaving a photograph of his other mistress in one of the pockets. Its discovery threw Simone into a state of utter despondency.

She bought the gun — or so she afterwards claimed — with the intention of taking her own life, but decided to go and see him again before doing so. It was then that the encounter which resulted in Pierre's death took place.

When Simone Soursas was brought to trial, the case for the prosecution was presented with more restraint than it might otherwise have been, the Advocate General conceding that the accused was 'worthy of commiseration'. She was found guilty only of manslaughter with extenuating circumstances and given a suspended sentence of five years' imprisonment. She was therefore set free.

While in jail she had given birth to her child — a little girl who was surprisingly pretty. The child was given to her as she left the court.

149

Body of Christopher Sabey discovered, 1968

On the morning of 20 May 1968, Christopher Sabey, the eight-year-old son of a publican, was found strangled near a disused gravel pit 200 yards from his home in the village of Buckden, in Huntingdonshire. He had left his home by bicycle early the previous afternoon, and his sister had begun to make inquiries about him when he was not back by 8.30 p.m. Later, during a search organized by the village policeman, his bicycle was found on a local building site, leaning against a pile of bricks.

Christopher had evidently been killed as he lay on the ground, his attacker kneeling on him and gripping his throat with both hands. As his body was fully dressed — apart from one shoe, which was found nearby — there was no apparent motive for the crime. The police also had difficulty obtaining information about his movements, as almost all of the village's inhabitants had been watching the F.A. Cup Final on television on the afternoon of 19 May, when the crime was committed.

However, they soon found a suspect: a youth of nineteen named Richard Nilsson, who lived in the village and worked as a labourer on the building site where the dead boy's bicycle had been found.

Nilsson, together with others employed on the site, had been interviewed on 20 May, when it was noticed that he was sweating and kept swallowing hard. It was afterwards found that he had been officially cautioned for indecent assaults on small boys and also that he had tried to strangle another boy some months earlier. He was therefore questioned again and proved unable to account for his movements on the afternoon of the 19th satisfactorily. But the police had no evidence against him and so were obliged to let him go.

Later, after he had been questioned several more times, and had changed his story repeatedly, dog hairs found on his clothes — from his own golden Labrador — and others found on Christopher Sabey's jersey were sent to the Home Office Central Research Establishment at Aldermaston to be analyzed by the new method of neutron activation. They were found to have similar trace-element characteristics.

As this was not, in itself, considered strong enough evidence to secure a conviction, detectives began collecting samples of hair from all other dogs in the village which appeared to be the same colour. Of the 144 samples thus obtained, ninety were discarded after microscopic examination and the other fifty-four, which were similar in structure as well as colour, were sent to Aldermaston for analysis. The tests proved that the hairs found on the dead boy could have come from only three dogs in the village, one of them being Nilsson's.

Nilsson had already admitted having seen Christopher on the day of the murder, saying that they had been at the building site together until 1.45 p.m. On being told the results of the tests, he said that the boy had taken some cigarettes from his pocket, suggesting that that explained the hairs on his clothes.

Certain now that Nilsson was the murderer, the police renewed their inquiries among the villagers, and this time found a witness who had seen him with the victim later than he had admitted on the afternoon in question. Mrs Colleen Harries remembered looking out of her window shortly after 4.30 p.m. and seeing Nilsson riding his moped with Christopher following on his bicycle. She later saw Nilsson walking alone near the building site.

On being questioned further on 17 July, Nilsson said that he had been on the site with Christopher between 4.30 p.m. and 5.15 p.m., and had then left him there. Though this was yet another change in his story, he persisted in denying that he was the culprit the police were seeking. He was charged with the murder.

At his trial at the Nottingham Assizes he pleaded not guilty. 'I had nothing to do with Christopher Sabey,' he told the court. 'I did not kill him. I had nothing to do with his death at all.' But the jury decided otherwise and he was sentenced to life imprisonment.

Murder of Walter Dinnivan, 1939

On the night of 21 May 1939, Walter Dinnivan, a retired garage proprietor, was found unconscious and bleeding in his ground-floor flat on the outskirts of Poole, in Dorset. He had been savagely battered and was suffering from multiple head wounds and a fractured skull; his attacker had also attempted to strangle him. The discovery was made when his granddaughter — who lived in the same flat — arrived home with her brother, with whom she had been to a dance. The old man was taken off to hospital, where he died from his injuries the following morning.

In the room in which the crime had been committed the police found a beer bottle — with beer in it — a tumbler and a whisky-glass, all lying on their sides on an occasional table. A woman's hair-curler, made in France, and a bloodstained brown paper bag, folded diagonally, lay on the floor nearby. And four cigarette ends were found: one on the tablecloth, two underneath the table and one on a settee cushion.

It seemed obvious that the person responsible had been drinking with Mr Dinnivan prior to the attack, and Joseph Williams, who lived about ten minutes' walk from the scene of the crime and had known the dead man for some forty years, was soon suspected. Williams, who lived in one room, was in serious financial difficulties; he had visited Mr Dinnivan frequently, and admitted to having borrowed £5 from him a few days before the murder.

Some brown paper bags similar to the one left at the scene were found in Williams' room; his right thumb-print was found on the tumbler, and his saliva was found to be of the same group as that on the four cigarette ends. Moreover, his wife was known to have had a hair-curler of the type which had been found in Mr Dinnivan's flat. Joseph Williams was accordingly brought to trial in Dorchester in October 1939.

Surprisingly, he was acquitted, and left the court a free man. But a few hours afterwards he told Norman Rae, the well-known crime reporter, 'The jury were wrong. I did it, so now I claim to be the second John Lee of Babbacombe, the man they couldn't hang.' He then insisted on returning to Poole the same night, in order to parade himself in the town where he was well known.

By the early hours of the morning, however, his nerves were in a bad state. Norman Rae, who had retired for the night, was woken up by Williams banging on his bedroom door. 'I have got to tell someone,' he sobbed over and over again. 'The jury were wrong. It was me!'

He was almost certainly telling the truth, but there was nothing that could be done about it. Having already stood trial for his life and been acquitted, he could not, under English law, be tried again for the same crime. Joseph Williams therefore remained free until his death in March 1951. The story of his confession was then published in the *News of the World.*

Death of Martin Brown, 1968

MAY 25

On 25 May 1968, the body of Martin Brown, aged four, was found in a derelict house in a slum area of Newcastle. It appeared that he had died as a result of swallowing pills from a bottle found at the scene, but on 27 May, police investigating a case of vandalism at a nearby nursery school found four scribbled notes in a child's handwriting, one of them referring to the 'murder' of Martin Brown.

Two months later Brian Howe, aged three, was found strangled on a piece of waste ground in the same area, his stomach marked with small cuts and his legs with puncture marks. The pathologist who examined his body said that little force had been needed to kill him and that the person responsible could have been another child.

The police therefore asked 1200 children in the district to fill in questionnaires about what they had done on the day of Brian Howe's murder, and interviewed those who gave evasive or unclear answers. Among the children interviewed were two girls, Norma Bell, aged thirteen, and Mary Bell, eleven, who were not related to each other but were close friends. These were questioned a number of times, changed their statements twice, and gave the impression of knowing more about the crime than they cared to admit.

Mary Bell, the more assertive of the two, was an intelligent child, but a liar and an exhibitionist. At one point, she claimed to have seen Brian in the company of an older boy, and said that she saw this boy hitting him; she also said that the boy in question had had a pair of scissors with a broken blade. This detail was to place Mary strongly under suspicion when the boy she named was found to have been elsewhere, for — unbeknown to the public — a pair of scissors with a broken blade had been found at the scene of the crime.

Norma Bell then made a statement accusing Mary of having attacked the boy in her own presence, pushing him to the ground and struggling violently with him. She denied having taken part in the crime herself, saying that she had run away when Mary asked her to help. Later, she said, they went back to the waste ground together, and Mary marked the boy's body with the scissors and a razor. Mary, however, said that the statement was a lie and that it was Norma who had killed Brian.

The two girls were both arrested, and charged with murdering Martin Brown as well as Brian Howe. At their trial, which began at the Newcastle Assizes on 5 December 1968, Norma was overawed by the proceedings but Mary remained calm and self-possessed throughout. Norma was acquitted and Mary — who was said to be suffering from an abnormality of mind 'such as substantially impaired her mental responsibility for her acts and omissions in doing or being a party to this killing' — was convicted of manslaughter on both counts.

Sentenced to detention for life, Mary Bell was sent to a special unit of an approved school, as no mental hospital would accept her. In 1970 her house-master in this institution was brought to trial, accused of indecently assaulting her, but was acquitted when the evidence against him was found to have been fabricated. Then, in September 1977, she absconded from an open prison, in the company of another inmate, and was recaptured three days later.

She was released in 1980.

Suspicious illness of Mrs Amy Clements, 1947

On the evening of 26 May 1947, Mrs Amy Clements, the wife of a doctor living in Southport, Lancashire, was admitted to the Astley Bank Nursing Home, her husband having told a local colleague by telephone that she was dying of a cerebral tumour. When she arrived there, already in a coma, she was examined by the superintendent, Dr Andrew Brown, who formed the opinion that she was suffering from morphine poisoning. She died the following morning, without regaining consciousness.

A post-mortem was carried out on Dr Brown's instructions by Dr James Houston, a young pathologist at the Southport Infirmary. Houston found no evidence of a cerebral tumour, nor did he notice any signs of morphine poisoning. His report stated that Mrs Clements had died of myeloid leukaemia, and he made out her death certificate to that effect. But Brown refused to accept this finding and informed the area coroner of his dissatisfaction.

Police inquiries followed and Mrs Clements' funeral was postponed at the last minute — after mourners had gathered at the church — so that a second post-mortem could be performed. The dead woman's husband, Dr Robert Clements, was now suspected of having murdered her.

Clements, a sixty-seven-year-old Irishman and a Fellow of the Royal College of Surgeons, had been married four times and each of his first three wives had also died. In the case of the third Mrs Clements, who died in 1939, the cause of death had been given as tuberculosis, but a woman doctor — a friend of the deceased — was suspicious of this and gave information to the Chief Constable of Southport which led to a post-mortem being ordered. But by the time the order was made the body had been cremated, so nothing more could be done.

Amy Clements had, like two of her predecessors, been a wealthy woman whose money had enabled her husband to live extravagantly. The police learnt that for several weeks her skin had been gradually turning yellow and that she had frequently lapsed into unconsciousness, with her husband apparently knowing when this was about to occur. They found, too, that Clements had had his telephone disconnected, thus preventing his wife keeping in contact with her friends. He had also been writing prescriptions for morphine sulphate tablets for patients who never received them and did not know that they had been prescribed.

After the postponement of the funeral, Clements was found unconscious in the kitchen of his flat, with a note which said: 'To whom it may concern — I can no longer tolerate this diabolical insult to me.' He died a few hours later, his death having been caused by an injection of morphine.

The second post-mortem on his wife revealed that she had also died of morphine poisoning, as Dr Brown had suspected.

Appalled at his own mistake, Dr James Houston took his own life on 2 June, with a massive dose of sodium cyanide. He left a note saying, 'I have for some time been aware that I have been making mistakes. I have not profited by my experience. I was convinced that Mrs Clements died of leukaemia, and accordingly destroyed the vital organs after completing my autopsy.' The destruction of the organs in question had made the second post-mortem an extremely difficult task to perform.

A coroner's inquest found that Mrs Clements had been murdered by her husband. The police suspected that Clements had murdered each of his other wives as well. However, they decided not to investigate these cases in view of the fact that he, too, was now dead.

Murder of Agnes Walsh, 1950

MAY 27

On the morning of 27 May 1950, the body of a naked woman was found in a boarding-house in Sussex Gardens, Paddington. She had been punched six times in the face during the course of a fierce struggle — two of her injuries suggesting that her attacker had worn a ring — and had also had a handkerchief thrust into her mouth and pressed against the back of her throat. Afterwards, when she was already dead, one of her own stockings had been tied round her neck, so that it appeared at first that she had died from strangulation. The discovery was made about 10 a.m., when the rooms were being cleaned — by which time the woman had been dead for several hours.

The body was found to be that of Agnes Walsh, a known prostitute aged twenty-two, who had frequented the Piccadilly area in search of clients. She had arrived at the boarding-house the previous evening with a young man, who had entered their names in the visitors' register as 'Mr and Mrs Davidson' and given an indecipherable address in County Durham — though even this was only made out later, when the entry was subjected to close scrutiny. Her underclothes were neatly folded on a chair — showing that she had removed them herself — and although certain valuables were missing, the contents of her handbag had not been touched.

Margaret Walsh, the dead woman's sister — who was also a prostitute — told the police that she had seen Agnes in Piccadilly the previous evening, speaking to a man who was a stranger to her. She was unable to give a good description of this man, and inquiries among other prostitutes who had been in the area at the time revealed only that he had been a sad-faced, softly-spoken man with an accent. However, these details were circulated to all the main police stations in London, and printed in the *Police Gazette*, together with a sketch of a cocktail watch on a snake bracelet known to have been stolen from the dead woman. At the same time the police in County Durham were asked to make inquiries about a man named Davidson.

No further information was obtained for some days, and a search for the wanted man in London proved unavailing. But suddenly the police in Houghton-le-Spring, County Durham, sent news of the disappearance of a local man named Donald Davidson, aged twenty-nine, who had driven off in his sports car that morning, wearing bakers' clothes and a sports jacket, and had not been seen since. His departure had followed the publication of newspaper reports the same morning, stating that Scotland Yard officers were making inquiries in Durham about the murderer of Agnes Walsh.

Davidson's description was circulated to the police in neighbouring counties, but a few hours later he was found dead near Finchley Priory, just a few miles from his home. He had shot himself.

It was later learnt that Davidson and a friend had arrived in London on 25 May, while on a fortnight's motoring holiday, and had booked into a hotel in Euston. The following evening Davidson had gone out alone, returning on the morning of the 27th with his face and hands badly scratched. He explained his injuries to his friend by saying that he had been involved in a drunken brawl.

He remained in the hotel that day — though he had previously intended to go to Epsom for the Derby — but sent out several times for newspapers, claiming that he was interested in the horse-racing news. Later the two friends left London to return home, Davidson insisting that they should drive through the night.

Davidson was generally a quiet man who rarely drank, but was known to have a quick temper. It was assumed by the police that on the night in question Agnes Walsh had given offence to him in some way and that he had attacked her while he was drunk, and stolen some of her possessions to make it appear that robbery had been the motive for the crime. Then, having returned home, he had worked in his parents' bakery for a few days until his fear of arrest became so intense that he decided to take his own life.

On the day of his death he drove to an empty caravan at Finchley Priory, where he attempted to gas himself with the use of the stove but succeeded only in causing an explosion, as the gas was not poisonous. Blown out through the doorway into a field, he found himself badly burnt and bleeding, and it was only after falling into some bushes as he staggered about that he finally shot himself.

At the inquest on the body of Agnes Walsh a senior police officer, on being asked what he would have done if he had found Davidson alive, replied, 'I would have apprehended him and brought him back to London on a charge of murder.' But this was not proof that Davidson had killed her, and the jury returned a verdict of murder by some person or persons unknown.

Murder of Gladys Hosking, 1942

MAY 28

On 28 May 1942, an Australian woman, Gladys Hosking, was found strangled in a street in Melbourne. There was no obvious motive for the murder, which was the third such crime in Melbourne that month. But when a serviceman who had been on sentry duty at a US army camp heard the news, he provided police with information which led to the arrest of the person responsible.

The soldier, an Australian, reported that on the night in question he had challenged a GI arriving back there in an untidy state. The GI, who was out of breath and wearing a dirty uniform, was only allowed to enter the camp after explaining that he had fallen down in a nearby park, said the sentry. His report led to all US troops in the camp being called out on parade, so that he could identify the GI concerned.

The GI was found to be Edward Joseph Leonski, a Texan, whose tent-mate gave police further information about him. Leonski, said the tent-mate, had lately become very emotional on occasions, and had told him, 'I'm a Dr Jekyll and Mr Hyde! I killed! I killed!' He was also known to have been keeping newspaper reports about the Melbourne murders.

Leonski was taken into custody and confessed that he had killed all three women, saying that he had done so because he wanted 'to get their voices'. In one case — that of the second woman, Pauline Thompson — he said that his victim had sung to him as they walked through the streets together, her voice so sweet and soft that he could feel himself 'going mad about it'. It was found that there was a history of mental instability in his family.

Edward Leonski was tried by court-martial, a defence of insanity being made on his behalf. Despite the ludicrous reason which he had given for his crimes, he was convicted and sentenced to death, the newspapers which had earlier compared the murders with those of 'Jack the Ripper' now calling him 'the Singing Strangler'. He was hanged at Pentridge Jail on 9 November 1942.

Barbara Songhurst found murdered, 1953

JUNE 1

On the morning of 1 June 1953, Barbara Songhurst, aged sixteen, of Teddington in Middlesex, was found dead in the River Thames near Richmond, Surrey; she had been battered over the head, stabbed and then raped before being thrown into the water. The discovery led to fears that eighteen-year-old Christine Reed (who, like Barbara, had been missing since the previous afternoon, when they had gone out cycling together) had also been murdered, and these fears which were confirmed when Christine's body was found in the same river at Richmond five days later. She, too, had been raped after being murdered in a similar manner.

It was learnt that on the evening of 31 May the two girls had been in the company of three youths who were camping on the river bank, and that they had been attacked shortly after leaving to cycle home. Other people camping on the bank reported hearing screams about 11 p.m., and one witness claimed to have seen a man riding a woman's bicycle along the towpath about 11.20 p.m. But no clue to the man's identity was discovered until several weeks later, when Alfred Charles Whiteway, a twenty-two-year-old building labourer, came to the attention of the police officers conducting the investigation.

Whiteway was a married man who, because of housing difficulties, had been living with his parents at Teddington while his wife stayed with hers at Kingston in Surrey. He had a criminal record for theft and was already in custody for attacking a woman and a girl on Oxshott Heath, not far from Kingston. It was for this reason that he was questioned in connection with the murders.

He denied being the person responsible, saying that he had been with his wife on the evening in question, but admitted that he had known Barbara Songhurst, as she had once lived near him in Sydney Road, Teddington. Some weeks afterwards, while being questioned at New Scotland Yard, he confessed that he had killed the two girls — only to deny the offences when he was formally charged on 20 August.

At the time of his arrest Whiteway had had an axe in his possession, but this was not realized, and he managed to conceal it under the seat of a patrol car in which he was being taken to Kingston police station. A constable cleaning the vehicle the following day found the axe, took it home and chopped wood with it, unaware of its importance until a month later. It was then found to match head injuries which the two murdered teenagers had received.

Whiteway was brought to trial at the Old Bailey in October 1953, charged with the murder of Barbara Songhurst. The axe was produced in evidence against him, his fifteen-year-old sister telling the court that it was similar to one that was missing from their home. The prosecution also produced a knife, which the prisoner — whose hobby was knife-throwing — had allegedly confessed to using during the course of the crime, together with a bloodstained shoe which he had been wearing that evening.

Though he denied having confessed to the murders, claiming that his statement had been fabricated by the police, Whiteway was found guilty and sentenced to death. He was hanged at Wandsworth Prison on 22 December 1953.

Three executed at San Quentin, 1955

JUNE
3

On 3 June 1955, Barbara Graham, a thirty-two-year-old murderess, and two male accomplices were executed in the gas chamber of San Quentin Prison, California, for the murder of an elderly woman in Burbank two years previously. The executions received much publicity, and a controversial film based loosely on Barbara Graham's life story — *I Want to Live*, starring Susan Hayward — was released a few months afterwards. This gave the impression that she was innocent of the crime for which she had been sentenced, which was not the case at all.

The crime had been committed on 9 March 1953, when Barbara Graham, her two fellow-condemned, John Albert Santo and Emmett Perkins, together with a third man named John True, forced their way into the home of sixty-two-year-old Mrs Mabel Monahan, a former vaudeville star whom they beat savagely in an attempt to discover the whereabouts of a large sum of money rumoured to be hidden there. When this got them nowhere — for there was no truth in the rumour — they ransacked the house, then killed their victim in cold blood before leaving empty-handed.

A fourth accomplice, Baxter Shorter, had at first kept watch for them outside, but fled on realizing what had happened to Mrs Monahan. He later agreed to testify against the others, but was abducted at gunpoint and killed before any charges could be brought against them. His body was never found.

Barbara Graham was an occasional prostitute and a drug-taker who already had a record for various offences; she had been married four times, each of the first three marriages ending in divorce. Though it was her involvement which attracted most of the publicity to the case, she had only been asked to take part because the others needed a woman to induce Mrs Monahan to open her door. But she did so without any qualms, and was as violent as the rest of them.

As Shorter could not be produced to give evidence against the others, Barbara was given an opportunity to do so, but scornfully refused. She was later tricked by a police officer into agreeing to pay for an alibi: a fact revealed with devastating effect during the course of the trial. In the meantime, John True, a deep-sea diver, was given the chance to appear as a prosecution witness — and he agreed to do so.

165

The three defendants were convicted and sentenced to death in September 1953. Santo and Perkins were afterwards convicted of the murder of a gold-mine proprietor in December 1951, and also of the murders of a supermarket owner and three of his children in October 1952.

Shortly before her death Barbara Graham confessed her guilt to the warden of San Quentin, but this was not made known to the public until several years later.

Baxter Shorter was declared legally dead in 1960, seven years after his disappearance.

Body of Albert Greenfield discovered, 1961

JUNE 4

On 4 June 1961, the body of Albert Reginald Greenfield, a blacksmith aged forty-one, was found under an old shed standing alongside the Domain Baths in Sydney; he had been stabbed over thirty times and his genitals had been hacked off in a frenzied attack during the course of the previous night. The gruesome nature of the mutilation led police officers to believe that the crime had been inspired by jealousy, and that the culprit would prove to be an outraged husband or lover. They did not anticipate difficulty in bringing him to justice.

However, they made no headway with the investigation, and the case was still unsolved on 21 November, when a second corpse, similarly mutilated and with many stab wounds, was found in a public lavatory in Moore Park. The victim this time was

Ernest William Cobbin, also aged forty-one, a married man with two children who had been living apart from his family. This second murder was clearly the work of the person who had killed Greenfield, so police officers had to abandon their original theory. This time, they decided that the killer was 'a psychopath homosexual . . . killing to satisfy some twisted urge'.

But still they failed to identify him, and on 31 March the following year Frank Gladstone McLean, a war pensioner with a number of convictions for minor offences, was found lying in the gutter in Little Bourke Street, in the suburb of Darlinghurst. He had been stabbed in the neck a number of times and mutilated, and was in too bad a state to give any information about his attacker before he died. The couple who found him told the police that their baby had been crying as they arrived at the scene, and that they thought this may have warned the killer of their approach.

These 'Mutilator Murders' were by now causing much concern. As the police were still unable to catch the person responsible, the Government, which had earlier offered a reward of £1000, now offered £5000 for information leading to his arrest. But this was likewise to no avail, and it was not until May 1963 that he was finally arrested. Even then, it was only after an extraordinary sequence of events.

In November 1962 a man was found dead under a shop in Burwood Road, in the suburb of Concord. The body, which was badly decomposed, was identified as that of Alan Edward Brennan, an employee of the postal service in Alexandria, south Sydney, where he had given the shop address as his own, and it was under that name that it was buried, in spite of misgivings on the part of the coroner. But in April 1963 another post office employee reported seeing Brennan alive, and a belated examination of clothes found beside the body was carried out. This resulted in the discovery of prison markings, showing that they had been issued to Patrick Joseph Hackett, a man who had served a short sentence in October 1962 for using indecent language.

Further reports were received, confirming that Brennan was still alive, and it was now accepted that the dead man was Hackett. But a garage owner whose business was next door to the place where the body had been found said that he had seen Brennan inside the shop with another man on the evening before his disappearance. The following day there had been a notice in the shop, saying that the owner had cut his hand and would be away for three weeks.

After an extensive search the missing man was found in Melbourne, where he was working as a railway porter. On being arrested, he said that his real name was William MacDonald, and that he was an English immigrant, aged thirty-nine. He agreed to return to Sydney to stand trial, rather than face extradition proceedings, and was charged with all four murders. When he appeared for trial the Crown proceeded with the charge of murdering Patrick Hackett on 3 November 1962.

MacDonald admitted that he had killed Hackett, saying that he had met him while under the influence of drink and feeling a compulsive urge to kill. In the opinion of three psychiatrists, he was a paranoid schizophrenic, but the jury rejected their evidence and found him guilty of murder. Sentenced to life imprisonment, he was later transferred to the Morisset Hospital for the Criminally Insane.

Two police officers shot dead, 1961

JUNE 6

On 6 June 1961 a man went to West Ham police station in London with a loaded pistol in his pocket after hearing that his wife had made a complaint about him. John Hall arrived in a sports car and gave a general impression of being well-off. He was seen by Inspector Philip Pawsey and Sergeant George Hutchins, who informed him that a warrant had been issued for his arrest on a charge of causing grievous bodily harm.

Hall, however, had no intention of being arrested, and when an attempt was made to search him he pulled out the pistol and forced the police officers to keep their distance while he moved towards the door. He fled from the building with Pawsey, Hutchins and PC Charles Cox in pursuit, and soon began firing at them. The inspector and the sergeant were both killed, and PC Cox was seriously injured.

The chase was taken up by other officers, some of whom had police dogs with them. Even so, it lasted for eight hours, with further shots being fired — though there were no more casualties — before the culprit finally took refuge in a telephone kiosk three miles away. He then turned the gun on himself and fired, wounding himself fatally; he died in hospital eight days later.

John Hall was a man of no settled occupation; he had been a lorry-driver, a mechanic, a commercial traveller, a book-keeper and the proprietor of a pet-shop. He was keen on activities such as surf-riding, speedboat-racing and flying, as well as pistol-shooting.

He had been married — for the second time — less

than two months earlier, his first marriage having been dissolved two years previously.

Second life sentence for Kiernan Kelly, 1984

JUNE
7

On 7 June 1984, a fifty-four-year-old Irish tramp who told police that he had killed nine people in thirty years, was sentenced to life imprisonment at the Old Bailey for the second time in a fortnight. Kiernan Kelly, an alcoholic, had been convicted of manslaughter, having killed a fellow vagrant in a police cell in Clapham, south-west London, the previous August. He was said by a psychiatrist to be 'incorrigible in penal terms and incurable in medical terms' — a description which the trial judge said was 'plainly right'. His earlier life sentence had been for the murder of a drinking companion — a crime committed in 1975.

Kelly, who had been living rough in England since his arrival from the Irish Republic in 1953, had forty-one convictions for drink-related offences. In 1977 he was charged with killing another tramp in Kennington Park, south London, but when he appeared for trial the jury acquitted him. Then, in the summer of 1983, he was charged with attempted murder, after allegedly trying to push yet another tramp under an underground train. This time the jury could not agree, so a re-trial was ordered — and Kelly was again acquitted. The crime in the police cell took place not long afterwards.

The victim was fifty-five-year-old William Boyd,

who was sharing the cell with another man when Kelly was locked in with them. Kelly, who had been arrested for drunkenness and robbery, became incensed when Boyd began shouting and swearing during the course of the night and, making a ligature with his socks and shoelaces, used it to strangle him. The crime was followed by his confession that he had killed nine people, one of them being Hector Fisher, a sixty-seven-year-old retired printer who had been stabbed to death in a Clapham churchyard eight years previously.

The information contained in Kelly's fifty-two-page statement was not very detailed, and police suspected him of exaggerating the number of people he had killed. But after investigating the matter they were satisfied that he had killed at least five times, and in the case of Hector Fisher they felt justified in charging him with murder. It was for this offence that he was given his first life sentence, the judge telling Kelly that he was a dangerous man, particularly when he was drunk.

At his manslaughter trial two weeks later Kelly was said to have a violent temper and to have developed obsessions about other tramps. 'This conviction for a second killing confirms that the view of the consultant psychiatrist who says that you are incorrigible in penal terms and incurable in medical terms is plainly right,' said the judge on this occasion. In passing sentence, he went on to remark that Kelly might be considered too dangerous ever to be released.

On the afternoon of 8 June 1957, Emily Pye, an eighty-year-old spinster, was beaten to death in her corner shop in Gibbet Street, Halifax, during the course of a thunderstorm. Her murderer escaped with a small amount of money from the till, leaving a much larger sum untouched in her living quarters. The crime was reported by the victim's niece and her husband, who found the body in the back room, partly covered by a rug. A few hours later the Chief Constable of Halifax requested the assistance of Scotland Yard.

Though Miss Pye's attacker had smashed her skull with a fire-iron, the pathologist who carried out a post-mortem on her body found that most of her injuries had been inflicted with fists. Detective Superintendent Herbert Hannam, the Scotland Yard officer in charge of the case, afterwards claimed that the nature of the injuries suggested that her killer suffered from mental abberation.

The police began interviewing local people, at the same time making public appeals for information from anyone who had visited the shop on the day of the murder. It was suspected that the culprit was a local man, who may even have been one of Miss Pye's customers. However, little progress was made, and before long Hannam complained at a press conference that 'vital information' was being withheld. He believed that somebody was shielding the perpetrator of the crime.

A request was made to Interpol to trace three people known to have been in Halifax on 8 June, who had since left the country. While awaiting the results of this Hannam held a conference with officers who had investigated two similar crimes in the same county: one in Bradford two years earlier, the other in Leeds seven years before that. The interviewing of local people continued.

Then in August, after 15,000 statements had been taken, a search was made for eight men whom Hannam said he wanted to interview. And on 10 August it was announced that 'considerable progress' had been made on the case. Yet no arrest followed, and some months afterwards — following several other optimistic statements to the press — the investigation was terminated. The case remains unsolved.

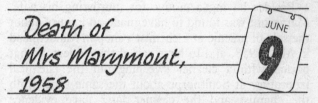

Death of Mrs Marymont, 1958

JUNE 9

On 9 June 1958, Mrs Mary Helen Marymont, the forty-three-year-old wife of an American army sergeant stationed in Britain, was rushed to the US Air Force hospital in Sculthorpe, Norfolk. She was in a state of collapse after becoming ill the previous day, and her husband, Master Sergeant Marcus Marymont, was warned that her condition was so grave that she might not recover.

Marymont appeared to be unconcerned about this, and tried to draw the hospital's general medical officer into a discussion about his marital problems. His wife died shortly afterwards, and a post-mortem was carried out against his wishes. Her organs were then sent to Scotland Yard's Forensic Laboratory, where it was found that she had been poisoned with arsenic.

Marymont, who was six years younger than his wife, was found to have been having an affair with Cynthia Taylor, a young married woman living in Maidenhead, Berkshire, and letters found in his desk showed that he had had a motive for his wife's murder.

Mrs Taylor, who was separated from her husband, managed a local garden stores. Marymont had met her at a Maidenhead club two years earlier, and within a few months they had become deeply involved with each other. Marymont, pretending to be divorced, asked her to marry him, and she said that she would when she was free to do so. She was waiting for her own divorce with this in mind at the time of Mrs Marymont's death.

Besides having a motive for murdering his wife, Marymont was found to have made an inquiry about the sale of arsenic at a chemist's shop in Maidenhead in May 1958, and to have raised the subject of that poison with a cleaner sweeping out the chemical laboratory at Sculthorpe about the same time. Both the chemist and the cleaner later gave evidence against him.

Marymont was arrested just over a month after his wife's death, and in December 1958 he was tried by a US General Court Martial in Denham, Buckinghamshire, for murder and adultery — the latter being a punishable offence under American military law. The trial lasted ten days, with Cynthia Taylor giving evidence for seven and a half hours; it resulted in the prisoner being convicted on both charges and sentenced to hard labour for life.

Later his conviction for adultery was set aside, and his life sentence — which he was serving in Fort Leavenworth Prison, Kansas — was reduced to thirty-five years.

Murder of Zoe Wade, 1984

On 13 June 1984, firemen found the naked body of Zoe Wade, an unmarried woman aged forty-two, in the bedroom of her council flat in Bradford, Yorkshire. She had been raped and strangled, and her killer, twenty-six-year-old James Pollard had splashed cleaning solution on her body before setting fire to the place. Pollard was a known offender with a grudge against Miss Wade, and police suspected right from the start that he was the culprit. On being arrested shortly afterwards, he made a confession.

Miss Wade, a shy, nervous person who liked to keep herself to herself, had been raped and beaten by the same man after he had forced his way into her home in January 1982. A former neighbour, Pollard had warned her on that occasion, 'Don't call the police, or I will kill you!' He had afterwards been sentenced to four and a half years' imprisonment, having pleaded guilty to a charge of rape at the Leeds Crown Court, but served only sixteen months before being released on parole.

His victim, in the meantime, had suffered a great deal as a result of the crime. She was frightened to go out, and could not stand the company of men; she was also worried about what would happen when Pollard came out of jail — so worried, in fact, that she asked her local Housing Department to move her to a different address. But this request was made in vain, and when Pollard was released nobody told her about it. Miss Wade, who worked as a machinist, was therefore taken by surprise when she arrived home on the day of the murder, and her attacker was once again able to force his way into her flat without difficulty.

An examination of Pollard's clothes led to the discovery of incriminating fibres, and Miss Wade's purse — with his fingerprints on it — was found in the men's lavatory of a public house just across the road from her home. Pollard claimed that he had only gone to see her because she had failed to reply to a letter of apology which he had sent to her from prison; he also denied that he had raped her again, saying that he had killed her unintentionally while trying 'to shut her up'. He even pretended that the fire at her flat had been caused by accident.

Needless to say, he was not believed, and charges of rape and murder were brought against him. Pollard duly appeared for trial in Leeds on 5 February 1985, this time denying both offences. Under cross-examination, he admitted going to Miss Wade's flat, but denied that he had intended to kill her, saying, 'I wanted to talk to her ... I wanted to say I was sorry.'

Miss Wade had invited him in, and taken off her clothes of her own accord, he continued. At this, he had told her to get dressed again, but she, on hearing a loud noise from the direction of the front door, had looked startled, and given him the impression that she was about to scream. As a result, he had grabbed hold of her round the neck, but released her while she was still alive. 'I threw a bottle of Ajax at her because I was frightened and mad,' he said.

He admitted that he had taken off his trousers, but denied that this had been for the purpose of having sexual intercourse. 'There was no reason,' he said. 'I just took them off.'

The jury retired for an hour and twenty minutes before returning a verdict of guilty on both counts. The judge then told the prisoner that he was dangerous and vengeful, adding, 'In my view, you will remain dangerous for many years to come.' Pollard was then sentenced to life imprisonment for the murder and ten years' imprisonment for the rape, the judge informing him that he would remain in jail for at least twenty years, and perhaps a lot longer.

Even so, the news that a rapist had been released after serving only sixteen months — in spite of having threatened to kill his victim — caused much disquiet, as was only to be expected.

Murder of Countess Skarbek, 1952

Late at night on 15 June 1952, a woman was stabbed to death in the foyer of the Shelbourne Hotel in London's Earls Court. The crime was witnessed by members of the hotel staff, and the police were called to the scene without delay. The killer, forty-one-year-old Dennis Muldowney, made no attempt to escape. 'I built all my dreams around her, but she was playing me for a fool!' he said self-piteously.

The victim, an attractive woman in her thirties, was Polish by birth but spoke English and several other languages fluently. Though generally known as Christine Granville, she was, in fact, the Countess Krystyna Skarbek, a wartime British Intelligence agent whose exploits in Occupied Europe had brought her fame which she did not want.

She had met Muldowney the previous year while she was working as a stewardess aboard an ocean liner, and a friendship had developed between them. They continued to see each other when Muldowney left the ship and became a night porter at the Reform Club in London. But he was possessive about her, resenting her association with other men, and when she suddenly became engaged to an old wartime colleague, Muldowney began following her.

On the day of the murder Christine had spent the evening with some Polish friends at a café not far from her hotel; one of them afterwards saw her to the hotel door, where he stood talking to her for a few minutes. Muldowney, hiding in the shadow of the basement steps, heard her say that she would soon be going to Belgium for a short holiday, and when the friend left he rushed into the hotel after her.

'You're not leaving me!' he cried. 'Not now!'

He immediately drove the dagger five inches into her chest, then sat staring at her body as it lay at his feet.

Christine's funeral was attended by wartime heroes from both sides of the Iron Curtain. Medals found in her hotel room, including the George Medal and the Croix de Guerre, were displayed beside the grave.

Brought to trial at the Old Bailey, Dennis Muldowney pleaded guilty to her murder and was sentenced to death, the proceedings lasting a mere three minutes. He was hanged at Pentonville Prison on 30 September 1952.

Double murder in Bignell Wood, 1956

JUNE
17

On 17 June 1956, a motorist driving through the New Forest near Cadnam, Hampshire, stopped to help an injured man who was leaning over the bonnet of a parked car. The man, who had a four-inch knife wound in his stomach, staggered towards him and claimed to have seen a murder — which he also described as 'a fight with two women' — in a nearby wood. The motorist summoned help, and Albert William Goozee, a thirty-three-year-old labourer and former merchant seaman, was rushed to hospital.

A policeman went into Bignell Wood to investigate and found two bodies near the remains of a picnic. Mrs Lydia Leakey, aged fifty-three, of Alexandra Road, Parkstone, near Poole in Dorset, had been stabbed and also struck with an axe; her daughter Norma, a girl of fourteen, had stab wounds in her chest and stomach. There was a wood fire still burning, tea in an aluminium teapot, and warm water in a tin kettle. The knife with which all the stab-wounds — including Goozee's — had been inflicted was later found in the injured man's car.

Goozee told the police that he had been Mrs Leakey's lover for over a year, having moved into her home as a lodger in January 1955. At that time Mrs Leakey had slept with Norma in one bedroom, while her husband, a machine operator who had lost one leg, slept in another. But as soon as she started her affair with Goozee, Mrs Leakey began to spend her nights with him, returning to the room she shared with her daughter just before her husband's alarm clock woke him up.

The situation was further complicated by the fact that Norma, who was also attracted to Goozee, went on frequent outings with the couple, and sometimes joined them in bed.

Eventually, in December 1955, Goozee joined the army, signing on for twelve years, and was sent to Catterick, in Yorkshire. Mrs Leakey wrote to him almost every day, begging him to return, but for some time he refused. She then threatened to tell the police that he had had sexual intercourse with Norma, who was still only thirteen — and who, in fact, was still a virgin at her death, as the post-mortem revealed. Not long after that, however, Goozee returned to Mrs Leakey as both lodger and lover, she having given him the money to buy himself out of the army.

This time the affair was even more complicated than before, because Norma insisted on being present when the couple made love, and threatened to tell her father of their relationship if they tried to prevent her doing so. Then Mr Leakey suddenly left home — only to move back into the house a few weeks later and order Goozee to leave. And when Goozee did this, Mrs Leakey once again persuaded him to return.

Thereafter, Goozee was frequently told to leave and just as often induced to stay, until the first week of June 1956, when he moved into other lodgings in Parkstone. Even then, Mrs Leakey continued to pursue him and persuaded him to take Norma and her for a picnic, saying that she had something she wanted to tell him.

As for what actually happened at that picnic, Goozee gave several different accounts, the last of them in December 1956, when he was on trial in Winchester. In this he stated that after sending Norma off to pick bluebells, Mrs Leakey had asked him to make love to her, promising that it would be for the last time. But while they were lying together on a rug beside the car, Norma reappeared and, calling her mother 'a dirty rotten beast', attacked her with the axe which they had brought along to chop firewood. Mrs Leakey, whose head was bleeding, afterwards stabbed first Goozee — while he was trying to help her — and then Norma, who had managed to get between them.

But no credence could be given to this story, because most of the blood on the knife-blade matched samples of Goozee's own blood, which was of a different group from that of Mrs Leakey and her daughter and showed that he had been stabbed *after* them. It was therefore contended that he had killed them both, intending to

180

commit suicide afterwards.

Convicted of murdering Norma Leakey, Goozee was sentenced to death. His sentence was later commuted to life imprisonment.

Reading Shop murder, 1929

JUNE
22

Shortly after 6 p.m. on 22 June 1929, Alfred Oliver, a sixty-year-old tobacconist, was found lying on the floor of his shop in Reading, Berkshire, suffering from head injuries. He had been attacked during the previous few minutes — while his wife was out walking their dog — and his assailant had snatched the contents of the till. Mr Oliver was unable to give a clear account of what had happened, and died of his wounds the following day.

Suspicion fell on Philip Yale Drew, an American actor in a touring company which was performing a play called *The Monster* in a local theatre that week. Drew was a man of distinctive appearance, and several witnesses claimed to have seen him near the shop about the time of the murder.

Though no charge was brought against him, Drew was subjected to a searching examination at the subsequent inquest, the coroner — a friend of the dead man — treating him almost as though he was a prisoner on trial. But the evidence was far from convincing, and after hearing about sixty witnesses the jury brought his ordeal to an end by returning a verdict of 'murder by person or persons unknown'.

This was greeted with approval by crowds thronging the streets, and the coroner's own conduct became the subject of much criticism. Even so, the affair ruined Drew's career, and he later became destitute.

The crime was never solved.

Murder of Florence Dennis, 1894

On the evening of 24 June 1894, Florence Dennis, a young single woman, left her sister's home in Southend, Essex, to meet James Canham Read, a married man with eight children who worked as a clerk at the Royal Albert Docks in Woolwich. Read had formerly been her lover, and Florence had written to him five days previously, asking what 'arrangements' he had made in view of the fact that she was pregnant. He turned up to meet her with a revolver in his pocket, took her for a walk and then shot her. Florence's body was found in a ditch near the village of Prittlewell the following day.

Her sister, Mrs Ayriss, knew Read personally. He had been her lover, too, and in fact had had a child by her: it was as a result of this liaison that he had met Florence in 1892. So when her sister failed to return, Mrs Ayriss sent him a telegram, asking what had become of her. This worried Read so much that — having replied that he had not seen 'the young person' for eighteen months — he stole £160 from his employers and absconded from his home in Jamaica

Road, Stepney. Mrs Ayriss, in the meantime, had reported her sister's disappearance to the police.

Read was discovered a fortnight later at Mitcham, in Surrey, where he was living with another woman and child and known as Edgar Benson. It was then learnt that while living with his own wife — and having an affair with Florence Dennis — he had been spending almost every weekend with 'Mrs Benson', explaining his absences from this second home by pretending to be a commercial traveller. He was arrested for murder, and also charged with the theft from his employers.

Read denied having killed Florence and claimed that he was not responsible for her pregnancy; he had met Mrs Ayriss on the evening in question, and she had informed him that a soldier was the child's father, he said. However, he had been seen with Florence in the Prittlewell area, and letters had been discovered proving that he had had an affair with her. Moreover, he was known to have possessed a revolver of the type used for the crime, though this could not be found.

Convicted of murder at the Chelmsford Assizes, James Canham Read was sentenced to death, his execution taking place on 4 December 1894. His brother Harry, who had also been arrested in connection with the theft, committed suicide a few days later.

On 26 June 1926, Louie Calvert, a thirty-three-year-old petty criminal, was hanged at Strangeways Prison, Manchester, for the murder of Mrs Lily Waterhouse, a widow aged forty, three months earlier. Mrs Waterhouse — with whom the prisoner had been lodging for three weeks prior to the crime — had been battered to death at her home in Amberley Road, Leeds, on the evening of 31 March, shortly after complaining to the police that her lodger had stolen some of her possessions. During the investigation which followed it was found that the culprit's brief stay at the victim's home had been part of an extraordinary plan to dupe her own husband.

Arthur Calvert, a Leeds nightwatchman living in Railway Place — about two miles from Amberley Road — had engaged Louie as a housekeeper in 1925, and later married her after she had told him that she was pregnant. At the time he believed her to be a widow with two children — a boy who stayed with her and a girl who lived with her sister in Dewsbury, seven miles away — and must therefore have been surprised when she described herself on her wedding certificate as a spinster. During the months which followed she failed to show any signs of pregnancy, and Calvert became impatient for reassurance that a child was on the way. Eventually Louie embarked on her incredible course.

Pretending that she was going to stay with her sister for 'the confinement', she left for Dewsbury on 8 March 1926, but after sending her husband a telegram to advise him of her arrival she returned to

184

Leeds and went into lodgings at the home of Mrs Waterhouse. A few days later, as a result of an advertisement in a local newspaper, a seventeen-year-old unmarried mother agreed to let Louie adopt her baby daughter, and the child was given to her on 31 March. Later the same day, having murdered her landlady in the meantime, she returned to her husband and pretended to have given birth to the child herself.

Early the following morning, before the body was discovered, Louie went back to the house in Amberley Road and stole a number of articles which had belonged to her victim. She was seen leaving the house and arrested shortly afterwards, the police having discovered her identity from a letter which she had left behind. On being confronted at her home in Railway Place, she was found to be wearing Mrs Waterhouse's boots, which were several sizes too large for her. A suitcase containing crockery, cutlery and household linen stolen from the victim's home was discovered in her living-room.

Louie Calvert was known to the police as Louie Gomersal, an occasional prostitute. She was convicted at the Leeds Assizes in May 1926, and while awaiting execution confessed to another murder: that of John William Frobisher, an elderly man for whom she had also worked as a housekeeper. Frobisher's body — with his boots missing — had been recovered from the canal near his home in Leeds on 12 July 1922. An open verdict was recorded at the inquest, but the police saw no reason to investigate the matter.

On 27 June 1981, thirty-five-year-old Michael Barber, of Westcliff-on-Sea, Essex, died in a west London hospital after an illness lasting some weeks. Though his death was at first attributed to pneumonia and kidney failure, the pathologist conducting the post-mortem suspected paraquat poisoning and sent parts of his organs to be tested by the National Poisons Units at New Cross Hospital. When his suspicions were confirmed, the police were informed, and Michael Barber's death was treated as a case of murder.

The following April Barber's twenty-nine-year-old wife Susan, who had been left £15,000 in her husband's employment insurance policy, was arrested and charged with the crime, and Richard Collins, a younger man with whom she had been having an affair at the time, was charged with a lesser offence in connection with it. The case came before Chelmsford Crown Court in November 1982, both defendants pleading not guilty.

The court heard that Michael and Susan Barber, who had three children, had been incompatible and quarrelled frequently. Susan went out to parties a lot, had a succession of lovers and twice left home; returning on each occasion because her husband begged her to do so. Then in May 1981 Michael Barber arrived back at their house in Osborne Road after cutting short a fishing trip, and found Susan and Richard Collins — his best friend and fellow darts player — making love in the bedroom. He chased Collins out of the house and gave his wife a beating.

The following day Susan made him a steak and

kidney pie but, according to the prosecution, added a spoonful of weed-killer from a can in the garden shed before giving it to him. When he became ill, she gave him more of the poison by putting it into medicine which his doctor had prescribed. Michael Barber was admitted to Southend Hospital soon afterwards, and later removed to Hammersmith after failing to respond to treatment for suspected pneumonia.

When the dead man's body was cremated Susan Barber put on a display of grief, throwing herself onto the coffin as it moved along the conveyor belt. But Richard Collins, already discarded as a lover, had begun to tell friends what had happened, and evidence of this was given to the court.

'Richard was very upset and crying,' said one witness. 'I said he did not want to believe something like that, but he said it was true. He told me that he had a photograph of Susan coming out of the garden shed, taken with a zoom lens, and it showed her with the poison. I told him he couldn't say things like that, but he told me he could prove it.'

Susan Barber told the court that she had not intended to kill her husband; she said that she gave him the poison to punish him for hurting her, without realizing that it could be fatal. She was, however, convicted of murder and sentenced to life imprisonment, while her twenty-five-year-old former lover was given two years' imprisonment for conspiracy to murder.

In July 1983 Susan Barber was allowed out of Holloway Prison briefly in order to marry a divorcee aged thirty-seven. The man had stood by her during the trial and, on hearing that the Home Office had given permission for the ceremony to take place, was reported to have said, 'I love Susan very much. I am overjoyed that we can get married.' It was also stated that he was living in her house in Osborne Road and had adopted her three children.

On 28 June 1964, two boys looking for fishing bait in Bracknell Woods, Berkshire, discovered a man's body in a mound of earth. The body was lying face upwards, fully clothed and with its head wrapped in towelling; it was covered in maggots and extensively decomposed. Professor Keith Simpson, the pathologist, said that the man had been dead for at least nine or ten days and that he had died as a result of a blow — perhaps a karate chop — across the throat. The body was identified from fingerprints as that of Peter Thomas, a forty-two-year-old unemployed man with a criminal record.

Peter Thomas was found to have been living alone — on unemployment benefit — in a wooden bungalow at Lydney, in Gloucestershire. Though he pretended to be poor, he had, in fact, inherited £5000 from his father three years earlier, and letters found in his home revealed that he had made a six-month loan of £2000 to a man named William Brittle, of Hook in Hampshire, at 12½ per cent interest. This loan, which had been made as a result of a newspaper advertisement, was due to be repaid about the time of Thomas' disappearance on 16 June.

Brittle was a salesman who, according to his advertisement, had wanted the loan for the sake of an 'agricultural prospect'. On being questioned by police, he said that the money had already been repaid: he had driven to Lydney with it himself on 16 June, he said. But there was no proof of this, and when asked how he had managed to raise such a large sum, Brittle said that he had won it betting on horses. The police officers then spoke to bookmakers and betting-shop employees in the district, showing them a photograph of Brittle, and found that none of them recognized him.

Brittle's car was examined and a beech leaf was found under the driver's mat. This was of interest to the investigators, as sprays of beech wood had been found over the dead man's body, though there were no beech trees in the vicinity. Bloodstains on Brittle's coat were of little value as evidence, as his blood group was the same as Thomas'. But it was also learnt that while in the army Brittle had attended a course in unarmed combat.

The police officers working on the case were sure that Brittle had visited Lydney on 16 June, and were able to trace a hitch-hiker to whom he had given a lift on the return journey. But they believed that he had gone there to kill Thomas rather than to repay the loan, and that he had afterwards concealed the body in the boot of his car.

However, no further evidence came to light to support this theory, and after the investigation had gone on for four months, a nylon-spinner named Dennis Roberts claimed to have seen Peter Thomas in Gloucester on 20 June. Though Professor Simpson insisted that this could not be true, the nylon-spinner's statement was seen as undermining the case against Brittle, and the Director of Public Prosecutions decided against having him committed for trial.

A coroner's inquest was then held in Bracknell, lasting seven days, and at the end of it the jury surprised everyone by naming Brittle as Peter Thomas' murderer. Brittle was therefore committed for trial, and appeared at the Spring 1965 Assizes in Gloucester.

The case against him was still no stronger than it had been when the Director of Public Prosecutions decided against committal proceedings, and two further witnesses had since come forward to say that they had seen Peter Thomas alive several days after the date of his disappearance. But the jury was more impressed by the evidence of Professor Simpson, who explained the various stages of development of maggots of the bluebottle fly, and insisted that those found on the body were at a stage which could not have been reached in less than nine or ten days.

William Brittle, who was not called to give evidence himself, was accordingly found guilty and sentenced to life imprisonment.

Murder of the Stubbe brothers, 1901

On 1 July 1901, a shocking double murder was committed on the island of Rügen, in the Rostock district of north Germany (now in the German Democratic Republic). Hermann Stubbe, aged eight, and his six-year-old brother Peter, the two sons of a carter living in the village of Göhren, had been out alone during the afternoon and failed to return home by dusk. A search was therefore started in the extensive woodland nearby, but by this time they were already dead.

Both boys had been battered over the head with a large stone discovered near the scene of the crime. Their heads, arms and legs had then been cut off, their bodies cut open and their internal organs cut out and scattered through the woods. The discovery of the bodies, on 2 July, horrified the inhabitants of Rügen and was quickly followed by the arrest of Ludwig Tessnow, a journeyman carpenter from another village who had been seen talking to the boys the previous afternoon.

Tessnow, a native of Rügen who had spent some years travelling all over Germany before returning to the village of Baabe, denied having had anything to do with the murders. But a new suit and other articles of clothing found in his wardrobe appeared to be bloodstained, and it was also learnt that Tessnow had been suspected of the unsolved murder of two girls in a village near Osnabrück in September 1898. Moreover, he was identified by a local shepherd as a man seen running away from a field near Göhren on the night of 11 June 1901, when a number of sheep were killed in a revolting manner.

Tessnow denied that he had killed either the children or the animals, and insisted that stains found on his clothes were not bloodstains but spots of a woodstain used in his work. The examining magistrate in charge of the inquiry, though convinced of his guilt, was therefore far from certain that he would be convicted if brought to trial. But the case against Tessnow was greatly strengthened when his clothes were sent to Paul Uhlenhuth, a young serologist at the University of Greifswald, for examination.

Uhlenhuth, using tests which he had only recently devised, was able to show that while Tessnow's working clothes were free of bloodstains of any sort, the better clothes from his wardrobe had been stained in various places — by both human and sheep's blood. The tests were so impressive that they ensured Tessnow's conviction and were immediately recognized as a great advance in forensic medicine. The mad carpenter of Rügen was sentenced to death, but this sentence was afterwards commuted on the grounds of his insanity. He died in the 1920s.

Execution of Dr. Robert Buchanan, 1895

On 2 July 1895, Dr Robert Buchanan, a New York medical practitioner, was executed in the electric chair at Sing Sing Prison for the murder of his second wife. The offence had been committed in 1892, the victim's death being caused by morphine poisoning. It had been inspired by the case of Carlyle Harris, a medical student who had been tried for a similar crime earlier the same year.

Buchanan, who had qualified as a doctor in Edinburgh, set up his practice in New York in 1886. It was initially successful and prosperous, but he was discontented with his home life and paid regular visits to brothels. When his first marriage ended in divorce in 1890, he married Anna Sutherland, the keeper of one of these establishments, who afterwards worked as his receptionist.

A wealthy woman, many years his senior, the new Mrs Buchanan had already made a will in which her husband was named as chief beneficiary. But her presence in his consulting-rooms was an embarrassment to him, and his patients began to take their ailments elsewhere.

When Carlyle Harris was brought to trial in January 1892 the case made headline news. It was the first known case in which murder had been committed with the use of morphine in New York, and the victim's death had only been properly investigated as a result of disclosures made in the *New York World.*

Buchanan, who was vain and boastful, expressed the view that Harris was a fool: the preparation of an undetectable poison could easily be accomplished, he

TRUE CRIME DIARY

TOP
Search for clues on wasteland near Dennis Nilsen's home.

SYNDICATION INTERNATIONAL

INSET
Dennis Nilsen

PRESS ASSOCIATION

BOTTOM
Martin Hunter-Craig, a homosexual prostitute and close friend of Nilsen.

SYNDICATION INTERNATIONAL

TRUE CRIME DIARY

TOP
 Henri Désiré Landru, the French 'Bluebeard' on trial.

POPPERFOTO

BOTTOM
 The body of Mafia boss Albert Anastasia in the barber's shop where he was shot.

ALDUS ARCHIVE/N.Y. DAILY NEWS

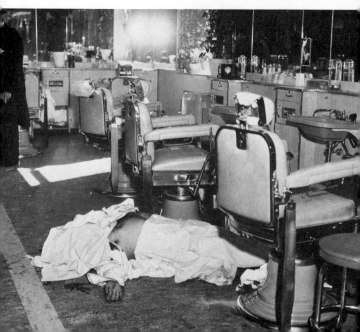

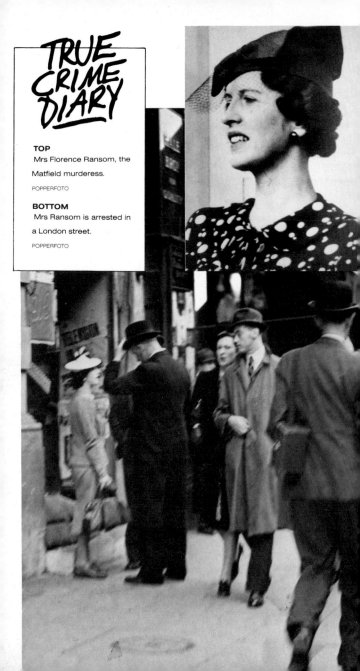

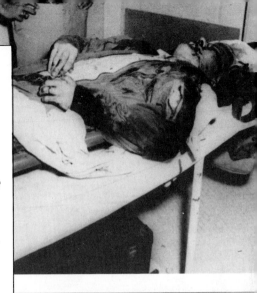

TRUE CRIME DIARY

TOP
The body of Charles Whitman, a twenty-five-year-old mass murderer of Austin, Texas.

BOTTOM
Edmund Kemper, the 'Co-ed murderer' smoking after his appearance in court.

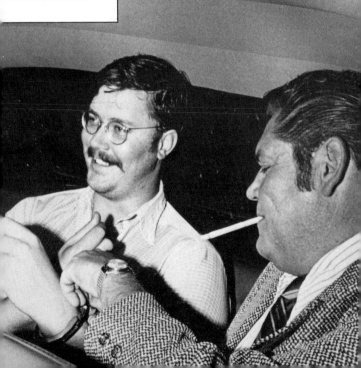

TRUE CRIME DIARY

TOP
Charles Manson giving a
television interview.

POPPERFOTO

BOTTOM
Manson leaving the
courtroom after being
convicted of seven
murders.

POPPERFOTO

TRUE CRIME DIARY

TOP

Jacques Mesrine, in some
of his disguises.

THE KEYSTONE COLLECTION

BOTTOM

Mesrine took these
photos of journalist
Jacques Tillier after
knocking him unconscious
and shooting him three
times.

ASSOCIATED PRESS

Grigori Rasputin, the 'Holy Devil' whose powers of survival have been the subject of speculation.

POPPERFOTO

declared. When his own wife died on 23 April, her death was thought to have been caused by a cerebral haemorrhage, but Buchanan's behaviour gave rise to suspicion and, as luck would have it, the reporter who had exposed Carlyle Harris decided to look into the matter.

Having inherited $50,000 from his second wife, Buchanan drew further attention to himself by remarrying his first less than a month later. This led to an exhumation of Anna Buchanan's body, a post-mortem being carried out by Dr Rudolph Witthaus — who had also examined the body of Harris' victim. In this case, although he found morphine in the body, the doctor also reported that the most important sign of morphine poisoning — contracted pupils — was absent.

This puzzled everyone concerned until the *New York World* reporter, questioning Buchanan in a saloon, suddenly remembered an observation which he had made during his schooldays, and realized that the contraction of the pupils could be counteracted by putting belladonna into the victim's eyes. This flash of insight caused him to request a further examination of the body, as a result of which traces of belladonna were found.

Buchanan was arrested and charged with murder, being brought to trial in March 1893. During the course of the proceedings, a cat was killed with morphine so that the effects of belladonna on its pupils could be witnessed. Even so, it was only the unconvincing answers which he gave under cross-examination that ensured Buchanan's conviction. Had he taken the advice of his counsel and declined to give evidence, he may well have been acquitted.

Kidnapping of Graeme Thorne, 1960

On the morning of 7 July 1960, eight-year-old Graeme Thorne disappeared after setting out for school from his home in the Bondi district of Sydney. A few days earlier his parents, Bazil and Freda Thorne, had won the £100,000 first prize in the Sydney Opera House Lottery, and it was immediately feared that the child had been kidnapped. Shortly afterwards a man with a foreign accent telephoned their home, saying that he had Graeme and demanding £25,000 for his return.

The call was answered by a detective, who pretended to be the boy's father but was unable to draw the man into conversation. Bazil Thorne and his wife afterwards told the police that they were willing to pay the whole of their £100,000 to get their son back safely. But they were never to be able to do so, for after a second telephone call, the kidnapper made no further contact with them.

On 16 August Graeme's body was found wrapped in a rug on a patch of waste ground in Seaforth, about ten miles from the family's home. His hands and feet were tied and a silk scarf was knotted round his neck. He had died from strangulation and a fractured skull.

It was not long before police began to suspect Stephen Leslie Bradley, a naturalized Australian who, at the time of the kidnapping, had lived in a nearby neighbourhood with his wife and their three children. Bradley, an electroplater, was Hungarian by birth: his name had originally been Istvan Baranyay, but he had changed it by deed poll. Since the crime he had altered his appearance, and he and his family had left their house. It was learnt that they were about to

194

leave the country.

Bradley owned a car which was similar to one seen near Graeme Thorne's home on the morning of 7 July; it was also discovered that he had not been to work that day. Further evidence was provided by an examination of leaves and hairs attached to the rug in which the body had been wrapped: some of the leaves were similar to those of an unusual type of shrub growing at the house which Bradley had left, and some of the hairs were identical to those of his dog. The rug was eventually identified as one which Bradley had owned.

By the time the police were ready to arrest him, Bradley was on his way to London by sea. He was arrested in Colombo on a provisional warrant, and extradition proceedings were started against him. These resulted in his being returned to Australia, where he confessed that he had abducted Graeme Thorne and threatened to 'feed him to the sharks' unless he was paid £25,000 for his return. He denied having struck the child, and said that he had been accidentally suffocated in the boot of the car. He (Bradley) had then become frightened and hidden the body.

On being brought to trial, Bradley withdrew his confession, but the evidence against him was overwhelming. He tried to gain sympathy by telling the court that he and his wife had both been in concentration camps during the Second World War, and that he on one occasion had survived a firing squad. But this did not help him, either, and he was convicted of murder. The announcement of the jury's verdict was followed by noisy scenes in the courtroom, with one spectator shouting, 'Feed *him* to the sharks!'

As murder was no longer a capital offence in New South Wales, Bradley was sentenced to penal servitude for life. This was not generally considered a harsh enough punishment for what had clearly been a callous crime, and many people resented the fact that he could not be hanged.

Triple murder at Matfield, 1940

On the afternoon of 9 July 1940, three women were murdered in the grounds of a cottage at Matfield, a village about seven miles from Tonbridge in Kent. Mrs Dorothy Fisher and her nineteen-year-old daughter Freda had both been shot in the back in an orchard screening the cottage from the Tonbridge road; their maid, Charlotte Saunders, aged about forty-eight, had been shot as she ran from the cottage after dropping a tray of crockery.

The cottage had no other occupants — for Mrs Fisher and her husband had separated in October the previous year — and the murder weapon had not been left at the scene. Although there was a great deal of disorder inside, with jewellery, money and other valuables strewn all over the different rooms, the broken crockery, when pieced together, made up four cups, four saucers and four plates — which strongly suggested that Miss Saunders had been preparing tea for four people when the murders took place. If so, the identity of the fourth person was unknown.

The police officers working on the case also discovered a lady's white hogskin glove, which could not be immediately identified, on the ground between the bodies of Mrs Fisher and her daughter. A lady's bicycle, belonging to Mrs Fisher, was found in a ditch near the entrance to the cottage.

It seemed likely that the culprit was a woman, and Detective Chief Inspector Beveridge, the Scotland Yard officer in charge of the investigation, soon learnt that a woman had been seen behaving suspiciously outside the cottage on the afternoon in question. The same woman had been seen walking along the road from Matfield to Tonbridge, where she had boarded a train to London at 4.25 p.m.

The witnesses — and there were several of them — all agreed on this woman's description, and said that she had been carrying a long, narrow object wrapped in brown paper. This was undoubtedly the murder weapon, for the pathologist Sir Bernard Spilsbury was certain that all three of the victims had been killed with a shotgun. The woman was found to be Mrs Florence Ransom, a young widow who lived with Mrs Fisher's husband Lawrence on a farm at Piddington, near Bicester in Oxfordshire.

In addition to being a farmer, Lawrence Fisher was in business, and travelled to London every day. He had remained on good terms with his wife — who had a lover of her own — and often went to Matfield to see her, as well as their daughter.

Mrs Ransom, who was known locally as 'Mrs Fisher' — and to Mr Fisher as 'Julia' — was an attractive red-haired woman, described as domineering and dictatorial by one of the servants employed at the farm. She had, according to the same man, been learning to fire a shotgun owned by the farm's cowman, and also trying — not very successfully — to learn to ride a bicycle. It was later discovered that the cowman was Mrs Ransom's brother and that an elderly housekeeper at the farm was her mother. But Mr Fisher did not know that either were related to her, and although they both admitted it to the police, Mrs Ransom strenuously denied it.

The cowman agreed that he had been teaching Mrs Ransom to fire his shotgun. He said that she had borrowed it from him on 8 July and returned it two days later, saying that it needed cleaning. Mrs Ransom was then picked out by a number of witnesses at an identification parade, and afterwards asked to try on the hogskin glove. It fitted her perfectly, though the other one of the pair could not be found. A graze on one of her knees indicated that she may have fallen off Mrs Fisher's bicycle while trying to leave the scene of the crime in a hurry.

After an investigation lasting just a few days — during the course of which desperate air battles were fought over Kent — Mrs Ransom was charged with the three murders. She was tried at the Old Bailey in November 1940, her mother and brother both telling the court that she appeared to be missing from the farm during the daytime on 9 July. Mrs Ransom denied the offence — and continued to deny that the housekeeper and cowman were related to her — but was found guilty and sentenced to death. She was later certified insane and sent to Broadmoor.

Yukio Saito declared innocent, 1984

JULY 11

On 11 July 1984, Yukio Saito, a fifty-three-year-old man who had spent nearly twenty-seven years on Japan's Death Row, was set free after a court had reviewed his case and declared him innocent of the crime for which he had been sentenced. The crime, a quadruple murder, had been committed in 1955, and Saito had confessed to it after being arrested later the same year. He afterwards retracted the confession but was convicted and sentenced to death in 1957.

The crime had taken place in Matsuyama, near Sendai, the victims being a farmer and three relatives. Saito claimed that the police had forced him to confess to it after he had been arrested in connection with a different offence, and Judge Takehiko Kojima of the Sendai district court — 185 miles north of Tokyo — accepted that they had used illegal methods of interrogation in order to make him do so.

It was Japan's third such case in twelve months. On 15 July 1983, Sakae Menda, aged fifty-seven, was released from jail in south-western Japan after an appeal judge had found him innocent of two murders committed thirty-two years previously. He, too, had said that he was forced by police to confess, but previous appeals had been dismissed. Then, in March 1984, Shigeyoshi Taniguchi, who had spent thirty-four years on Death Row, was similarly released.

A year after Saito's release a Japanese woman who had died in 1979 was posthumously cleared of a murder for which she had served thirteen years in prison. Miss Shigeko Fuji had been convicted of the murder of her common-law husband, Kamesaburo Saegusa, on the evidence of two youths who worked in the victim's radio shop. The youths later retracted their evidence, saying that it had been given under pressure, but Miss Fuji withdrew an appeal against her conviction because she was afraid that the proceedings would use up the money which she needed to pay for the education of her children.

She was granted a retrial a year after her death, and her name was finally cleared thirty-two years after the crime had been committed. It was the first such retrial in Japan's history.

On 12 July 1906, the body of a young woman was found on the shore of Big Moose Lake, a holiday resort in the Adirondack region of New York State. It seemed at first that she had been drowned in a boating accident, and later, when an upturned rowing-boat was discovered in the water, with a man's straw boater nearby, it was assumed that another death had occurred at the same time. But an examination of the body revealed that the woman had been pregnant and that injuries which she had suffered were not consistent with a drowning accident. It was therefore suspected that she had been murdered.

The woman was found to be twenty-year-old Grace Brown, from Cortland, in the same state. It was learnt from her friends that she had been having an affair with Chester Gillette, the superintendent of the skirt factory where she worked, and from hoteliers in the Adirondack lake resorts that she had been on holiday there with a young man who sometimes signed his name as Carl Graham and sometimes as Charles George — registering Grace as his wife on each occasion. It was this man, wearing a straw boater and carrying a heavy suitcase, who had hired a rowing-boat on 11 July and failed to return it.

Police officers went to look for Chester Gillette at his lodgings in Cortland, but he was not there. Instead, they found a batch of letters which he had received from Grace Brown, telling him that she was desperate to hide her pregnancy from her parents and begging him to help her. A search was then started for him in the Adirondacks, and he was apprehended at

Arrowhead on Fourth Lake. On being charged with murder, he claimed that he had accidentally over-turned the rowing-boat while leaning out to pick a water lily, and that Grace had been drowned in spite of an attempt which he had made to rescue her.

Gillette, aged twenty-three, was brought to trial in November 1906, the case lasting twenty-two days and attracting much publicity. Medical evidence was produced to show that Grace Brown had been struck in the face, probably with the prisoner's tennis racket, and that she had been drowned while unconscious. But Gillette continued to deny that she had been murdered, saying now that she had committed suicide after they had discussed their circumstances in the boat.

Found guilty of first-degree murder, Chester Gillette was sentenced to death. A number of appeals were made, but all were dismissed and he was finally executed in the electric chair at Auburn Prison on 30 March 1908. Theodore Dreiser, who had been a spectator at the trial, was so inspired by it that he based his famous novel, *An American Tragedy*, on the case.

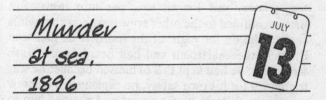

Murder at sea, 1896

JULY 13

On the night of 13 July 1896, a triple axe murder was committed aboard the *Herbert Fuller*, a sailing ship bound for Argentina carrying timber from Boston. Two of the victims, Captain Charles Nash and his wife Laura, were discovered almost immediately afterwards — while Nash was still alive — but the body of Second Mate August Blomberg was not found until later. The dying captain was on the floor of the chartroom; the body of his wife was in her bunk. They were found by Lester Monks, the ship's only passenger, who had gone to investigate after hearing screams above the sound of the wind.

Monks told the first mate, Thomas Bram, of his discovery, but Bram at first seemed unwilling to believe him. He said that he would not rouse Blomberg because the second mate had been inciting the crew to mutiny, then suddenly burst into tears and begged Monks to protect him. When Blomberg's body was eventually found in his cabin, Bram, who by this time had assumed command of the ship, drew attention to an axe which he appeared to have discovered. Saying excitedly that this was the murder weapon, he threw it into the sea before anyone could stop him.

Bram then sought to have the three bodies thrown overboard — a proposal which was resisted by the crew. Against his wishes, the crew also insisted that the *Herbert Fuller* should return to the United States. But for the six days that it took to reach port, an air of terror hung over the ship.

Bram convinced the crew that one of their number, a fellow named Charley Brown, had been acting suspiciously, and Brown was put into irons. But Brown confided to the other crew members that while at the helm on the night of the murders he had seen Bram in the chartroom and had heard Laura Nash screaming; he had kept this to himself because he was frightened for his own safety, he explained. The crew then accused Bram of the crimes and chained him to the mast.

In December 1896 Thomas Bram was brought to trial in Boston, charged with murder. The prosecution produced evidence that he had often approached fellow sailors with the idea of killing a ship's officers and stealing its cargo, and that he had also boasted of having looted other ships in which he had served: he was convicted and sentenced to death. But as a result of procedural errors, a retrial was ordered, and on being convicted for the second time in 1898, he was sentenced to life imprisonment.

Bram was pardoned in 1919, after the mystery writer Mary Roberts Rinehart had managed to convince President Woodrow Wilson that he was innocent, and he later became a successful businessman.

Crimmins children reported missing, 1965

JULY
14

On the morning of 14 July 1965, a man telephoned the police in Queens, New York City, to report the disappearance of his two children: a boy aged five and a girl a year younger. Edmund Crimmins was separated from his wife Alice, with whom the children had been living in a ground-floor apartment. He said that his wife, on finding that they were missing from their bedroom, had called to ask him whether he had taken them.

Detectives went to investigate the matter, and Alice Crimmins, an attractive woman of twenty-six, showed them the children's bedroom, where the beds were rumpled and the window stood open. She said that a latch on the door prevented it being opened from the inside — to ensure that her son did not go to the refrigerator while she was asleep — and that this had been in use the previous night. She also said that she had last seen the children before going to bed herself about 4 a.m.

That afternoon the girl, Alice Marie, was found strangled on a vacant lot, and it appeared from undigested food in her stomach that she had died about seven hours before her mother claimed to have last seen her. So Alice Crimmins — who had already given the impression of being far less distressed than might have been expected in the circumstances — now seemed not to have been telling the truth. The boy, Edmund Jr, was found dead on a piece of waste ground over a week later, his body in an advanced state of decomposition.

The police learnt that during the early hours of 14 July a neighbour looking out of her window had seen Mrs Crimmins in the company of a man; she was carrying a bundle wrapped in blankets under one arm and holding a small boy with her free hand. As she and her husband were in the process of getting divorced, it was suspected that she had killed the children herself because she feared losing custody of them. Nearly two years after the crimes had taken place Alice Crimmins was charged with her daughter's murder.

She was brought to trial in May 1968, the case attracting much attention — mainly as a result of evidence concerning the promiscuity of the accused. She was convicted of first-degree manslaughter and given a sentence of five-to-twenty years' imprisonment, but was released on bail shortly afterwards to await the outcome of an appeal. This resulted in the sentence being quashed and a fresh trial ordered.

In 1971 she was tried for the murder of her son and the manslaughter of her daughter. As at her previous trial, she screamed abuse at witnesses who appeared against her: one of these outbursts occurred when a former lover testified that during a night spent at a motel with him Alice Crimmins had confessed that she was the killer of her children. According to this witness, she had said that she preferred to see them dead rather than allow her husband to get custody of them.

Alice Crimmins was convicted on both charges and this time she was sentenced to life imprisonment. But further appeals followed, and in 1975 her conviction for murder was quashed. In January 1976 she was transferred to a residential work release establishment in Harlem.

Shooting of two police officers, 1951

JULY
15

During the early hours of 15 July 1951, police officers surrounding a farmhouse in Yorkshire heard the sound of shots and found two of their number fatally injured. The shooting took place at Whinney Close Farm, Kirkheaton, near Huddersfield, the home of thirty-six-year-old Alfred Moore and his family. Moore, a poultry farmer, was suspected of burglary, and the party of policemen had been awaiting his return in the hope of catching him in possession of stolen property.

The two wounded men were taken to hospital, Detective Inspector Duncan Fraser, who had been shot three times, dying before they got there. Others remaining at the scene of the crime believed that Moore was now inside the house, but no attempt was made to arrest him until armed reinforcements arrived. Moore then gave himself up, pretending to have been in bed at the time the shots were fired.

A search of the farmhouse and the adjoining yard resulted in the discovery of a pair of wet shoes, some live ammunition, discharged cartridge cases, a large assortment of keys — including skeleton keys, safe keys and car ignition keys — and certain items of value, such as gold and silver cigarette cases, which appeared to have been stolen. There were also the remains of hundreds of postage stamps and dollar bills which had been burnt in a fireplace after the shooting had occurred.

At the Huddersfield Royal Infirmary PC Arthur Jagger, the other man who had been shot, was able to make a statement. He said that he had seen Moore walking towards his home just before 2 a.m. and tried to arrest him after Moore had dived into a hedge. At this, the farmer pulled a gun from his pocket and shot him, causing him to fall to the ground. The shooting of Detective Inspector Fraser took place immediately afterwards, as Jagger lay watching but unable to move.

As Jagger was unlikely to recover, an identification parade was held at his bedside later the same day, and Moore was picked out as the culprit. A special court was then convened before a local magistrate, Jagger remaining in bed as he gave evidence. When Jagger died the following day Moore was charged with the murder of both men.

The search of the farm went on for several weeks, but the murder weapon was not discovered, even with the use of mine-detectors. Alfred Moore was nonetheless brought to trial at the Leeds Assizes in December 1951, and the jury took only fifty minutes to find him guilty. He was hanged at Armley Prison on 6 February 1952.

JULY 16

Murder of Alice Wiltshaw, 1952

On 16 July 1952, Mrs Alice Wiltshaw, the sixty-two-year-old wife of a pottery manufacturer, was beaten to death by an intruder at her fourteen-room house in the village of Barlaston, in Staffordshire. The person responsible got away with jewellery worth several thousand pounds, leaving the murder weapon — a heavy, old-fashioned poker — near the body. The crime was discovered by the victim's husband, Frederick Cuthbert Wiltshaw, when he arrived home from work shortly afterwards.

The property had been entered by way of an overgrown path — unlikely to have been used by a stranger — and there were no signs of a forced entry to the house. Moreover, the servants employed by Mr and Mrs Wiltshaw had all been off duty and out of the house at the time the murder took place. It therefore seemed that the culprit was somebody familiar with the building and household routine — and probably known to the victim.

Before long police began to suspect Leslie Green, the Wiltshaws' twenty-nine-year-old former chauffeur, who had been sacked two months previously for using one of the family cars for his own purposes. Green, a married man with a six-year-old daughter, had been missing from his home in nearby Longton since the beginning of July, but came forward seven days after the murder in response to a public appeal.

He denied knowing anything about the crime, saying that he had been at the Station Hotel in Stafford — twelve miles from Barlaston — during the afternoon and evening of 16 July, and had then left

207

for Leeds by train. A number of people with whom he had been associating could give him an alibi, he said.

This at first appeared to be true, but it was later found that a train leaving Stafford at 5.10 p.m. arrived in Barlaston at 5.35, and another, leaving Barlaston half an hour later, arrived in Stafford at 6.26. If Green had caught both of those trains, he would have been in Barlaston long enough to have committed the murder — and none of his associates had seen him at the Station Hotel during that particular period of time.

It was also learnt that Green, pretending to be unmarried, had become 'engaged' to a twenty-year-old nurse in Leeds, with whom he had been in close contact since leaving his wife. But she evidently suspected him, too, for she had returned two rings which he gave her after the murder, and it was in the hope of convincing her that he was innocent that he went to the police on 23 July.

Not long afterwards an RAF macintosh which Green had worn on 16 July was located in a railway lost property office. One of the pockets contained a letter mentioning an address in Leeds, and led to the discovery of the rings which the nurse had returned. As expected, they were found to have been among the valuables stolen from Mrs Wiltshaw. The rest of the jewellery was never recovered.

Leslie Green was charged with murder and tried at the Stafford Assizes. Pleading not guilty, he then claimed that the crime had been committed by two other men, who had given him the rings the following day. But a footprint found at the scene matched the sole of one of his shoes, and a bloodstained glove which had also been found there had a hole corresponding with a recently-healed cut on one of his thumbs.

On being found guilty, he was sentenced to death. His execution took place at Winson Green Prison, Birmingham, on 23 December 1952.

208

Danuta Maciejowicz found dead, 1964

On 23 July 1964, the naked corpse of Danuta Maciej-owicz, a girl of seventeen, was found in a park in Olsztyn, 160 miles north of Warsaw; she had been raped and the lower part of her body had been horribly mutilated. The crime had taken place the previous day — one of Poland's national holidays — and Danuta's parents had reported her missing when she failed to return home after going to watch a parade in the town's main street.

The discovery of the body was followed by an unsigned letter in red ink, received by a Warsaw newspaper editor, in which the writer stated that he had 'plucked a rose in bloom in the gardens of Olsztyn' and would do it elsewhere on another occasion. The letter was in the same spidery handwriting as another which had been sent to a different newspaper three weeks earlier, in which the writer had warned that he would give 'cause for weeping'. But the police were unable to trace the person responsible.

Then, on 17 January 1965, Anna Kaliniak, a sixteen-year-old girl from a Warsaw suburb, failed to return home, also after attending a national-holiday procession. Police were still searching for her when they received a letter, again in red spidery handwriting, telling them to go to a factory opposite Anna's home. There, in the basement, they found her body; she had been strangled with a piece of wire, stripped naked, raped and then mutilated, her killer leaving a metal spike stuck in her vagina. Once more, the police were unable to find the culprit.

Nine and a half months later, on 1 November —

All Saints' Day — there was another such murder. An eighteen-year-old hotel receptionist named Janina Popielska left her home in Poznań, 200 miles from Warsaw, and set out on foot towards a nearby village, a distance of three and a half miles. Her killer, whom she met on the way, suffocated her with a pad soaked in chloroform, then tore off her clothes and raped her three times behind a packing-shed before stabbing her to death with a screwdriver. Finally, her body was mutilated in a revolting manner and left in a packing-case at the scene of the crime.

A letter, in the now-familiar red spidery hand-writing and this time containing a quotation from a Polish epic written in 1928, was received by the editor of a Poznań newspaper the following day. But the police still had no idea who the killer could be.

On May Day in 1966, when celebrations were taking place all over the country, he struck yet again. Marysia Gałązka a seventeen year-old student living in the Warsaw suburb of Zoliborz, was found dead in the tool-shed of her family's back garden after she had gone out to look for her cat; she had been stripped naked, raped and disembowelled.

This fourth outrage led to a search of records of all other unsolved murders in Poland during the previous few years, and it was learnt that a further fourteen crimes, all committed since April 1964, had features similar to those already attributed to the unknown Polish Ripper. They had all taken place within a group of towns which formed a rough circle round Warsaw, no fewer than six of them in or near Poznań. But this discovery did not prevent two further murders occurring before the culprit was arrested.

On 24 December 1966, the body of seventeen-year-old Janina Kozielska, wearing only a leather mini-skirt, was found on a late-night train in Kraków; both the mini-skirt and the lower part of her body had been slashed repeatedly, and she, too, had been raped. A letter, in the usual red spidery handwriting, was found in the mail-van, stating briefly, 'I have done it again.' The killer was not among the passengers.

Janina Kozielska was found to be the sister of Aniela Kozielska, a girl of fourteen who had been murdered while on a visit to Warsaw to see her grand-mother in 1964. Her parents had no idea who had committed either of the murders, but mentioned that both girls had been associated with an academy of art in Kraków, called the Artlovers' Club — Janina as a part-time model, Aniela as a part-time student.

This was of interest to the police officers working on the case, as laboratory reports on the anonymous letters revealed that they had not been written in ordinary red ink but in a home-made solution containing artists' paint. They therefore began inter-viewing all 118 members of the club — people from a variety of professions, students, and even housewives — and eventually decided that Lucian Staniak, a twenty-six-year-old translator with a preoccupation with red paint and a locker full of knives, was the person they wanted.

Staniak, a native of Katowice, was not at his home when police went to see him on 31 January 1967; he was arrested at dawn the next day. In the meantime Bożena Raczkiewicz, an eighteen-year-old student, had been murdered in a railway-station shelter in Łódź. Her clothes had been cut off with a knife, then she had been raped twice and mutilated with a broken bottle.

Staniak, who had spent the night drinking, confessed to having committed twenty sex murders in less than three years. He was charged with all of them and, on being convicted, sentenced to death. Later, however, the 'Red Spider', as he had become popu-larly called, was declared insane and sent to an asylum in his home town.

Death of Edward Gein, 1984

On 26 July 1984, Edward Gein, a ghoulish murderer, body-snatcher and necrophile, died in an American mental institution at the age of seventy-seven. He had been in such institutions since 1957, when the remains of fifteen women were found at his farm in Plainfield, Wisconsin. It was Gein's activities which inspired the novel on which Alfred Hitchcock's famous horror film *Psycho* was based.

The events leading to Gein's arrest began on 16 November 1957, when relatives of Bernice Worden, a fifty-eight-year-old widow who ran a hardware store in Plainfield, realized that she was missing. Gein's pick-up truck had been seen near the store twice that day, and a sheriff's deputy called at his farm to see if he knew anything of her whereabouts. The farmer was not at home.

Calling again later, the deputy found that Gein was still not there. But this time he looked into a lean-to at the side of the house and saw Mrs Worden's decapitated corpse, hanging by the heels. Gein was located in the town shortly afterwards and taken into custody.

A search of the farmhouse resulted in the discovery of preserved human heads, many organs, a soup bowl made from a sawn-up skull, and lampshades and bracelets made of human skin. The relics were mainly of women whose corpses had been dug up after burial, but the remains of a woman who had been murdered three years earlier — as well as those of Mrs Worden — were also found.

Gein had a morbid interest in female corpses, particularly after the death of his mother, for whom he was said to have had an abnormal love and who had always managed to restrain him from showing a more natural interest in the opposite sex. It was because of this curiosity that he had taken initially to body-snatching and then to murder.

According to his own statements, both Mrs Worden and the woman murdered in 1954 — a middle-aged tavern keeper named Mary Hogan — had borne a resemblance to his mother, and he had killed them for this reason. He admitted acts of cannibalism as well as necrophilia, and also said that he found it sexually gratifying to drape the skin of corpses over his own body.

Though Gein was judged to be unfit to stand trial by reason of insanity, the revulsion caused by his practices was so intense that his farm was burnt to the ground by other members of the local community.

Gein was sent to the Central State Hospital at Waupon, where he remained until 1978; he was then transferred to the Mendota Mental Health Institute in Madison, where his last six years were spent. After his death, it was stated that he had not been a problem at either of these institutions, and that while at Central State he had worked as a carpenter, a mason and a hospital attendant.

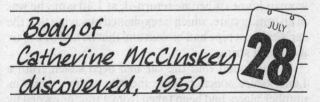

Body of Catherine McCluskey discovered, 1950

JULY
28

During the early hours of 28 July 1950, the body of Catherine McCluskey, a forty-year-old unmarried mother, was found lying in a road on the outskirts of

Glasgow, apparently the victim of a hit-and-run driver. She had, however, been run over twice by the same car — the second time when she was already dead — and a large bruise on her right temple, caused by a blow from a blunt instrument, indicated that she had been knocked unconscious beforehand. This was confirmed by the absence of any of the usual signs of a violent collision, such as broken glass and chipped paint, at the place where the body was found. It was therefore clear that Catherine McCluskey had been the victim of a murder.

The dead woman's body was identified by a friend with whom she had left her two children the previous evening. The friend, Mrs Rose O'Donnell, told police officers that the children — one aged six, the other three months — had been left with her several times when their mother went out, and that she had never before failed to collect them; she also said Miss McCluskey had told her that she was going out with a policeman. Further inquiries among the dead woman's neighbours in Nicholson Street, and at the Glasgow Assistance Board, revealed that a policeman — presumably the same one — was the father of Miss McCluskey's younger child.

PC James Robertson, a thirty-three-year-old married man with two children, soon came to the attention of the investigating officers. On the night of the murder he had left his beat at 11.15 p.m. and driven off in his black Austin car, saying that he was going to take a woman home. When he returned, at 1.10 a.m., he was in an untidy state, which he explained by saying that the car's exhaust pipe had broken and that he had had to tie it on with string.

It was found that the car had been stolen from a Lanarkshire solicitor some months earlier, while its number plates had been taken from a tractor owned by a farmer in Aberdeenshire. There were no signs of a collision on the body of the vehicle, but traces of blood, skin and hair were found on its underside. It was discovered, too, that marks on the surface of the road where the crime had taken place had been made by the broken exhaust pipe as the car went over the body.

On being questioned, Robertson said that he had found the car abandoned and had since been using it himself, having changed its number plates for those taken from the tractor. He admitted that he had killed Catherine McCluskey, but said that her death had been the result of an accident. He had agreed to drive her to the home of some friends because she said that she had been turned out of her lodgings, but on the way an argument started and he told her to get out and walk. The accident occurred when he drove towards her in reverse after relenting, he claimed.

Robertson was arrested and found to be carrying a heavy rubber truncheon which was not part of his regulation equipment. At his trial, at the Glasgow High Court, it was contended that Catherine McCluskey had been his mistress and that he had turned to murder as a means of terminating their relationship. Robertson denied that he had ever been intimate with Miss McCluskey, but was convicted and sentenced to death. His execution took place at Barlinnie Prison on 15 December 1950.

First murder of David Berkowitz, 1976

On 29 July 1976, two teenage girls were sitting in a stationary car in the Bronx, New York City, when a man walked over, pulled a gun out of a paper bag and

fired five shots at them. Donna Lauria, an eighteen-year-old medical technician, was killed and Jody Valenti, a student nurse aged nineteen, was wounded in the thigh. There was no motive for the crime and police quickly became convinced that the culprit was a madman who killed for pleasure.

Three months later, on 23 October, Carl Denaro, aged twenty, was sitting in his sports car in front of a tavern in Queens, Long Island, in the company of his eighteen-year-old girlfriend Rosemary Keenan, when the same man fired at them through the rear windscreen. Denaro was wounded but recovered in hospital; his girlfriend was not injured.

The connection between the two crimes was not discovered until some time afterwards, and in the meantime a third was committed. This was the shooting of another two girls — both of whom were wounded — also in Queens, on 27 November. Donna DeMasi and Joanne Lomino, who had been sitting outside a house together when the crime occurred, were found to have been shot with the same gun that had been used in both of the other cases.

Further crimes followed. On 30 January 1977, again in Queens, shots were fired at a young couple sitting in a car: the girl was fatally injured, but her companion was not hurt at all. Then, on 8 March, a female student was shot dead as she made her way home on foot in the same district. And on 17 April a couple were shot in a parked car in the Bronx: Valentina Suriani died instantly, Alexander Esau died later in hospital.

After this last attack a letter was found at the scene of the crime. It read: 'Dear Captain Joseph Borelli, I am deeply hurt by your calling me a women-hater. I am not. But I am a monster. I am the Son of Sam. . . .' A further note, signed 'Son of Sam', was sent to a New York columnist. The killer naturally became known by this name.

There were two more shootings: the first on 26 June in Queens, when a young couple were both shot and wounded in a stationary car, the other on 31 July, when another couple were shot in similar circumstances in Brooklyn. In this last case the girl, Stacy Moskowitz, aged twenty, died in hospital; her companion, Robert Violante, who was the same age, was blinded. But after the shooting an incident occurred which led to the killer's arrest.

A parking ticket was placed on his own car, which had been left near the scene of the crime, and when he returned to it, he screwed up the ticket, got into the car and drove off. This was witnessed by a woman walking her dog, who also noticed that he was holding a gun. When the matter was reported the police were able to trace the culprit from their own records, and he gave himself up without a fight.

The killer who had terrified the inhabitants of New York City for several months turned out to be David Berkowitz, a mentally-ill postal worker aged twenty-four, who lived in a Yonkers apartment block, harbouring feelings of rejection and persecution. He was shy of women, believing that they found him ugly, and claimed to hear demons telling him to kill. He also said that after a murder he felt 'flushed with power'. He was nonetheless judged to be sane, and sentenced to 365 years' imprisonment shortly afterwards.

He later became a celebrity and made a great deal of money from the sale of his life story.

Charles Whitman's first murder, 1966

JULY
31

On 31 July 1966, Charles Whitman, a twenty-five-year-old architectural engineering student of Austin, Texas, typed a note in which he said that he intended to kill his wife. He was interrupted by friends before he could do so, and spent the next few hours in their company, giving no cause for concern. But later, about midnight, he went to see his mother in her nearby apartment, where he stabbed her and then shot her in the head. He afterwards wrote a note saying that he loved her.

It was the first of many murders, and in the early hours of the following morning he carried out his original intention by stabbing his wife to death. Just a few hours after that, heavily armed, he went to the local university campus, where he climbed the observation tower, killed the receptionist on the twenty-seventh floor with a blow of his rifle butt, then shot three other people, killing two of them. Finally, just before noon, he began firing from the top of the tower at people below.

During the next hour and a half Whitman, an ex-Marine, killed another sixteen people and wounded many more. The tower was surrounded by police, and at one point a marksman tried to shoot him from a light plane — but this attempt was called off when Whitman returned the fire. The shooting then continued until three policemen stormed the tower and killed him.

Whitman had appeared to be quite normal until some months earlier, when his mother suddenly left his father after years of ill-treatment. This disturbed

Whitman in some way, and not long afterwards he went to see the campus psychiatrist, complaining of severe headaches and manic rages, which sometimes resulted in assaults on his wife.

In his typewritten note of 31 July, he said that he could not understand his violent impulses. 'I am prepared to die,' he said. 'After my death, I wish an autopsy on me to be performed to see if there is any mental disorder.' Later he wrote a note, '12.00 a.m. — Mother already dead, 3 o'clock — both dead.' He also said that he hated his father and that life was not worth living.

Following his death, a tumour was found on Whitman's brain, but medical experts did not regard this as the cause of his violent rages. The twenty-one murders which he committed in little more than thirteen hours are therefore inexplicable.

Double Axe Murder in Fall River. 1892

AUGUST

4

About 9.30 a.m. on 4 August 1892, Mrs Abby Borden, the sixty-five-year-old second wife of a wealthy businessman, was brutally murdered as she dusted the spare bedroom of her home on Fall River, Massachusetts. Her attacker struck her over the head with an axe while she was kneeling on the floor, then went on to strike another eighteen blows when she was already dead. The body lay undiscovered until much later in the morning — and in the meantime the victim's husband was killed in the same way.

Andrew J. Borden, aged sixty-nine, had gone out

after breakfast to attend to business matters. On returning just before 11 a.m., he settled down to have a rest in the living room, unaware that he was now a widower. A few minutes afterwards he, too, was attacked and killed, the culprit in his case striking ten blows. In view of the fact that an hour and a half had elapsed between the two crimes, it was naturally suspected that the killer was another member of the household.

Before long suspicion fell upon Lizzie, Andrew Borden's second daughter by his first marriage. Lizzie, an unmarried woman of thirty-two, had been in the house all the morning, and shortly after 11 a.m. had sent for the local doctor, saying that her father had been killed. Nothing was said at this stage about her stepmother's death, and when a neighbour asked where Mrs Borden was, Lizzie replied, 'I'm sure I don't know, for she had a note from someone to go and see somebody who is sick.' However, she then made the extraordinary remark, 'But I don't know perhaps that she isn't killed also, for I thought I heard her coming in.' It was shortly after this, when the neighbour and another woman began a search of the house, that the second body was found.

Lizzie Borden had borne her stepmother a good deal of ill-will and resented her father's meanness. She was strangely calm after the discovery of the bodies, but also made statements which contradicted each other. The police learnt that members of the household, including Mr and Mrs Borden (but not Lizzie), had been ill with food poisoning during the days preceding the murder, and that Lizzie had tried unsuccessfully to buy prussic acid on 3 August. A search of the cellar led to the discovery of a recently-cleaned axe-head, which they supposed to have been part of the murder weapon.

Following the inquest, which was held in secret, Lizzie was charged with the crimes. Her trial, which took place in New Bedford in June 1893, aroused nation-wide interest, and although the case against her at first seemed very strong, some of the evidence — of the prisoner contradicting herself at the inquest, for example — was not allowed, and her elder sister and the family's maid both played down Lizzie's hatred of Mrs Borden. Lizzie gave a good impression of herself, appearing refined and modest; it did her case no harm when she fainted in the courtroom, or even when she declined to give evidence on her own behalf. At the end of the ten-day trial she was acquitted.

She returned to Fall River, where she bought herself a larger house. Her sister shared it with her for a while, but moved out after a quarrel. Lizzie then lived alone for the rest of her life, dying in 1927.

The murders for which she had been tried were never officially solved, for Lizzie was the only real suspect, and it is generally believed that she was, in fact, guilty. The case has inspired many books, as well as five stage plays and a ballet. The American authoress Victoria Lincoln argues in *A Private Disgrace* that the crimes were committed while Lizzie was suffering from an attack of temporal epilepsy.

Death of Mary James, 1935

AUGUST 5

On 5 August 1935, Mary James, the fifth wife of Robert James, a barber's shop proprietor, was found dead in the lily pond at the couple's bungalow in Los Angeles. She had apparently drowned in just a few inches of water, and it was assumed that this had been the result of an accident. Little notice was taken of a grotesque swelling of her left leg, which was thought at the time to have been caused by an insect bite. But a few weeks later, when Robert James was reported for accosting a woman in the street, the police began to make further inquiries about him.

James, whose real name was Raymond Lisemba, was a native of Alabama, married for the first time in 1921. Three of his first four marriages had ended in divorce, James being a pervert who enjoyed whipping his partners as well as being whipped himself. But his third marriage had ended in circumstances which the Los Angeles police found to be of greater interest than that. Winona James had drowned in her bath only a short while after the marriage had taken place, and as a result her husband had collected $14,000 insurance money. This was particularly suspicious because James had profited in the same way — though to a lesser extent — from Mary's death.

Detectives also learnt that Charles Hope, who had worked for James in his barber's shop, had bought two rattlesnakes from a Long Beach snake farm in July 1935, returning them less than two weeks later with the comment that they 'didn't work'. When Hope was questioned about this, he said that the snakes, named Lethal and Lightning, had been purchased on James' behalf, and went on to declare that Mary James had been murdered by her husband — but not in the manner in which he had intended to murder her. The statement led to Robert James being arrested and brought to trial, with the snakes exhibited in court in a glass cage.

Hope, who was allowed to turn State's Evidence, told the court that James had offered him $100 to find two such snakes, as he wanted to have somebody bitten by them. Hope had agreed to do this, and Lethal and Lightning were actually the third pair that he had acquired on James' behalf, the first two pairs having proved unable even to kill rabbits. On the night of the murder, he said, he took the snakes to the couple's bungalow in a box, but did not produce them until Mary James, who was pregnant, had drunk so much whisky that she had become insensible, and so was unable to resist when the two men undressed her and held her down on the kitchen table.

The box was then taken into the kitchen, and the lid pushed back far enough for Mary's foot to be inserted, continued Hope. But although she was bitten several times, and her leg was badly swollen, she remained alive and began to recover from her drunken stupor. Her husband then became impatient and drowned her in bathwater, afterwards drying and dressing the body to avoid suspicion. Finally, Hope helped him to carry it out to the lily pond, where it appeared that she had accidentally fallen and drowned.

The trial, which took place during the summer of 1936, naturally attracted a great deal of attention. On being found guilty, 'Rattlesnake' James — as he became popularly called — was sentenced to death, his accomplice being given a life sentence. A series of appeals followed, but each of them was turned down, and eventually, on 1 May 1942, James became the last person to be hanged in California. Subsequent executions in that state were carried out in the gas chamber.

Execution of William Kemmler, 1890

On 6 August 1890, William Kemmler, a convicted murderer, was executed in the electric chair in New York's Auburn Prison. He was the first person to be put to death by this method, which the state had adopted in the expectation that it would prove to be more humane than hanging. The death chamber was a large room, with seats provided for officials, reporters and witnesses, but the apparatus was controlled from an adjoining room, where the executioner was hidden from view.

Kemmler, a short, black-haired man wearing a new suit, had murdered his mistress, Tillie Zeigler, with a hatchet in March the previous year. Having been ushered into the room by the warden, Charles F. Durston — who introduced him to the spectators in the manner of a master of ceremonies — he sat down calmly and made a short statement. The newspapers had been saying a lot of things about him which were untrue, he said. However, he wished everyone good luck and concluded, 'I believe I am going to a good place.'

He then had to take off his coat before he could be strapped to the chair and the electrodes fitted into place — one to his head, the other to his back, where his shirt had been torn to expose the flesh.

When all was finally ready the warden knocked twice on the door of the adjoining room, and the executioner threw the switch. The current was kept on for seventeen seconds, until the doctors present ordered it to be switched off. They then gathered round the chair, supposing Kemmler to be dead.

What happened next was described by the *New York World*'s reporter as follows:

'Suddenly the breast heaved. There was a straining at the straps which bound him ... The man was alive. Warden, physicians, everybody, lost their wits. There was a startled cry for the current to be turned on again. Signals, only half understood, were given to those in the next room at the switchboard. When they knew what had happened, they were prompt to act, and the switch-handle could be heard as it was pulled back and forth, breaking the deadly current into jets.'

Though Kemmler was unconscious, and therefore unaware of what was happening, it was accepted that the execution had been bungled, and at the second attempt the current was kept on for four minutes before the prisoner was pronounced dead.

The execution made headline news and there was much criticism for its 'unnecessary brutality': one English newspaper declared that it had 'sent a thrill of horror around the globe'. But New York was unwilling to return to 'the barbarism of hanging', and the electric chair was soon in regular use.

It is not known for certain who officiated at this first execution by electricity, but it was probably Edwin F. Davis, a wiry little electrician with a drooping black moustache, who was employed at the prison and known to have supervised the chair's construction.

Davis, at any rate, became New York's official executioner soon afterwards and later operated in New Jersey and Massachusetts, too. He carried out about 240 executions altogether before retiring in 1914.

Double execution at Darwin Jail, 1952

On 8 August 1952, two young immigrants were hanged at Darwin Jail, in Australia's Northern Territory, for murdering a taxi-driver. Jerry Koci, a twenty-year-old Czech, and his Rumanian accomplice, Jonas Nopoty, aged nineteen, had killed and robbed their victim, George Grantham, after asking him to drive them out of Darwin on the evening of 20 April previously. They left his body hidden in a patch of scrub off the Stuart Highway, and made off in his dark green Plymouth sedan.

George Grantham was a cheerful man, well known in the Darwin area. Shortly before his death he told his wife over the telephone that he had 'a job a bit out of town, with a couple of fellows', and so would not be home until after midnight. He also said that he had won over £600 at the Tennant Creek races earlier the same day.

When his disappearance was reported police started a search for him, asking aircraft pilots to report all cars seen in desolate areas and motorists to look out for car tracks leading off main roads. It was as a result of these appeals that the body was discovered by two other Northern Territory residents.

Grantham had been shot in the back of the head and stabbed in the region of the heart. The brutality of the crime shocked and angered the inhabitants of Darwin, and friends of the dead man threatened to form lynch mobs. 'You get the murderer and leave him to us,' they said to police officers. 'We'll do the hanging.'

Koci and Nopoty were apprehended while travelling in the stolen Plymouth in the direction of a small town in north-west Queensland. Nopoty then revealed that it was for the sake of his vehicle that Grantham had been murdered.

Koci had earlier been involved in a car accident in which a small boy had been killed. Because of this, he was frightened of being arrested, and therefore proposed a desperate course of action. 'We'll get hold of a car and then kill the driver,' he said. 'Then we can get to Melbourne and get a ship back to Europe.'

This, at least, was Nopoty's explanation of the crime, and Koci did not deny that it was true. He refused to make a statement of any sort.

The two men were taken back to Darwin, where police officers had to guard the jail in order to prevent them being lynched. When they appeared for trial the streets outside the courthouse were full of people, and it was no secret that they intended to take the law into their own hands in the event of the prisoners being acquitted. The residents of the Northern Territory afterwards made it known that they would not tolerate commutations of sentence, either.

It was only when the executions were carried out that the danger of a lynching was averted.

Murder of Shavon Tate, 1969

AUGUST
9

On 9 August 1969, three members of a hippie commune broke into the Los Angeles home of the film producer Roman Polanski and killed five people — including his twenty-six-year-old pregnant wife, the actress Sharon Tate. Four of the victims (Sharon Tate and three guests) were stabbed repeatedly; two of these were also shot — one in addition to being battered over the head with a blunt instrument. The fifth victim was a youth of eighteen, who was shot four times after stopping his car in the drive. Before leaving the scene the murderers daubed the slogan 'PIG' on the front door in Sharon Tate's blood.

The following night the same group, together with others — including Charles Manson, the commune leader — murdered Leno LaBianca, the forty-four-year-old president of a chain of grocery stores, and his wife Rosemary, aged thirty-five, also in Los Angeles, in a similar fashion. They broke into their victims' home, stabbed both of them many times and daubed slogans in blood on two of their walls and on the door of their refrigerator. One of the slogans on this occasion was 'HEALTER SKELTER', which was evidently a mis-spelling; the others were, 'DEATH TO PIGS' and 'RISE'. A further slogan, 'WAR', was scored on Leno LaBianca's body.

There was no known connection between the two sets of victims, and while the Los Angeles Police Department investigated the 'Sharon Tate Murders', the other crime was left to the Los Angeles Sheriff's Office. Neither was able to find out who the culprits were until many weeks later, when it was learnt that a young woman in custody on a different charge had told other prisoners that she had taken part in both crimes. Twenty-one-year-old Susan Atkins was then questioned and gave information which led to charges of murder and conspiracy to murder being brought against herself, Charles Manson and four other people.

Manson, who was thirty-five years old and only five foot two inches tall, was a violent man with a long record of crime. He lived with his hippie band in shacks on a movie ranch in the Simi Hills, thirty miles from Los Angeles, where they took hallucinogenic drugs and held sex orgies. But although his followers saw him as a Christ-like figure, and obeyed his orders without hesitation, Manson envied people who were rich and successful, and had a list of 'pigs' to be killed in a general day of reckoning which he referred to by the code-name 'Helter Skelter'.

According to Susan Atkins, he had ordered the murders of 9 August because another member of the group had been arrested in connection with a different one, and was then so pleased with the panic which they caused that he planned and personally took part in those of the following day.

Manson, Susan Atkins and two other members of the commune — Patricia Krenwinkel and Leslie Van Houten — were brought to trial in Los Angeles on 15 June 1970. Of the others who had been indicted, Linda Kasabian had been accepted as a prosecution witness, as she had not killed anybody herself — at Polanski's home, for example, she had stayed outside while the three main culprits broke in and murdered the people they found there — and Charles Watson was in Idaho, resisting extradition.

During the course of the trial, which lasted nine months, there were many sensations. On one occasion Manson hacked a cross into his forehead, and this inspired the three girls to burn similar marks onto theirs. On another he leapt ten feet over the counsel table and tried to attack the judge — which caused the judge to begin carrying a revolver. Eventually three of the prisoners were each convicted on seven counts of murder in the first degree and one of conspiracy to murder; the fourth — Leslie Van Houten — was found guilty on two counts of murder in the first degree and one of conspiracy. All four prisoners were sentenced to death.

Charles Watson was tried separately in 1971, and he, too, was sentenced to death after being convicted on seven counts of murder in the first degree and one of conspiracy. Manson, Susan Atkins and other members of the commune were subsequently convicted of other murders.

All of the death sentences passed in connection with these crimes were automatically commuted to life imprisonment when the California Supreme Court, in February 1972, voted to abolish the death penalty for murder.

Beginning of Transvaal Poisoning case, 1925

AUGUST
10

During the early hours of 10 August 1925, a middle-aged couple living in the northern Transvaal village of Koster, thirty-six miles from Rustenburg, were awakened by their son-in-law's mistress, who told them that their daughter, Anna Nortje, was ill. Mr and Mrs du Plessis accompanied the woman back to Anna's home, where they found their daughter dead and their son-in-law, Jan Christian Nortje, in tears. Nortje said that Anna, who was fully dressed except for her shoes, had died after being suddenly taken ill. She had complained of a pain in her back.

Mr and Mrs du Plessis were immediately suspicious. Anna had been to their home with her four young children the previous afternoon and had been in good health and spirits when she left. Besides that, their son Adrian — the husband of Nortje's mistress — had died mysteriously a year earlier, at the age of twenty-seven. They therefore called in the district surgeon, Dr Theodore Radloff, and insisted that this second death should be investigated more thoroughly than the first.

Nortje then became evasive about the symptoms which had preceded his wife's death, protesting that he had been 'too overcome with grief to notice (them)', so a post-mortem was carried out and the dead woman's organs were sent to a medical research institute for analysis. It was thus discovered that Anna Nortje had been poisoned with strychnine.

At the inquest which followed Nortje said that his wife had suffered from pains in her chest and back for some time, and hinted that village gossip about his affair with her sister-in-law, Dirkie Cathrina du Plessis, had driven her to suicide. On 9 August, when the children had been put to bed, Anna had cooked an evening meal for the three of them — for Dirkie frequently stayed overnight at their home — then went to bed herself. Shortly afterwards he found her to be unwell, and not long after that she was dead. Nortje also claimed that a note left by Anna, saying that her heart was 'sore and full of grief', had been destroyed by the children.

Dirkie, a mother of two, gave a slightly different account, stating that she had gone to fetch Mr and Mrs du Plessis while her sister-in-law was at the point of death, and that Anna was dead by the time she returned with them. Nortje, at this point, was strangely quiet, claiming to have seen an inexplicable purple light — which he took to be a 'premonition of evil' — outside the house.

Although there was no evidence against them, Nortje and his mistress were widely suspected of having poisoned Anna and the police were criticized for failing to arrest them. A search of Nortje's home on 1 September resulted in the discovery of a broken poison bottle, and inquiries revealed that during the month of July Nortje had obtained strychnine from a chemist in the village, darting out of the shop before he could be asked to sign the poison register. The police also learnt of other occasions on which either Nortje or Dirkie had tried to acquire poison. When the two lovers were arrested in December written evidence of their liaison was found at Dirkie's home.

At their trial in Rustenburg in June 1926 the prosecution produced evidence of a confession which Nortje had allegedly made to another prisoner. Nortje, however, denied having been Dirkie's lover, or having bought or attempted to buy poison. He said that his wife had complained of being in pain during the late afternoon of 9 August and had not eaten much of the evening meal because she 'felt bad'. Under cross-examination, he admitted that Anna had been ill for about five hours before her death, and that neither he nor Dirkie had done anything to help her. Dirkie later admitted having attempted to buy poison pills, saying that she wanted them to use for killing dogs.

On being found guilty, both prisoners collapsed and the judge had to adjourn the court before passing sentence of death. Some weeks later Dirkie's sentence was commuted to a long prison term by the Executive Council, but Nortje was told that in his own case the death sentence would be carried out.

From his cell in Pretoria Central Prison, he then wrote a long letter to the Minister of Justice, once more declaring that he was innocent of his wife's murder. As this was delivered just a few hours before he was due to be hanged, a brief postponement was ordered so that the matter could be considered afresh. This time, though no credence could be given to his statement, it was decided that mercy should be shown. Nortje's sentence was accordingly commuted to life imprisonment.

On 11 August 1954, William Sanchez de Pina Hepper, an artist and former BBC news translator aged sixty-two, was hanged at Wandsworth Prison, in London, for the murder of Margaret Spevick, the eleven-year-old daughter of a friend of his wife's. The crime had been committed at Hepper's flat in Hove, Sussex, where the victim was found raped and strangled six months earlier. Margaret, who attended the same London school as his own daughter, had been staying with Hepper for a few days in order to convalesce after breaking her arm.

Hepper, who had once suffered head injuries in a car accident — it was for this reason that he had resigned from the BBC — rarely saw his wife and claimed to be haunted by dreams of her infidelity. It had been his idea that Margaret should stay with him, and shortly after her arrival she had sent her mother a postcard, saying that she was having 'a splendid time'. After her death an unfinished portrait of her was found on an easel near her body.

The crime was discovered by Mrs Spevick on the evening of 7 February, when she went to the flat to see her daughter, whom she had expected to meet earlier in the day in nearby Brighton: she had to get the caretaker of the block to let her in, as nobody had opened the door to her. Hepper had already fled the country by this time, and was arrested a few days later in Spain, where he had once been a spy. The following month he was extradited to Britain.

At his trial at the Lewes Assizes in July he pleaded insanity. He told the court that he had bouts of amnesia and hallucinations, and it was suggested on his behalf that in assaulting the child he had been under the impression that he was attacking his wife.

But on being asked why he had left the country without informing Margaret's parents, the prisoner could only reply, 'I did not do things properly because I was not in a normal condition.' And a Hove psychiatrist, who told the court that the accused had regarded the crime as a hallucination, was obliged to admit that he could not explain Hepper's sudden flight.

The jury therefore rejected the plea of insanity and the prisoner was found guilty of murder.

Execution of Richard Brinkley, 1907

AUGUST
13

On 13 August 1907, Richard Brinkley, a fifty-three-year-old jobbing gardener, was hanged for the murder of a middle-aged couple at their home in Croydon, Surrey, on the night of 20 April previously. Richard and Annie Beck had both died after drinking oatmeal stout poisoned with prussic acid which Brinkley had intended for their lodger, Reginald Parker. Daisy Beck, the couple's twenty-one-year-old daughter, had also drunk some of the stout but had recovered after being rushed to hospital.

On 17 December 1906, Brinkley, who lived in Fulham, south-west London, had tricked Parker into signing a forged will, pretending that it was a list of people invited to go on a picnic outing during the spring. The will was ostensibly that of his own land-

lady, an elderly German woman named Mrs Blume
— who had also been tricked into signing it — and
stated that he was to receive her home and furniture,
together with all her stocks and cash. The second
'witness' was a man named Henry Heard, who had
presumably been tricked as well.

When Mrs Blume died on 19 December, a
coroner's jury accepted that her death was the result
of a cerebral haemorrhage. But when Brinkley
produced the will — after the inquest had taken place
— Mrs Blume's relatives decided to contest it. This
meant that both Parker and Heard would be questioned about the document at some stage, and that
Brinkley would be sent to prison.

Brinkley, keeping up the pretence of friendship,
then started visiting Parker at home almost every
evening and tried repeatedly to murder him — always
by putting poison into his food or drink after asking
him to go out and fetch a glass of water. But on each
occasion Parker — who now suspected that his was
one of the signatures on Mrs Blume's will — managed
to outwit him by declining to touch anything which
had been left in Brinkley's presence.

On the evening of 20 April Brinkley arrived with
the bottle of stout and, in spite of the fact that he was
normally a teetotaller, drank some of it himself before
offering any to Parker. There was no prussic acid in it
at that stage, but shortly afterwards Brinkley asked
Parker for the usual glass of water and poisoned the
stout while he was out of the room. Unfortunately for
him, Parker was no less suspicious than on other
occasions, and on returning refused to drink any more
of it.

The two men later took Parker's dog out for a
walk, leaving the unfinished bottle on his table. The
Becks, who had also been out for part of the evening,
found it there when they came indoors, and for some
reason thought they were entitled to help themselves

to the contents. They were thus poisoned by accident because their lodger realized that Brinkley was trying to poison him.

Surprisingly, though Parker had been in fear of his life for several months, he had made no attempt to avoid seeing Brinkley and had not sought the aid of the police. But on hearing what had happened to Mr and Mrs Beck, he revealed all that he knew of the affair. Brinkley, who had parted company with him in the street, was arrested in Fulham the following day.

He denied all knowledge of what had happened, saying that he had not seen Parker for three weeks. But a boy working in a Croydon off-licence remembered selling him the bottle of stout on the evening in question and a railway inspector who knew him by sight was certain that he had bought a rail ticket to Croydon on the same evening. It was also discovered that Brinkley had obtained prussic acid from a doctor's dispenser in Manor Road, South Norwood.

Though no evidence of poisoning was found during a second examination of Mrs Blume's body, there was enough evidence against Brinkley to ensure his conviction not only for the murder of Mr and Mrs Beck but also for the attempted murder of Daisy Beck and Reginald Parker.

His trial took place at the Guildford Assizes, and his execution at Wandsworth Prison.

William Rowe found murdered, 1963

AUGUST
15

On the morning of 15 August 1963, William Garfield Rowe, a sixty-four-year-old recluse, was found murdered on his farm near the village of Constantine, in Cornwall. His skull had been shattered, there was a gash in his throat, his jaw was fractured, and he had suffered many other injuries to his scalp and chest. The farmhouse had afterwards been ransacked, his killer or killers missing some £3000 which Mr Rowe had had hidden there. Mr Rowe had last been seen alive about 9.15 the previous evening.

Following the discovery of the body, road-blocks were set up in the area, and on 16 August a twenty-three-year-old man named Russell Pascoe, who had been stopped while riding a motor-cycle in the village, was questioned about his movements on the night of the murder. He said that he had been at a caravan near Truro, about fourteen miles away, with his friend Dennis Whitty and three teenage girls. But he admitted having known the victim and said that he had worked for him three or four years earlier.

Pascoe, Whitty and the three girls were taken to Falmouth police station for questioning, and the girls then told the police that on the night of the murder the two men had left the caravan on Pascoe's motor-cycle to 'do a job', taking a starting-pistol, an iron bar and a knife. They had returned in the early hours of the morning, Pascoe downcast and frightened-looking and his companion grinning. Later, after Whitty had confessed that he and Pascoe were responsible for Mr Rowe's murder, both men warned the girls that they would suffer the same fate if they revealed this to anyone else.

On being charged, Pascoe, a builder's labourer, admitted that he had been present at the crime, but said that he had 'only' hit the deceased on the head with the iron bar: it was Whitty who 'went mad with the knife', he claimed. He then gave an account of what had happened, stating:

'We went on my motor-bike and knocked on (the farmhouse) door at about 11 o'clock. Old man Rowe answered the door. Dennis was standing in front of the door and said he was a helicopter pilot and had crashed, and wanted to use the phone. I then hit Rowe on the back of the head with a small iron bar — I meant only to knock him out, that's all.

'He (Whitty) took the iron bar and went for him. I had to walk away, honest I did. I went inside and found £4 under a piano. Dennis took a watch and two big boxes of matches, and some keys from the old man's pockets. We shared the £4, and I've spent mine.'

Later, giving further details, Pascoe said, 'I didn't kill him — that was my mate. He went mad, he did. I didn't stop him in fear he would stick me. I had to walk away. I couldn't stop him. He said he finished him when he stuck the knife in his throat. I only knocked him on the head with a bar. I just knocked him out.'

Dennis John Whitty, aged twenty-two, then blamed Pascoe for what had happened. 'Pascoe made me stick him,' he said. 'I stabbed him in the chest. Pascoe was going to hit me, so I stuck him in the neck.

On 29 October the two men appeared for trial at the Bodmin Assizes, the crime being described by the prosecution as 'one of the most horrible and gruesome murders ever known in this county or this country'; both pleaded not guilty. Whitty's counsel claimed that his client had acted under 'the influence, fear and pressure of Pascoe', who three years earlier had burgled the farmhouse and stolen £200, together with jewellery which had belonged to Mr Rowe's mother; the court was also told that Whitty suffered from hysteria, black-outs and 'strange and unnatural things', such as doors opening of their own accord and a figure with wings appearing in the sky early in the morning.

However, the jury returned verdicts of guilty against both men, and they were sentenced to death.

On 17 December 1963, Pascoe was hanged at Bristol and Whitty at Winchester.

William Rowe had been a First World War deserter whose parents had hidden him for over thirty years at their farm in the fishing village of Porthleven, in Cornwall. When his father died, his mother and brother moved to Constantine, with Mr Rowe hiding under a pile of clothing in a cart. But after he had lived in secrecy for thirty-nine years — with everyone outside his immediate family believing him to be dead — an amnesty was declared and William Rowe was able to emerge as a living person.

Besides the £3000 which his murderers had missed, he had had other large sums hidden in the farm grounds — one in a safe buried in the floor of a cowshed, another in a large glass jar buried elsewhere. These were eventually found as a result of directions in a diary which he had left, written in Esperanto.

Execution of Santo-Geronimo Caserio, 1894

On 16 August 1894, a young Italian anarchist was executed in front of the Prison Saint-Paul in Lyons. Santo-Geronimo Caserio, who had assassinated the French President, Sadi Carnot, was far from fearless — indeed, he was terrified, and moaned inarticulately all the way from his cell to the guillotine. At the last minute, however, he managed to pull himself together for one final act of defiance. 'Courage, comrades —

and long live anarchy!' he called out in a weak voice. As he did so, the blade fell.

Caserio, a native of Motta-Visconti, near Milan, had been born in 1873, and apprenticed to a baker at the age of thirteen. He became an anarchist in 1891, and not long afterwards was given a sentence of eight months' imprisonment for distributing revolutionary literature to soldiers at a Milan barracks. He left Italy in the spring of 1893 to avoid military service, and arrived in France from Switzerland in July the same year.

For several months prior to the assassination, Caserio lived in Cette, a seaport on the Mediterranean, staying at the home of a baker named Viala, who was also his employer. He left Viala suddenly, bought himself a dagger, then made his way to Lyons, where the crime was committed. He had apparently been planning to strike 'a staggering blow' against the existing social order for quite some time.

Carnot was murdered on the evening of 24 June 1894, while he was in Lyons attending the Universal Exhibition. He was being driven to the theatre in a carriage when Caserio dashed out of the crowd lining his route and stabbed him in the chest. He died three hours later.

Caserio, who had been arrested at the scene, admitted that he was the person responsible and identified the weapon without any sign of remorse. He said that he had planned and carried out the crime on his own, without confiding his intention to anyone. At his trial at the beginning of August he described it in detail.

'When I saw the carriage approaching, I drew my dagger from my pocket, overturned two young people in front of me, threw aside the sheath, and then sprang forward,' he said. 'I grasped the carriage door with my left hand, and with my right I struck downwards with all my force.'

He went on to say that after striking the blow, he cried, 'Long live the revolution!' And he added, 'When I had stabbed the President, he looked me fixedly in the face and then sank back.'

The defence claimed that the prisoner was an epileptic and that his crime had been committed as a result of 'some mysterious and irresistible force'. It was also argued — to his own indignation — that he had been merely the 'striking arm' of others. But all this was to no avail: the jury retired for only ten minutes before finding him guilty without extenuating circumstances.

Though overcome with emotion after being sentenced to death, Caserio managed to shout a number of slogans before being taken from the court-room.

Post Office massacre in Oklahoma 1986

AUGUST
20

On the morning of 20 August 1986, Patrick Sherrill, a forty-four-year-old part-time postman, entered the Edmond, Oklahoma, post office armed with three pistols and began shooting his fellow workers. In the space of just eight minutes, beginning at six minutes past seven, he killed fourteen people and wounded others. He then remained trapped in the building for an hour and a quarter, finally killing himself as police burst in.

Sherrill, who had been working at the post office for about eighteen months off and on, was a solitary man with a sense of grievance. He had been an object of derision for much of his life — he was reputed to be a Peeping Tom, for one thing — and had a violent temper which caused him to be known locally as 'Crazy Pat'. He appeared to have been deteriorating mentally since his discharge from the US Marine Corps over twenty years earlier.

'He was sick in the head,' one of his neighbours said afterwards. 'He should have been put away long ago. He was always angry at something — like he didn't know what he was angry about.' The same woman, whose eleven-year-old son had once been threatened by Sherrill, also remarked, 'We're black — and he didn't like blacks. He didn't like much of anything.'

But Sherrill had a keen interest in guns, and was a firearms instructor in the Oklahoma Air National Guard. A few weeks before the massacre he had been sent to Britain, to help supervise the training of US service personnel stationed at RAF Mildenhall, in Suffolk, and at the end of August he was due to take part in a national competition in Little Rock, Arkansas. His conduct while on National Guard duty had always been exemplary.

As a postman, however, he left much to be desired; his performance ratings were unfavourable and he was often in trouble; only the day before the shootings he had been threatened with dismissal. He confided his problems with his supervisors to a young female employee, telling her, 'They'll be sorry — and everyone's going to know about it. Everybody's gonna know.' Thirty-eight-year-old Richard Esser, one of the supervisors concerned, was the first person to be killed the following morning.

When police officers went to Sherrill's home they found amateur radio equipment, a computer, piles of clothes, books, paramilitary and sex magazines, two air pistols, an air rifle and boxes of ammunition. They also discovered that the hallway had been used as an indoor shooting-range, with mounted targets in one of the bedrooms. But there was only one chair in the whole house — a sure sign that visitors hadn't been welcome.

Though post office union officials in Edmond were as shocked as everyone else by what had happened, they were quick to point out that there had recently been a lot of friction between rank-and-file workers and their supervisors as a result of pressure to increase productivity. In their view, this pressure had often amounted to harassment, and it was not really surprising that a disturbed man like Sherrill should have reacted in such an extreme way.

Murder of Rose Render, 1911

AUGUST
21

During the early hours of 21 August 1911, a nineteen-year-old waitress named Rose Render was stabbed to death in the Clerkenwell district of London. A passer-by heard her cries of 'Don't, Charles! Don't!' — followed by screams — but made no attempt to help her. It was not until later in the morning, when a milkman going through Wilmington Square found her body lying on the pavement, that the crime was brought to the attention of the police.

The girl was found to have been living with a man named Charles Ellsome until shortly before her death. Ellsome, aged twenty-two, described himself as a labourer, but Rose had, in fact, been keeping him and had taken to prostitution on his account. On being confronted in a café in Soho the day after the

243

murder, Ellsome gave his name as Brown, but told police officers, 'It's me you want.' He later claimed that all he had meant by this was that he knew he would be suspected of the crime.

Ellsome was charged with murder and appeared at the Old Bailey on 13 September, his trial lasting less than a day. A friend of the accused, a man named Fletcher, told the court that on 21 August Ellsome had woken him up between two and three o'clock in the morning and said that he had killed Rose, declaring. 'She drove me to it!' He went on to say that he had threatened her with his knife, and that Rose had thrown up her arms, saying, 'Here you are, then — do it!' He had then stabbed her eight or nine times in a fit of anger.

Fletcher was hardly the most impressive of witnesses. Under cross-examination he admitted that he suffered from epilepsy and that he had had a fit the day before the murder. Worse still, he boasted: 'I thieve for my living, and I'm proud of it!' However, it was proved that Ellsome had bought a long-bladed chef's knife a few days before the crime, and the victim's father accused him of trying to intimidate her. The jury took only half an hour to find the prisoner guilty, and on being asked whether he had anything to say before sentence was passed, Ellsome raised his eyes towards the ceiling, remarking, 'I have only got one Judge.'

The trial judge, Mr Justice Avory, was not taken in by this display of piety. 'The prisoner has been living the most degraded life that a man can live,' he said. 'I cannot doubt that he took away the life of the girl, not from jealousy that she loved another man, or that another man loved her, but from jealousy that another man should reap the benefit of her immoral life. For the crime of which he has been convicted, he must die.'

However, in his summing-up Avory had inadvertently misdirected the jury. Reminding them that they should not accept Fletcher's evidence without corroboration, he had intimated that such corroboration was provided by a statement made by that witness immediately after the murder. As the statement to which he was referring had not been introduced as evidence, the Court of Criminal Appeal was obliged to set aside the conviction — the first time it had done so in a case of murder. The prisoner had therefore to be released, as the court had no power to order a retrial.

Murder of an elephant-keeper, 1928

AUGUST
24

On the night of 24 August 1928, London Zoo's chief elephant-keeper, Sayed Ali, was battered to death by his assistant, a young Burmese named San Dwe. The two men shared rooms above the Tapir House, near the Outer Circle of Regent's Park, and it was there that the crime was committed. It was later claimed that the blows had been struck with 'a ferocity that was beyond belief'.

As far as the police were concerned, this unusual case began when two officers on patrol in the area heard groans coming from the back of the building and stopped to investigate. San Dwe, who was lying on the ground with a wounded foot, said that four men had broken into the place and killed Sayed Ali with a pick-axe. They had tried to kill him, too, but he had managed to escape, he added excitedly.

The police officers went inside the building and found

Sayed Ali's body; he had died of head injuries. His room had been ransacked and a wooden box broken open, but nothing had been taken. Two bags of copper coins were found, together with a wallet containing £36; a bloodstained pickaxe and a sledge-hammer were also found at the scene. However, the wounded man's story was not believed and, on being discharged from hospital, he was arrested.

San Dwe had arrived in London from Rangoon the previous year in charge of a white elephant. The elephant did not take to the English climate, and so was sent back to Burma not long afterwards. But San Dwe stayed on at the zoo as Sayed Ali's assistant, and deputized for him when he went for several months' holiday in his native Calcutta — as he did every year. During those months San Dwe received up to thirty shillings (£1.50) a week in tips from visitors whose children had had rides on the elephants in his care, and he was entitled to keep all this money himself.

Even so, he was not happy in England; he fretted over the loss of the animal which had been sent back to Burma, and longed to rejoin it there. Moreover, with the return of Sayed Ali from India, he had only minor duties to perform and lost his extra source of income. It seems that he killed his chief in the hope of stealing money, but then lost his nerve or suffered from feelings of guilt.

At his trial, which took place in November 1928, San Dwe was convicted of murder. His death sentence was later commuted to penal servitude for life, but he remained in jail only until 1932, when his case was considered by a special board. On his release, he was sent back to Burma.

Murder of Charles Fox, 1933

AUGUST 27

During the early hours of 27 August 1933, Charles William Fox, a twenty-four-year-old metal worker living in West Bromwich, Staffordshire, was woken up by his wife, who said that she had heard a noise coming from downstairs. He went to investigate, with Mrs Fox following, and, on looking into one of the downstairs rooms, found the window open. He immediately went to close it, unaware that the person who had opened it was in the room.

At that moment the candle which he was holding went out, and Mrs Fox heard a scuffle and a groan in the darkness. She called out to her husband, to go back upstairs with her, then returned to the bedroom alone. But a moment later, as she stood there trembling, he staggered into the room with a knife stuck in his back. Unable to speak, he threw his arms round her, then fell to the floor and died.

Mrs Fox threw open the bedroom window and screamed for help. Shortly afterwards two policemen arrived at the house, but by that time the intruder had fled. It was found that he had cut out one of the panes of the sash window by which he had entered, and left bloodstained glass both inside and outside. A doctor called to the scene found that the dead man had been stabbed seven times, one of the blows piercing his lung.

Not long after the murder had taken place a burglary was committed at the home of a butcher named Newton, half a mile away. In this case, in addition to stealing a few pounds in cash, the culprit stayed at the scene to have a shave — using the butcher's razor — and also made use of a needle and cotton which he had found in a work-basket. He eventually left, though not without leaving his fingerprints on a milk bottle. These were found to match others on file at Scotland Yard, identifying him as Stanley Eric Hobday — a man already known to the local police.

A few hours after the burglary, a farm labourer near High Legh, Cheshire, about seventy miles away, heard the sound of a crash and saw a car turn a complete somersault in a nearby lane — after which the damaged car was abandoned. The vehicle had been stolen from a private garage in West Bromwich, and one of Hobday's fingerprints was found on the starting-handle. A suitcase containing some of his belongings was also found.

In their search for Hobday, the police were assisted by the BBC, using radio for the first time to broadcast a description of somebody they wanted to interview. Three days later he was arrested near Gretna Green, in Dumfriesshire.

Hobday was a little man, whose extraordinarily small shoes — they were size four — matched plaster casts of footprints found in the soil outside Charles Fox's window. A cut in one of the sleeves of his jacket — with bloodstains round it — had been darned with black cotton identical to that found in the needle used at Mr Newton's home; it was also found to correspond with an unhealed cut on Hobday's elbow.

Hobday told the police that he had hidden the suitcase just before the murder, and afterwards found it to be missing from its hiding place. A sheath knife which he was known to have owned had been inside it at the time of its disappearance, he claimed. But his fingerprint on the starting-handle of the stolen car proved that this story was untrue; the suitcase had been in his possession at the time of the accident, and the knife had not been among the items found inside it.

Hobday was charged with all three crimes: the murder, the burglary and the car-theft. In respect of the two lesser crimes, he was clearly guilty, but this — according to the defence when he appeared for trial in Stafford — proved that he could not have been the murderer of Charles Fox.

'Is it conceivable that any man, woman or boy, after foully murdering another human being, and with his hands still bearing the stains of blood, could calmly go off to Mr Newton's house and commit a burglary, sit down and shave himself, his nerves so calm that he could thread a needle and sit down and mend his clothes, and then go off and commit another burglary — the theft of a motor-car?' Sir Reginald Coventry asked the jury. It was a fantastic story, he declared.

But Hobday's tiny shoes proved the opposite, and after a three-day trial the jury took only forty-five minutes to find him guilty. He was duly hanged at Winson Green Prison, Birmingham, on 29 December 1933.

Disappearance of Edwina Taylor, 1957

On the afternoon of 31 August 1957, Edwina Taylor, a pretty girl aged four, disappeared from her home in Upper Norwood, south-east London. A search was organized by the Metropolitan Police — it proved to be one of their biggest searches ever — and various people came forward, claiming to have seen her. But none of these reported sightings led to the child's discovery, and for several days the police could find no sign of her.

Before long a second person was found to be missing from the same district: a thirty-one-year-old factory labourer named Derrick Edwardson, who lived only a quarter of a mile from Edwina's home. As Edwardson was an unstable person with a criminal record — he had indecently assaulted one little girl and threatened to murder another — it was feared that the two disappearances might be connected.

This fear was confirmed on the afternoon of 5 September, when two police officers entered the cellar beneath Edwardson's ground-floor flat and found the missing girl's body lying on a heap of coal. It was immediately clear that she had been strangled, but the post-mortem, carried out by Professor Francis Camps, revealed that she had also been sexually assaulted and struck on the head and face with a heavy blunt instrument.

Forensic evidence was found inside Edwardson's flat, linking him with the crime. Bloodstains from Edwina's group were found in his kitchen and on his suit, and fibres from her coat were found in the turn-ups of his trousers. Hairs from his dog were found to be identical to others on the child's cardigan and sandals. Moreover, a search of Edwardson's locker at the factory where he worked resulted in the discovery of a note which he had written, confessing that he had murdered the missing girl.

He had taken her to his flat and strangled her — 'with the intention of raping her after death' — but had afterwards felt ashamed of himself and thrown the body into the cellar, the note revealed. It also said that he had not interfered with the child — which the post-mortem findings showed to be untrue.

Shortly afterwards, on giving himself up, Edwardson admitted responsibility for Edwina's death. He said that he had enticed her to the flat by giving her sweets — 'just to assault her and take her home again' — but had then knocked her unconscious with the blunt end of an axe which he had bought for cutting firewood. Then, according to this account, he strangled her by accident while trying to revive her.

Haunted by the thought of the child's face, he later got up in the middle of the night to go and look at her. 'It made my hair stand on end, although I only looked at her feet,' he said.

Edwardson was charged with murder and brought to trial at the Old Bailey on 25 October 1957; he pleaded guilty and was sentenced to life imprisonment. His victim's father then wrote to the Home Secretary, asking for known sex offenders to be kept under stricter control.

beginning of the 'Pyjama Girl' case, 1934

SEPTEMBER
1

On 1 September 1934, the body of a young woman, dressed in pyjamas and partly burnt, was found in a culvert a few miles from Albury, New South Wales. Her death had been caused by savage blows to the skull with a blunt instrument — though there was also a bullet wound in her face — and had taken place anything from one to four days previously. She was apparently an Englishwoman, aged between twenty-two and twenty-eight, but her identity was unknown. Her most distinctive feature was her ears, which were an unusual shape and had no lobes.

The body was taken to Sydney University, where it

was preserved in a tank of formalin for the next ten years. Various people identified it as the body of Mrs Anna Philomena Coots, the twenty-three-year-old wife of a writer, but finally, in 1944, it was established that the 'Pyjama Girl' was Mrs Linda Agostini, an Englishwoman married to an Italian waiter. In the meantime the unsolved crime had received a good deal of publicity, and an amateur investigator — a doctor named Palmer-Benbow — had accused the New South Wales police of protecting the person responsible.

Linda Agostini, an attractive but jealous woman who drank excessively, had been living with her husband Tony in Melbourne prior to her disappearance in August 1934. When her husband was interviewed by police in July the following year he said that she had left him after a quarrel — an explanation which he had already given to friends. On being shown photographs of the dead woman at this time, he denied that she was his wife.

But in 1944 the corpse was taken out of the formalin, so that its face could be made up in a fresh attempt to solve the mystery. After that seven people said that it *was* Linda Agostini, and her husband was questioned again. Tony Agostini, who had been interned as an alien for part of the Second World War, then confessed that that was so and that he was the culprit.

He claimed that he and his wife had been unable to get on together, and that one morning she had threatened him with a gun while they were still in bed. He managed to get the gun away from her, he said, but then killed her accidentally in a struggle. The next day he drove the body to the culvert near Albury and set fire to it in order to prevent identification.

When Agostini was brought to trial in June 1944 the prosecution produced medical evidence to show that the dead woman's skull injuries had been inflicted while she was still alive, thus disproving the story that she had been shot dead by accident. The prisoner was therefore convicted of manslaughter and sentenced to a term of imprisonment with hard labour. He was eventually deported to Italy.

Execution of Jimmy Lee Gray, 1983

SEPTEMBER 2

On 2 September 1983, Jimmy Lee Gray, aged thirty-four, was executed in the gas chamber of the state penitentiary in Parchman, Mississippi, for the murder of three-year-old Deressa Jean Scales. Gray, from Whittier, in California, had been convicted in 1976, but delayed the execution for almost seven years by means of a series of appeals. The last of these, to the United States Supreme Court, was rejected by a majority of six votes to three only a few hours before the sentence was carried out.

Gray entered the gas chamber just after midnight, and a few minutes afterwards the gas was released. Prison officials claimed that he was dead within two minutes, but other witnesses said that he was still convulsing and gasping for breath eight minutes later. It was the first execution in Mississippi for nineteen years.

Gray had kidnapped Deressa and taken her to a wooded area thirty miles from her home in Pascagoula. There he committed sodomy with her, then suffocated her by pressing her face into the mud. Finally, when she was dead, he threw her body off a bridge.

At the time of committing these offences, Gray was

on parole from a prison in Arizona, where he had served seven years of a twenty-year sentence. This had been imposed for the murder of his sixteen-year-old fiancée in 1968.

Shooting of Count Kamarowsky, 1907

On the morning of 3 September 1907, Count Paul Kamarowsky, a Russian nobleman on holiday in Italy, was shot at his villa on the Campo Santa Maria del Giglio, in Venice, receiving wounds from which he died three days later. The crime was committed by his young fellow-countryman, Nicolas Naumoff, who had arrived at the villa a moment or two earlier, claiming to have 'important business' to discuss with him. Naumoff escaped from the scene, but was apprehended in Verona soon afterwards.

Within a few hours of his arrest three other suspects were taken into custody: a beautiful but dissolute Russian countess named Marie Tarnowska, in whose favour Kamarowsky had insured his life, her companion Elise Perrier — a Swiss girl — and Donat Prilukoff, a solicitor from Moscow who had left his wife and abandoned his practice. Prilukoff immediately made a statement in which he said that Naumoff had committed the crime, but that the Countess had planned it; he also revealed that he, too, had been involved in the conspiracy to murder the Count.

Though Marie Tarnowska denied having had anything to do with the crime, letters and telegrams discovered by the police proved that Prilukoff's allegations were true. The Countess, who was separated from her husband, had had Kamarowsky, Naumoff *and* Prilukoff as lovers all at the same time, and had used each of them to suit her own purposes. However, it was not until two and a half years later that the prisoners were brought to trial.

They eventually appeared at the Criminal Court in Venice in March 1910, the trial attracting a great deal of attention. Nicolas Naumoff told the court that he had been infatuated with Maria Tarnowska, that he had been under her 'spell', and that he had shot Kamarowsky out of jealousy, knowing that he had been intimate with the Countess. Naumoff also told the court that he believed Elsie Perrier must have known of his intention to kill the Count.

Prilukoff likewise blamed the Countess, saying that he had been happily married, prosperous and held in high esteem before he met her. 'She was too strong for me,' he declared. 'There was nothing I would not have done at her command. Because she wished it, I left my wife, I robbed my clients, I sacrificed my honour — and once I even tried to kill myself.' He went on to confess that he and Marie Tarnowska had conspired to kill Kamarowsky, stating, 'We both considered that Naumoff would be the best man to do the job.'

Marie Tarnowska — 'the Russian Vampire' — admitted that she had had affairs with many men, including Kamarowsky, Naumoff and Prilukoff, but denied being responsible for Kamarowsky's death. She agreed that she had known of Naumoff's intention to kill Kamarowsky, but said that she was unable to warn the Count that his life was in danger because she was 'acting under the orders of Prilukoff'. Shortly after this a heated argument broke out between the Countess, Naumoff and Prilukoff over who was to blame for what had happened.

Although Prilukoff and Elise Perrier were believed

255

to be mentally quite normal, Naumoff was shown to be a degenerate and Marie Tarnowska a drug-addict of long standing who had suffered from hysteria and convulsions.

Naumoff was found guilty of premeditated murder, though with 'responsibility lessened owing to the fact that he was suffering from a partial mental collapse'; he was therefore given a prison sentence of only three years and four months. Marie Tarnowska was found guilty of helping him, though it was accepted by the jury that 'her mental faculties were partially destroyed'; she was given a sentence of eight years and four months. Donat Prilukoff was also found guilty of helping Naumoff, and in his case a sentence of ten years' solitary confinement was passed. Elise Perrier was acquitted.

Marie Tarnowska was sent to the women's prison at Trani, on the shores of the Adriatic, to serve her sentence, but was released in 1912. She died in Paris in 1923.

Disappearance of William Lavers, 1936

SEPTEMBER 5

On the morning of 5 September 1936, William Henry Lavers, a country storekeeper of Grenfell, New South Wales, mysteriously disappeared after getting up early to serve a motorist who required petrol. Later, when his wife went outside to look for him, she found the hose of one of the hand-operated petrol pumps on the ground, with the pumping handle bloodstained and a piece of wood — also bloodstained — lying nearby. The pump gauge showed that six gallons had been taken, and a quantity of oil was also missing. Further bloodstains were found on the wrappings of a new broom at the back of the store.

It appeared that the motorist had killed Lavers and taken his body away in the car. But a search organized by the Sydney police — with hundreds of volunteers taking part — revealed no further trace of it, and no clue to the culprit's identity. The crime was still unsolved ten years later, when a car-dealer reported that he had overheard a man named Frederick McDermott admit killing the missing storekeeper. As a result of this, McDermott was arrested in Dubbo, 185 miles north-west of Sydney, on 10 October 1946, and charged with Lavers' murder.

Frederick Lincoln McDermott was a sheep-shearer and general bush-worker who had several times been in trouble for minor offences. He lived with a half-caste Maori woman named Florrie Hampton, and the admission which led to his arrest had been made during the course of a quarrel with her. On being questioned, Florrie agreed that McDermott had admitted killing Lavers, and said that he had told her so on other occasions as well. Another woman, Doretta Williams, claimed that she, too, had heard McDermott admit to having murdered the store-keeper.

'Florrie said Fred hit Lavers on the head with a pump handle,' she told police. 'He put his body in the back of the car, drove out to the old Grenfell sheep-yard, and cut up the body with an axe. Then he put it in a bag and buried it.' She added that on hearing this McDermott had said, 'Of course I killed Lavers and cut up his body with an axe.'

A fresh search for the body was as unavailing as the first, and although a woman who called herself Mrs Essie King identified McDermott as one of two men she had seen in the vicinity of Grenfell on the day of the storekeeper's disappearance, she was the only witness to do so. And when McDermott was brought to trial he denied having made certain admissions of guilt which police officers claimed that he *had* made. Even so, he was convicted of murder and sentenced to death.

The sentence was afterwards commuted to life imprisonment, but McDermott was not satisfied with this and, although appeals against his conviction failed, his vehement protestations of innocence led to the appointment of a Royal Commission to inquire into the case in 1951.

'Mrs King' died before this body's proceedings started, but Charles Garrett — the former 'Mr King', whom she had married shortly before her death — gave evidence, revealing that his wife had been paid £25 by the Sydney police for her information about the case in question. It was then suggested that she had suffered remorse and even attempted suicide as a result of having given false evidence at McDermott's trial.

Florrie Hampton, who had not been called as a witness at McDermott's trial, now denied having told police that he had said he knew the whereabouts of Lavers' body, and claimed that she had signed a statement without reading it. She said that McDermott had sometimes denied killing Lavers, and at other times had said, 'If you say I killed him, I must have.'

She also said that the police had tried to get her to give information about a second man who had been named in connection with the storekeeper's disappearance — the man 'Mrs King' claimed to have seen with McDermott in the vicinity of Grenfell.

Moreover, it was proved almost conclusively that a car which had earlier been thought to have left tracks outside the store could not have done so.

In all, ninety-nine witnesses appeared before the Royal Commission — including McDermott, who broke down under cross-examination. The Commissioner, Mr Justice Kinsella, reported his findings on 12 January 1952, saying that while there was no truth in the allegations which had been made against 'Mrs King' and the police, fresh evidence which had been produced suggested that the jury at McDermott's trial had probably been misled by erroneous evidence. This did not prove that McDermott was innocent, but the law did not require him to prove his innocence, the Commissioner declared.

McDermott was released in accordance with the Commissioner's recommendations and given £500 compensation — which was considerably less than the sum for which he had hoped.

The other man named in connection with the case was never arrested, and the storekeeper's body has never been found. The crime remains unsolved.

Assassination of President McKinley, 1901

SEPTEMBER
6

On 6 September 1901, President William McKinley was shot and fatally wounded while attending the Pan-American Exposition in Buffalo, New York. The crime took place in the Temple of Music, a building normally used for organ recitals and concerts, while McKinley was shaking hands with members of the public. His murderer was Leon F. Czolgosz, a twenty-eight-year-old man of Polish descent who claimed to be an anarchist.

Czolgosz had joined the queue of people whom the President was greeting, and had wrapped a large white handkerchief round his own right hand in order to conceal the revolver that he was holding. Coming face to face with the President, he extended his left hand, as though the other had been hurt, and McKinley went to take it. But Czolgosz suddenly dashed the President's hand aside, lunged forward and fired through the handkerchief twice in quick succession.

McKinley, an affable and well-liked man, looked at Czolgosz in astonishment before slumping into the arms of those around him. One bullet had struck him in the chest, the other had passed through his abdomen. Before Czolgosz could fire again, he was knocked down by soldiers and secret service agents, who then beat him up.

The President was taken in an electric ambulance to an emergency hospital in the Exposition grounds. There surgeons operated on him for an hour and a half, but were unable to find the bullet which had caused the wound in his abdomen. McKinley died eight days later, the cause of his death — according to the autopsy report — being blood poisoning due to gangrene of the pancreas.

On being questioned at Buffalo police head-quarters, Czolgosz denied having had a grudge against McKinley. He made a confession in his own handwriting, in which he stated, 'I killed President McKinley because I done my duty. I don't believe one man should have so much service and another man should have none.' He later claimed that McKinley had been 'an enemy of the good working people' and that he had been 'going around the country shouting prosperity when there was no prosperity for the poor man'.

Czolgosz, a solitary man with no close friends of either sex, had been born in Detroit a few months after his parents arrived from Poland. He generally worked in factories, but had left his last regular job in August 1898 and since then, he had lived near

Warrensville, Ohio, on a farm which he and other members of his family had bought between them. Although he regarded himself as an anarchist, he was not a member of any recognized anarchist organization, and there was no evidence that anyone else had known of his intention to kill the President.

Following McKinley's death, Czolgosz was indicted for murder in the first degree. He was brought to trial before the State Supreme Court in Buffalo shortly afterwards, refusing to discuss the case with attorneys who had been appointed to represent him, or to take the stand himself. The trial ended on its second day, the jury bringing in a verdict of guilty after thirty-four minutes. Unrepentant to the end, Czolgosz was executed at Auburn Prison on 29 October 1901 — just forty-five days after the death of his victim.

'I killed the President because he was the enemy of the good people — the good working people,' he said as he was being strapped into the electric chair. 'I am not sorry for my crime.'

It was later discovered that Czolgosz had suffered from delusions. He had no real knowledge of anarchism, and various anarchist leaders whom he had met during the summer of 1901 refused to accept him as a comrade. In fact, only five days before the shooting, one of their newspapers published a description of him, warning its readers that he was a spy.

Perhaps if they had thought better of him, the crime would not have taken place.

On 8 September 1969, Beryl Waite, the forty-five-year-old wife of a chauffeur, died at her Warwickshire home after an illness lasting several months. One of the doctors who had attended her issued a death certificate, giving the cause of her death as acute gastro-enteritis — but then began to have doubts and advised the Warwickshire coroner that she may have been poisoned. The post-mortem which followed resulted in the discovery that Mrs Waite's body contained arsenic, administered over a period of more than a year. She had received no fewer than four doses — one of them massive — during the two days which preceded her death.

William Charles Waite, the dead woman's husband, was personal chauffeur to Lord Leigh, of Stoneleigh Abbey; he was four years her junior. On being questioned about the arsenic, he said that he did not know how it could have entered his wife's body, but suggested that she might have committed suicide. He afterwards admitted that he had been having an affair with a young woman working in the estate office at Stoneleigh Abbey, but denied that this gave him a motive for his wife's murder.

Mrs Waite, who was normally a healthy woman, had begun to suffer from various symptoms — loss of weight, listlessness, insomnia and loss of appetite — during the early part of 1968. Her condition improved a little when she started to receive medical attention in July, but in January the following year she had an attack of vomiting and complained of swelling ankles and numbness in her hands and legs.

Some weeks later, after she had been admitted to hospital, her illness was diagnosed as acute poly-neuritis, and during the month that she was away from home her health improved considerably. But it soon began to deteriorate again when she was discharged from hospital in April, and this time it was even worse than before.

Her husband seemed genuinely concerned about her, and began carrying her from room to room when she was unable to walk. But he destroyed articles connected with her illness as soon as her body was removed by the undertakers, and arsenic, in the form of a pesticide, was discovered at the estate garage where he worked. The police also found an empty dispenser containing traces of the same poison at the couple's home.

Six days after his wife's death Waite tried to kill himself with aspirin while staying with his parents at Home Farm, Stoneleigh Abbey. However, he re-covered in hospital and was arrested for his wife's murder. In February 1970 he appeared for trial at the Birmingham Assizes, the prosecution contending that he had killed his wife in order to be free to marry his mistress, twenty-year-old Judith Regan. He denied the charge.

Called as a prosecution witness, Miss Regan told the court of her affair with the accused, saying that she and Waite had started going out together in January 1968, and had become lovers shortly after-wards. She went on to say that once, after she had become a regular visitor to the couple's flat, Mrs Waite had asked her whether there was anything going on between the prisoner and herself, and she had replied that there was not. But the witness added that on three occasions Mrs Waite had threatened to commit suicide — the last time just four days before her death.

Although Miss Regan said that she had been

alarmed by these threats, one of the doctors who had treated Mrs Waite said that she had fully co-operated in her treatment and that he was sure she had wanted to get better. And the pathologist, Dr Derek Barrow-cliff, said he thought it inconceivable that the deceased should have used such an unpleasant, distressing and at times painful method of suicide. He had never met a suicide case which resembled chronic arsenic poisoning in twenty-five years' experience, he declared.

Waite gave evidence in his own defence, claiming that his wife had spoken of ending her own life because she did not want to be a burden to him and their two children, and his counsel, Mr James Ross, maintained that there were many inexplicable features of the case. But the jury, at the end of the fifteen-day trial, found the prisoner guilty of murder. He was sentenced to life imprisonment.

Murder of Bermuda's Police Commissioner, 1972

SEPTEMBER

9

On the night of 9 September 1972, George Duckett, Bermuda's forty-one-year-old Police Commissioner, was shot dead at his home in the Hamilton suburb of Devonshire, about half a mile from his office. He had just noticed that his back-door security light was out, and had gone to remove the bulb when he was shot from the darkness at close range. Other shots were fired into the kitchen, and Duckett's seventeen-year-old daughter Marcia was wounded in the chest.

There was no apparent motive for the crime, and

an investigation headed by Scotland Yard detectives made little headway for several months, in spite of the government offering a reward of 24,000 dollars for information about the culprits. Then, on 10 March the following year, Sir Richard Sharples, the Governor and Commander-in-Chief of Bermuda, and his aide-de-camp, Captain Hugh Sayers of the Welsh Guards, were shot dead in the garden at Government House. This time two black men were seen running away, but nobody could identify them.

Less than a month after that, on 6 April, two men who ran a shop in the Victoria Street, Hamilton, shopping centre were shot dead after being tied hand and foot with blue cord. In this case it appeared that the killers had concealed themselves on the premises before the shop closed and afterwards sawn through two iron bars at the back in order to make their escape. They also cut the telephone wires — as had happened at the home of George Duckett on the night of *his* murder.

These latest crimes caused the government to increase the reward it was offering to three million dollars, and the Metropolitan Police Commissioner to send a further team of detectives to the island. Intensive inquiries then revealed that on the night in question three black men had been seen running away from the shop in Victoria Street, one of whom had been recognized as Larry Winfield Tacklyn, a local man. Tacklyn's arrest was followed by a series of shooting incidents intended to obstruct the investigation.

Five months later a second local man, Erskine Durrant Burrows, was identified as the person responsible for two armed robberies: one at the Bank of Bermuda on 25 September, the other at a shopping complex called Pigley Wigley Plaza on 29 September. Although Burrows escaped on both occasions, a pair of wire-cutters found in his room were examined and the blades proved to be consistent with marks left on the cut telephone wires at George Duckett's home and the shop in Victoria Street.

Burrows was finally apprehended on 18 October, after being seen in the street carrying a sawn-off shotgun. People who had previously been frightened to give information to the police then began to do so, and both of the men in custody were found to have divulged information about the murders to associates. Before long Burrows made a written confession, claiming that he had wanted to make black people aware of the evils of colonial rule.

After much delay the two prisoners were brought to trial, both charged with each of the double murders, and Burrows alone with the murder of George Duckett. Burrows was found guilty on all charges, while Tacklyn was found guilty only of the shopping-centre murders. They were both hanged on 2 December 1977, their executions sparking off a wave of rioting and arson on the island. This led to the declaration of a state of emergency, and British troops were sent to reinforce the security forces until order was restored.

Body of
Agnes Brown
discovered, 1953

SEPTEMBER

11

On 11 September 1953, Mrs Agnes Irene Brown, an attractive middle-aged woman from south-east London, was found stabbed to death in a field in Chislehurst, Kent, a few hours after her husband had reported her missing. Mrs Brown, aged forty-eight, of

Passey Place, Eltham, had been to a restaurant in nearby Farnborough the previous evening in the company of twenty-seven-year-old William Pettit, her former lodger. Pettit, a labourer with a number of convictions for petty crime, was missing from his own home — also in Eltham — and a search was started for him.

Pettit was a very sick man. He suffered from tuberculosis and was mentally ill as well. He believed himself to be in love with Mrs Brown, and had threatened to kill her when her husband took him to court some months earlier; he had also threatened her on other occasions. Yet Mrs Brown had often been out with him, and at the inquest following her death a grave-digger at a Chislehurst cemetery — where Mrs Brown's parents were buried — spoke of seeing them there together.

'They used to be kissing and cuddling, and if we went anywhere near he used to call her "Auntie",' said Charles Badcock.

The same witness said that on 7 May the same year Mrs Brown had shown him a dagger which she said she had taken from Pettit.

At the restaurant where she and Pettit dined on the evening of 10 September Mrs Brown had played the piano for the benefit of other customers, while her companion watched sullenly. She afterwards told the proprietor that she was trying to help Pettit, as he was in trouble of some sort. The couple left to catch a bus about 8 p.m.

About two hours and twenty minutes later Mrs Brown's husband Arthur received an ominous telephone call.

'Hallo, old chap,' said Pettit. 'Your wife is quite all right, and everything should be all right now.'

Arthur Brown, a civil servant, asked where his wife was, and Pettit replied, 'We have had an argument or two about my future, but I am afraid it was all my fault. Everything should be all right now.'

'Where is my wife?' Mr Brown asked again.

'She has just gone across the road. She won't be five minutes.'

'Will you go and ask her to ring me up at once? She never asked you to ring me up.'

'Yes, she did — in a way.'

Pettit then rang off, and Arthur Brown stayed up all night, waiting for his wife to call him. He twice rang the restaurant in Farnborough in the hope of finding out what had happened to her, and at quarter to eight the following morning finally reported her disappearance. He did not tell the police about the telephone call from Pettit until after he had been shown his wife's body.

'One of the curious features of the whole case is that despite the summonses and threats and bindings-over, Mrs Brown still went out and was friendly with this man,' said the coroner. 'She went out with him knowing full well of the threats uttered against her over the past eight or nine months.'

The police carried on their search for Pettit for several weeks, and used the medium of television for the first time during the course of a murder hunt: photographs of the fugitive, full face and profile, were transmitted on 1 October, and a statement giving details of his description was read by John Snagge. It was thought that a man would be more suitable to read such a statement than the duty announcer, Sylvia Peters.

But by this time Pettit was dead. His body was eventually found in a bombed building in Budge Row, Cannon Street, in the City of London, and a piece of notepaper found on it bore a message to Arthur Brown: 'Forgive me for what I have done. I could have gone on living with Mr and Mrs Brown but not without Mrs Brown. I love her, I love her, I love her.'

Professor Keith Simpson, who carried out the post-

mortem, found that he had had advanced tuberculosis, and concluded that his death had probably
been due to natural causes.

Murder of Emily Jane Dimmock, 1907

On 12 September 1907, Emily Jane Dimmock, a
twenty-three-year-old prostitute known to her friends
as 'Phyllis', was found murdered in her lodgings in
Camden Town, north London; she was naked and her
throat had been cut. The discovery was made when
Bertram Shaw, a dining-car cook with whom she had
been living for the previous nine months, arrived
home from work about midday. It was established by
medical evidence that the crime had been committed
between four and six o'clock in the morning, while
Shaw was aboard a London-to-Sheffield train. He
was therefore not regarded as a suspect.

It was soon learnt that, unbeknown to Shaw — who
mistakenly believed that she had given up being a prostitute — Phyllis had regularly entertained men at their
lodgings while he was working, generally after picking
them up at a local public house called the Rising Sun.
One of her last clients had been Robert Percival
Roberts, a ship's cook, who admitted that he had spent
the nights of 8-10 September with her and said that she
had received a letter through the post just before he left
on the morning of 11 September.

The letter, which she had shown to Roberts, was
signed 'Bert', and asked Phyllis to meet the writer at
another pub in Camden Town the same evening.

Phyllis had burnt the letter, but only after showing Roberts a picture postcard — in the same handwriting but signed 'Alice' — which she had received on an earlier occasion. This suggested a meeting at the Rising Sun at 8.15 p.m. on the day of its receipt.

The police discovered pieces of the letter in the grate in which it had been burnt, and Bertram Shaw found the postcard by accident under the lining of a drawer. Three more cards bearing the same handwriting were found in an album which Phyllis had kept, and reproductions of all four were published in the hope that the writing would be recognized.

It was, in fact, recognized by an artist's model named Ruby Young, who lived in the Earls Court district, but she did not come forward of her own accord and was only questioned as a result of a rumour reported by a journalist. In the meantime a car-man named Mac-Cowan had given a description of a man he had seen leaving the house in question shortly before 5 a.m. on 12 September.

Ruby Young identified the writing on the postcards as that of Robert Wood, an artist who had been an occasional lover of hers for three years and who had asked her to give him an alibi for the evening before Phyllis' death.

Wood was arrested and put on an identity parade. He was picked out by witnesses who had seen him with Phyllis on the evening of 11 September; he was also identified by MacCowan as the man who had left the house early the next morning. It therefore seemed that the Crown would have little difficulty proving that he was guilty and on 12 December 1907, he was brought to trial at the Old Bailey. But the case against him was then found to be not very strong at all.

Edward Marshall Hall, defending, cast doubt on MacCowan's evidence and on the character of many of the other prosecution witnesses. The prisoner's attempt to arrange a false alibi for the evening of 11 September

— which he explained by saying that he had not wanted his family to know of his association with prostitutes — was argued to be proof that he was innocent, as he would otherwise have known that the crime had taken place several hours later. Finally, the judge summed up in Wood's favour, saying that the prosecution had not 'brought the case home against him clearly enough'.

The jury retired for only seventeen minutes before returning a verdict of not guilty. This was greeted with cheers from the spectators and a roar of approval from the crowds outside. Ruby Young, who was seen as having betrayed him, had to remain in the courthouse until late at night, in order to avoid an angry mob; she eventually left disguised as a charwoman.

Robert Wood later changed his name and vanished into obscurity.

Attack on Miss Wren, 1930

SEPTEMBER
20

A strange unsolved murder case began in Ramsgate, Kent, on the evening of 20 September 1930, when a girl of twelve was sent out to buy a packet of blancmange powder from a sweet-shop across the street from her home. The shop was kept by Margery Wren, a miserly eighty-two-year-old spinster who lived in squalid conditions in spite of owning property and having money in the bank. Finding the door locked, the girl looked through the window.

Miss Wren was sitting in her back room. When she

eventually got up and came to the door, the girl saw that she had blood streaming down her face and realized that she could only speak in whispers. But she let her into the shop, went behind the counter and got out some packets of blancmange powder to show to her. The horrified child ran home and told her parents what had happened, and soon Miss Wren was taken to hospital.

It was found that she had been the victim of an assault, and that she had suffered injuries to her head and face severe enough to have caused instant death. But she lingered for five days, making various statements and then contradicting them as her mind wandered — sometimes, for example, saying that she had been attacked, sometimes that she had had an accident. Then, on one occasion, she claimed that she knew her assailant but would not name him. 'I don't wish him to suffer,' she said. 'He must bear his sins ...' And finally, just before she died, she said, 'He tried to borrow ten pounds.' But she refused to elaborate on this.

The attack was known to have taken place during the half-hour before the girl went to the shop: that is, between 5.30 p.m. and 6 p.m., when there were other people going up and down the street and children playing nearby. Miss Wren's head and face injuries had been inflicted with her own fire-tongs, to which hairs were attached. But the post-mortem revealed that an attempt had also been made to strangle her.

It seemed that the door had been locked by her murderer, who must then have escaped by the back-yard, for Miss Wren normally kept the shop open after six o'clock. It seemed, too, that the culprit had been disturbed, for, although robbery was almost certainly the motive for the crime, nothing appeared to have been stolen.

Six people were regarded as suspects, and each of these was referred to at the coroner's inquest by a letter of the alphabet. The first three, *A*, *B* and *C*, were able to clear themselves, and the police officers heading the investigation became convinced that one of the remaining three, *D*, *E* and *F*, was the murderer. But there was not enough evidence to justify charging any of them, and before long the case was abandoned.

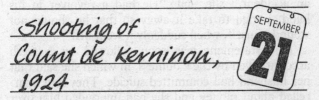

Shooting of Count de Kerninon, 1924

SEPTEMBER
21

On 21 September 1924, Count le Roux de Kerninon, a French nobleman, was wounded in a shooting incident at his home in Lannion, Brittany. His wife, stepson and stepson's wife all claimed that he had shot himself by accident, and this was generally believed. But the Count, who had been admitted to a nursing-home, confided to visitors — one of whom was his mistress Bernardine Nedellec — that it was his wife who had shot him. The Countess had tried to kill him, and he would 'settle with her' when he was well again, he said. Until then, he did not want her to be denounced.

After spending two days in the nursing-home, however, the Count died, the cause of his death being certified as 'a tumour on the lung, complicated by his wound'. His mistress then revealed what he had said to her about the incident, accusing the Countess of murder, and an investigation was started. But the widow's daughter-in-law, Madame Fleury, challenged the allegation, insisting that the shooting had been 'a terrible accident which has thrown us all into despair'.

'It was about 1.30 p.m., and we had just lunched,' she declared. 'My husband had gone back to his office, situated in a neighbouring house. The Count and Countess de Kerninon had gone to their room, which is on the first floor, overlooking the street. I was in the garden when I heard a shot.

'I came back to the house. I then saw Monsieur de Kerninon coming down the stairs, his hand and face covered with blood. My mother-in-law was leaning against the stair-railing in a fainting condition. "It's an accident," she said. "He had a revolver in his hand. I tried to take it away so that he should not wound himself, when suddenly it went off."'

This statement was soon followed by a fresh account given by the Countess, in which she said that her husband had committed suicide. They had quarrelled about money and she had upbraided him over his infidelity, she claimed. He had then taken a revolver and shot himself, she having tried unsuccessfully to prevent it.

But the medical evidence showed that this, like the earlier story, was untrue, for four bullet wounds had been found in the body: one in the neck, one in the cheek and two in the hands. Moreover, it was learnt that the Countess de Kerninon's son Emile, a public notary, had taken possession of the revolver, removing both the empty cartridge-cases and the unused bullets and throwing them into a cesspool.

The Countess, a domineering Algerian woman eight years older than her husband, had known of de Kerninon's affair with Bernardine Nedellec, and also of a will which he had made in Bernardine's favour. She had frequently uttered threats of violence against both of them, and had forced her husband to destroy the will just before his death. 'When he tore up the will made in my favour, the Count signed his death warrant,' Bernardine said afterwards.

On being brought to trial, Countess de Kerninon

persisted in her claim that her husband had committed suicide, in spite of the evidence against her. But the jury found her guilty of murder, though with extenuating circumstances — and on 8 May 1925 she was sentenced to eight years' penal servitude.

Suicide of Joe Ball, 1938

SEPTEMBER
24

On the night of 24 September 1938, the owner of a tavern on the outskirts of Elmendorf, a small town in Texas, was visited by police officers investigating the disappearance of one of his waitresses. Far from trying to assist them, Joe Ball, a big, muscular man, took a revolver from his cash register and shot himself in the head. His death led to the discovery that he had murdered not only the woman in question but various others as well.

Ball, an ex-bootlegger in his forties, had been married three times and divorced twice. He had employed many young, attractive women as waitresses at the Sociable Inn and had had affairs with most of them. But none had interested him for long, and he had resorted to murder without compunction when he felt that one of them was becoming a nuisance.

In the case of twenty-two-year-old Hazel Brown — the waitress whose disappearance had prompted the investigation — the affair had lasted several months and she and Ball were often seen out together. A week after she was seen for the last time a neighbour complained to Ball about a foul smell emanating from a rain barrel in the tavern grounds. But the tavern keeper pulled a gun from his pocket and threatened to shoot the neighbour if he did not get off his property at once.

Later, when a deputy sheriff went to see him about the incident, Ball laughed it off and said that he used the rain barrel to store meat for his five pet alligators, which he kept in an outdoor pool. But it served to draw attention to him and further enquiries were made.

Lee Miller, a Texas Ranger, found that nobody in Elmendorf had seen the missing waitress leave town. He also learnt that she had opened a bank account a few days prior to her disappearance, and that none of the money which she had put into it had since been withdrawn. Miller was one of the police officers who were present at Ball's suicide.

Clifford Wheeler, Ball's handyman, was questioned at length and eventually admitted that Hazel Brown had been murdered by his employer. Wheeler had been forced to dismember the body, putting the pieces into the rain barrel, and had later buried them on a nearby river bank after Ball had cut off the head. The handyman led the police officers to Hazel Brown's shallow grave.

Ball's third wife, who had left him some months previously, was found living in California. She told detectives of another murder which her husband had committed — and in which Wheeler had also been involved — saying that she had been afraid that he would kill her, too.

Wheeler confirmed the story of this earlier murder — the victim of which was a girl of twenty named Minnie Gotthardt — and he once more helped to locate the body. It had been buried on a beach near Ingleside, on the Gulf of Mexico.

A search of Ball's home led to the discovery of letters from several former waitresses. Some of them

— including Minnie Gotthardt — had found themselves to be pregnant after leaving the Sociable Inn; others merely resented the way in which Ball had discarded them. It was learnt that some of these women had subsequently returned to Elmendorf and that none of them had been seen since.

Some months after Ball's death the former owner of a ranch adjoining his property revealed that one night in 1936 he had had the misfortune to catch the tavern keeper in the act of cutting up a woman's body and throwing the pieces to his alligators.

Terrified by Ball's violence and threats of murder, the rancher had promised to say nothing about what he had seen and had taken his family to live in California without delay. The ranch had been sold in his absence, and he had not dared to return to Elmendorf during the tavern keeper's lifetime, he explained to Lee Miller.

It was suspected that Joe Ball had fed at least four other women's bodies to his alligators, but this could not be proved. The pool had already been drained, without any human remains being found there. The alligators, which had been taken to a zoo in San Antonio, nonetheless proved to be very popular with visitors.

As for Clifford Wheeler, the reluctant accomplice, he was sent to prison for five years as an accessory to murder. He did not go back to Elmendorf after serving his sentence.

Death of Ernest Westwood, 1948

On the morning of 25 September 1948, Ernest Westwood, a seventy-year-old Yorkshireman living in the village of Southowram, near Halifax, was found unconscious in a pool of blood, having been attacked by an intruder during the hours of darkness. He was taken to hospital, where a constable waited at his bedside until later the same day, when he died without regaining consciousness.

Mr Westwood, in spite of being well over the normal age of retirement, had been working full-time at a mill in Halifax, and had also worked as a debt-collector in the evenings. He had been out debt-collecting on the evening before the crime, and the police learnt that he had had £14 in his possession when he returned home. It appeared that this money had been stolen by his murderer.

Within hours of the crime the police started a search for twenty-seven-year-old Arthur Osborne, an unemployed man who lived in Bognor Regis, Sussex, but was missing from his lodgings. It was learnt that he had arranged to marry a woman in Chichester that very day, irrespective of the fact that he was already married, but had fled on discovering that he was wanted by the police. He was later arrested on a train which had been stopped at Sutton in Surrey.

Osborne, whose thumbprint had been found on one of Mr Westwood's window sills, was charged with murder. He admitted having killed the old man with a screwdriver after breaking into the house to steal his money, but said that he had only done so because the victim threw something at him and caused him to lose his temper.

Arthur Osborne duly appeared for trial at the Leeds Assizes, his counsel arguing that the charge should be reduced as his client had been provoked by having something thrown at him. But the judge said that he would be sorry to see a householder's attempt to prevent a burglary being accepted as sufficient reason to reduce murder to manslaughter, and the jury followed his advice.

Although a strong recommendation of mercy was added to the jury's verdict, the Home Secretary declined to intervene on the prisoner's behalf. Osborne was accordingly hanged on 30 December 1948, his execution taking place at Armley Prison.

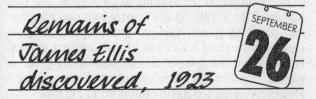

Remains of James Ellis discovered, 1923

SEPTEMBER 26

On 26 September 1923, the remains of a young soldier were found under some bushes in Long Valley, on the outskirts of Aldershot, in Hampshire. James Frederick Ellis, a twenty-one-year-old drummer in the Leicestershire Regiment, had been dead for four months, and little of his body was left apart from the skeleton. He had died of suffocation while tied up and gagged, with a greatcoat covering his face; the great-coat had been held in position by a military belt fastened round his head.

Ellis, a native of Hull, had disappeared from his quarters in Aldershot towards the end of May. It was believed that he had deserted, as a close friend of his, a lance-corporal named Albert Edward Dearnley, claimed to have heard him talking about emigrating to Australia. But Dearnley also said that Ellis had been missing since 23 May, whereas everyone else who was questioned was sure that he had not disappeared until the 24th. This divergence was seen as significant when the body was discovered.

On being questioned by a police officer, Dearnley said that he had last seen Ellis at the barracks about 5.30 p.m. on the day of his disappearance. He had then asked him where he was going, and Ellis had replied, 'I may be going for a drink, or I may be going to the pictures.' Dearnley later admitted that he and Ellis, who were generally the best of friends, had often come to blows, usually over a girl. Eventually he made a written statement, withdrawing all that he had said before and admitting that he was responsible for Ellis' death.

He said that on the evening of 24 May he and Ellis had gone for a walk on the nearby common together, and played a game, using a drum-rope as a lasso. Dearnley then tied Ellis up at his own request, but left him trussed and gagged in the bushes, in order to punish him 'for his having insulted my sweetheart'. However, he denied having intended to kill him.

Sir Bernard Spilsbury, who examined the remains, believed that the tying-up *had* been done at the victim's request, and regarded it as an act of masochism on his part. But he said that Ellis had been tied and gagged in such a way that air was excluded from his lungs and he could not move or cry out. He had therefore died of suffocation, probably within ten minutes.

The girl referred to by Dearnley revealed that on one occasion during the summer, when she mentioned Ellis to him, he had told her, 'You have no need to worry any more about Ellis. He is dead, and he is not a mile from here.'

Dearnley was arrested on a coroner's warrant and appeared for trial at the Winchester Assizes in

November. Giving evidence in his own defence, he then repeated his story of the game with the drum-rope, saying that Ellis had lassoed him first, but pulled the rope so tight that it hurt him. Then, when it was his own turn to be lassoed, Ellis asked to be tied up.

'He lay down on the ground, and I put the rope round his ankles and tied them in a knot,' the prisoner stated. 'His hands were behind his back, and I tied them to the ankles. He said, "Oh, that hurts!" I said, "Oh, no, it doesn't. Shut up!" And then I suddenly thought that I would take advantage of the fact that I had tied his hands and feet together, and give him some punishment for having insulted my young lady a few nights before. I said to him, "Tot, I am going to gag you." He said, "Don't do that." I said, "I am."'

Dearnley went on to describe how, having gagged Ellis, he had pulled the greatcoat over his head, fastened it with the belt, then pushed him into the bushes where his body was found. He then went off and left him, intending to release him early in the morning, but did not wake up until later than he had expected; by that time it was too late to leave the barracks, as he had to be on duty. He afterwards assumed that Ellis had worked himself free of his bonds and deserted.

The defence contended that Dearnley was guilty only of manslaughter, as he had not intended to kill Ellis, but the judge, Mr Justice Avory, advised the jury that if a person intending to do grievous bodily harm to another caused that other person's death, then he or she was guilty of murder. The prisoner left the court under sentence of death.

Dearnley's appeal was dismissed and preparations were made for his execution. When his coffin had been made, his grave dug, and the hangman and his assistant had arrived at the prison, a last-minute respite was granted, his sentence being afterwards commuted to penal servitude for life.

The coffin was used for another soldier named Abraham Goldenberg, who had also been convicted of murder (see 3 April).

Murder of Ivy Preston, 1985

SEPTEMBER
28

On the evening of 28 September 1985, Ivy Preston, a seventy-five-year-old spinster, was murdered in the living-room of her small terrace house in Bradford, Yorkshire. The crime was committed with much brutality, the victim being struck many times over the head with a hammer and then strangled. But there was no evidence of sexual assault and nothing seemed to be missing; the motive for the murder was therefore not immediately apparent.

Miss Preston had not been poor. She had worked for her living up to the time of her retirement ten years earlier, owned her own house and lived frugally. When police carried out a search of the premises they found almost £1000 in old, buff-coloured wage-packets which had never been opened. But there had been even more money in the house before the crime, as was soon to be discovered.

During the course of making routine enquiries police officers visited Allyson Kirk, Ivy Preston's nineteen-year-old great-niece, and her husband Ian, aged twenty-one, at their home in Todmorden, in the same county. The couple had visited Miss Preston on the evening in question, but were not at first regarded as suspects. Indeed, they seemed to be genuinely shocked by what had happened.

But the following day Detective Inspector Eddie Hemsley called at their house again and, finding them both out, went round the back and looked in their dustbin. There he found a T-shirt which had recently been washed, together with many small pieces of buff-coloured paper — torn-up wage-packets of the same type as those found at Miss Preston's house.

Shortly afterwards Allyson Kirk and her husband were arrested and £1465 was found in the glove compartment of their Volvo car. They both made confessions. 'Everyone used to laugh and say we'd all be better off if Auntie Ivy was dead,' said Allyson. 'I thought we had committed the perfect murder.'

When they appeared for trial at Leeds Crown Court in June 1986 the prosecution alleged that the couple, who had run up debts of over £8000 during the first six months of their marriage, had murdered Miss Preston for the sake of her life savings. It was Allyson Kirk who actually killed her, but her husband had driven her to the house — before going to a car-wash to establish an alibi — and had then returned to the scene of the crime to help his wife search for the dead woman's money. They found over £2000, and used £700 to pay off debts and buy food before being arrested.

Allyson Kirk pleaded guilty to the charge of murder and gave evidence against her husband; he admitted only a charge of impeding her arrest, know-ing that she had committed a crime. But according to Allyson's account, the couple had taken Miss Preston away on a caravan holiday during the summer of 1985, so that Ian could return to the house in her absence, break in and steal her money. And this scheme was only abandoned when he found himself unable to force open a window — after which they decided to murder Miss Preston instead.

Ian Kirk admitted having driven his wife to her aunt's house on the night in question. Under cross-examination, he also admitted that he had helped her to dispose of the hammer afterwards. But he claimed that he was innocent of the murder itself, as he had not known what his wife intended to do.

After retiring for nearly six and a half hours the jury returned a majority verdict of guilty. Ian Kirk was therefore — like his wife — given a sentence of life imprisonment.

A police officer said afterwards that the case was 'a classic example of the dangers of falling into debt'.

Murder at the Savoy, 1980

On the evening of 1 October 1980, Catherine Russell, a twenty-seven-year-old prostitute, was stabbed to death in an eighth-floor room at London's Savoy Hotel. The crime was discovered by a hotel employee, who had heard screams coming from the room about 10.15 p.m., and saw a young man emerging with blood on his clothes shortly afterwards. The victim, who was only partly dressed, had been stabbed fifty-five times with a clasp-knife.

The young man had booked into the hotel just an hour and a quarter before the screams were heard, claiming to be 'D. Richards' from Birmingham; afterwards, he left without paying his bill, unnoticed by other members of the staff. But a pocket diary found at the scene — together with the murder weapon and the culprit's fingerprints — showed that his real name

284

was Tony Marriott and give his address as Highland Avenue, Horsham, in Sussex.

A hunt was started for him and the following evening he was recognized by the landlord of a public house in Southend-on-Sea, Essex. On being taken into custody, Marriott, who was twenty-two years old, admitted the crime; he told police officers that he had invited Catherine Russell to his room at the Savoy because he wanted to murder a prostitute — and that, having stabbed her while she was getting undressed, he went on doing so, in a state of frenzy. He continued stabbing her even when she was dead.

Later, at another hotel, he made a half-hearted attempt at suicide by cutting his wrists.

'The real problem, I feel, is that I seem to develop a resentment of normal sexual relationships,' he informed the officers interviewing him.

Six months after his arrest Marriott was brought to trial at the Old Bailey, charged with murder. The defence contended that he was suffering from diminished responsibility, and evidence of 'a persistent psychopathic disorder, leading to abnormally aggressive behaviour' was produced. The plea was successful, and the prisoner was convicted only of manslaughter. He was sent to Broadmoor.

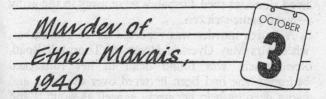

Murder of Ethel Marais, 1940

OCTOBER
3

On the evening of 3 October 1940, Mrs Ethel Marais, the wife of a South African soldier, was battered with a blunt instrument, sadistically assaulted and robbed not far from her home in Brockhurst Road, in the Cape Town suburb of Lansdowne. She was still alive when she was found behind a bush the following morning, but died of her injuries soon afterwards, without regaining consciousness. There was no clue to the identity of the person responsible, and police searched the neighbourhood for suspicious characters without success.

Nineteen days later a second murder was committed, the victim on this occasion being Mrs Dorothy Marie Tarling, of Prince George Drive, in the suburb of Wynberg. Mrs Tarling was similarly battered, abused and robbed, but in her own home, her murderer having entered the house through a window and taken her by surprise as she sat reading a newspaper. Thumb- and palm-prints found at the scene revealed only that the culprit had no criminal record, and a fresh search proved unavailing.

Then, on 11 November, the killer struck again in Wynberg, this time in Wetton Road, where Evangeline Bird, an unmarried woman of twenty-eight, was attacked and fatally injured at the front door of the house in which she lived, and dragged behind a shrubbery. In this case, unlike the others, the crime was committed in broad daylight, and the killer — a young man with a bicycle — was seen in the vicinity by two witnesses. But the police still failed to catch him, and the women of Cape Town — many of whom lived alone, as their husbands were away in the army — were panic-stricken.

A fourth murder was reported on 25 November, when Mrs May Overton Hoets, of Thornhill Road, Rondebosch, was found dead in her ransacked bedroom; she had been battered over the head and had a deep gash in her neck, as well as wounds and bruises on other parts of her body. This time both fingerprints and footprints were found, but several more weeks elapsed before the murderer was caught.

286

Even then, he only came to the attention of the police because he was seen in the street by the victim of a lesser offence.

Salie Linevelt, aged twenty, was arrested as he stood in a cinema queue in Wynberg. He had a ring stolen from Mrs Marais on one of the fingers of his right hand, and part of his left thumb had been cut off. It was found that he had mutilated himself with a chopper after newspapers had misleadingly reported — as part of a plan devised by the police — that the murderer's left thumb-print had been found at Mrs Tarling's home (where he had actually left a print of his other thumb). The chopper and the severed part of the thumb were among items found in a room he shared with his widowed father.

Elated at being the centre of attention, Linevelt soon confessed to all four murders. He said that he had beaten three of the women to death with a piece of piping — which he had afterwards hidden in the grounds of the house in Wetton Road — and killed the fourth with the chopper. But he denied having committed sexual acts against his victims, even though the state of the bodies indicated a sexual motive and in one case articles of underwear had been among the items taken.

'Why should I kill them to sleep with them?' he argued. 'I've been with lots of women. I'd been with a girl the night I was arrested.'

Inquiries revealed that this was not the truth: in fact, he did not seem to have associated with girls at all. But he continued to deny that the murders had been sexually motivated, saying that he had committed them because his 'boss' had ordered him to do so. It appeared from this that he was schizophrenic and had an imaginary character upon whom he could place responsibility for what had happened.

Linevelt was brought to trial before a judge and two assessors. He refused to allow a plea of insanity to be made on his behalf, and his counsel had no success in trying to prove mitigating circumstances, in spite of much attention being given to the prisoner's psychological make-up.

Mr Justice Davis, in his judgment, said that there was evidence that Linevelt 'had periods when he was moody and quiet, possibly even a little intractable', but that this — 'even taken in conjunction with his youth' — fell far short of what would be required to spare his life. He also rejected the suggestion that the number, brutality and unexplained character of the crimes were, in themselves, evidence of mitigating circumstances.

'Of course, the prisoner here is not entirely normal,' he said. 'One is thankful that normal persons do not act as he did. If he were entirely normal he could, and would, not have perpetrated these four horrible crimes. But, in saying this, I do not in the least suggest that any abnormality he may possess is such that would prove a mitigating factor in this case. In the court's view, it is rather the reverse.'

The prisoner, having continued to enjoy a great deal of attention, listened without concern as he was sentenced to death. During the last weeks of his life, in the condemned cell in Pretoria, he remained contented and cheerful; he had no wish to avoid being hanged, and seemed, if anything, relieved when the date of his execution was fixed. He died without trying to give any further explanation of his crimes.

OCTOBER
5

Gruesome discovery in Essex, 1974

A long and difficult murder investigation began on 5 October 1974, when an amateur ornithologist walking along the north bank of the River Thames near Rainham, in Essex, found the upper part of a male torso at the water's edge. It was the first of a number of gruesome discoveries, several other parts of the same body being found over a ten-mile stretch of the river during the next ten days. The pathologist who examined these remains was able to state that death had probably been caused by a head injury — though the head was still missing — and that dismemberment had been carried out with a saw and a knife. The various parts had all been immersed in water about five days before the first discovery.

The police suspected that the dead man was William Henry Moseley, a thirty-seven-year-old small-time crook from north London who was missing from his home. But the remains could not be positively identified at this time, as the hands were also missing, and a whole year elapsed without any further progress being made. In the meantime, on 7 September 1975, the body of Michael Henry Cornwall, a close friend of Moseley's and a member of the same gang, was found buried in a wood near Hatfield, Hertfordshire. Cornwall had died as a result of a gunshot wound in his right temple, but had been kicked or struck a number of times beforehand.

As it seemed almost certain that the two crimes were connected, a murder squad was set up to investigate them both. On 24 October a second post-mortem was carried out on the remains of the first victim, this time by Professor J.M. Cameron, who found evidence of torture: the nails of one foot had been pulled out before death, and the sole of that foot had burn marks on it. Cameron also succeeded in positively identifying the dead man as William Moseley — a task made possible by the discovery of gallstones for which Moseley had been receiving medical treatment.

Police inquiries later revealed that some days before any of the remains were found, Reginald Dudley, a fifty-four-year-old crooked jeweller, had been heard discussing Moseley's death with his fellow crook, forty-year-old Robert Maynard, and a third man at a family funeral. It was suspected that Dudley and Maynard were responsible for the murder, Dudley having been beaten up by Moseley some years earlier, after trying to thrust a broken bottle into his face during the course of a fight.

Cornwall, who was in prison at the time, had also suspected Dudley and Maynard, and it was known that he had tried to find them after his release. But on learning that Dudley and Maynard were looking for *him*, he had become frightened and gone into hiding. He was seen alive for the last time on or about 22 August 1975, and shortly afterwards it was rumoured that he had been killed.

The investigation of the two murders eventually led to the arrest of Dudley, Maynard and five other people, all of whom were committed for trial in April 1976. The trial, at the Old Bailey, lasted seven months, ending on 16 June 1977, when Dudley and Maynard were convicted of murdering both Moseley and Cornwall and sentenced to life imprisonment. Charles Clarke, a fifty-six-year-old greengrocer, was given two consecutive two-year sentences for conspiring to cause grievous bodily harm to both men, and Dudley's thirty-year-old daughter Kathleen was given a suspended prison sentence for conspiring to cause grievous bodily harm to Cornwall, who had been her lover and had actually shared a flat with her — unbeknown to her father — after Moseley's death.

Six weeks after the trial ended, Moseley's skull, which had evidently been kept in a refrigerator, was found thawing in a public convenience in Islington, north London. An examination of it confirmed the earlier opinion of both pathologists, that Moseley had died as a result of a head injury.

Double murder in Kenya, 1932

OCTOBER
6

On the evening of 6 October 1932, a youth of nineteen and two young women left the small town of Nakuru, in Kenya, in a blue Chevrolet. It appeared that they were all going to a cinema together and later, when they failed to return home, it was assumed that somebody they knew had put them up for the night. But when the next day passed without any sign of them, their parents and friends became anxious. The police were therefore informed, and an investigation began.

The youth, Charles William Ross, was found on the Eldama Ravine Road, some miles out of Nakuru, on the morning of 8 October, when his twenty-one-year-old brother Gordon went out on his motor-cycle to look for the missing party. He was dirty and untidy, as though he had been sleeping rough, and the Chevrolet was stuck in a ditch. But the two girls were not with him, and he denied knowing what had become of them: in fact, their disappearance did not

291

seem to concern him in the least.

Ross was taken into custody and a search was started in the area in which he had been found. The body of one of the missing girls — Margaret Keppie, a qualified chemist and druggist from Leeds — was then discovered at the bottom of a ravine, below a forty-foot cliff. She had been shot in the head.

After that the search was intensified, and the following day a camp was discovered in the bush, where fresh provisions, articles of women's clothing, toilet requisites, a revolver and two empty cartridge-cases lay near the remains of a fire. But there was no trace of the second girl — twenty-year-old Winifred Stevenson, with whom the prisoner was believed to have been in love — and the search continued for several more days without success.

Eventually, on 15 October, Ross directed police officers to a secluded spot near the Menengai crater, where the decomposed body of Miss Stevenson, who had also been shot, lay covered with leaves and grass within a mile of her own home. He afterwards made a confession, stating that he had killed both girls 'for nothing'.

'It happened at 9.30 on Thursday night,' he said. 'I shot Miss Keppie near the camp. She was sitting next to me at the time and grabbed at my revolver, which I kept in my left-hand pocket. I ordered her out of the car and took her about thirty yards from the camp. She was a yard from me when I shot her. I threw her down a sort of square pit nearby.

'After that I returned for Winnie. She was sitting in the car. When I took Miss Keppie away I had ordered her to get into the car. She had not moved when I got back. She was terrified. She wanted to go home. I told her I would lead the way and she could follow. When we were near her home she said she could not go any further. She lay on the grass under a tree. She did not know what was going to happen to her. I shot her in the side of the head.'

Ross was charged with both murders, and his trial, which began in Nairobi on 28 November, lasted four days; he pleaded insanity. Defence witnesses told the court of occasions when his behaviour had not been that of a normal person — when, for example, he had slashed open the carcasses of animals he had killed, in order to cover himself with blood. It was also stated that he had been suffering from a venereal disease, and that clothes he had worn on the night of 6 October bore traces of semen. Other evidence concerned the behaviour of his father, a soldier and big-game hunter who had committed many acts of brutality — including an attempt to put one of his own children on a fire.

In addition to all this, it was shown that the prisoner was mentally deficient, having an I.Q. of only 65.7. But the prosecution argued convincingly that none of the defence evidence proved insanity in the legal sense, and after retiring for fifty-five minutes the jury returned a verdict of guilty. The prisoner was accordingly hanged in Nairobi on the morning of 11 January 1933.

Body of George Heath discovered, 1944

OCTOBER 7

On the morning of 7 October 1944, the body of a murder victim was found in a ditch at Knowle Green, near Staines in Middlesex. George Heath, a thirty-four-year-old taxi-driver — 'the man with the cleft chin', according to the newspaper reports of the case

— had been shot in the back and robbed, and the culprits had taken his taxi-cab. The vehicle was found parked in a street in Hammersmith, west London, two days later — and a short while after its discovery an American GI was seen entering it.

Private Karl Gustav Hulten, aged twenty-two, had been absent without leave from his paratroop regiment for seven weeks. On being searched, he was found to have an automatic pistol in his left hip pocket and ammunition in one of his trouser pockets. He claimed to have found the stolen taxi abandoned near Newbury, in Berkshire, and to have spent the night of the murder in the company of a woman named Georgina Grayson, who lived in King Street, Hammersmith.

Georgina Grayson proved to be the stage-name of Elizabeth Maud Jones, an eighteen-year-old strip-tease dancer. When Hulten revealed where she lived, she was taken to Hammersmith police station to be interviewed, but was allowed to go home after making a statement, as she was not thought to have been involved in the crime. However, the same afternoon, while speaking to a War Reserve constable of her acquaintance, she made an indiscreet remark which suggested otherwise.

This was reported to detectives investigating the murder and Betty Jones was seen again a few hours later. She then made a fresh statement, saying that Hulten had shot George Heath in her presence, and that he had afterwards made her go through the dying man's pockets. The statement implied that she had taken part in the crime against her own will.

When Hulten was informed of this he, too, made a fresh statement. In this, he admitted having killed the taxi-driver, but said that he had done so by accident, and that Jones — with whom he had taken up only a few days previously — was herself to blame for the crime. 'She said she would like to do something exciting, like becoming a "gun moll", like they do back in the States,' said Hulten. He claimed that if it hadn't been for her, he wouldn't have shot Heath.

These statements also revealed that Hulten and Jones had committed other robberies, travelling at night in a stolen army truck, and that on one occasion they had attacked and almost killed a girl.

Hulten and Jones were both charged with murder. The consent of the American government had to be obtained before Hulten could be tried in a British court, but this was granted and both prisoners duly appeared at the Old Bailey on 16 January 1945. Betty Jones now claimed that she had only taken part in the crime because she was frightened by threats and violence, but at the end of the six-day trial the accused were both found guilty and sentenced to death.

Hulten was hanged at Pentonville Prison on 8 March 1945, five days after his twenty-third birthday. Betty Jones, whose sentence was commuted to life imprisonment, served nine years before being released in January 1954.

Multiple murder in New Zealand, 1941

On 8 October 1941, Constable Edward Best, of Hokitika, New Zealand, went to visit a farmer in the bush settlement of Kowhitirangi, some miles away, after it had been reported that he had been threatening neighbours with a rifle. Eric Stanley Graham, aged forty, was a sullen man with a violent temper, and received Best in such a hostile manner that the constable left the farmstead to call for assistance.

Best later returned with a sergeant and two other constables, the sergeant intending to take Graham to the police station for questioning. But Graham, who often felt persecuted, suddenly got out his gun and shot all four of them, killing the sergeant and the two other constables outright and gravely wounding Best. Then, after shooting a local volunteer and driving off two others, he shot Best again, this time killing him.

Graham then left the farmstead with food, firearms and ammunition, and fled into the bush. A search was started for him, with police being flown in from all parts of New Zealand, and troops from Burnham Military Camp, armed Home Guardsmen and civilians also taking part.

Several times during the next few days Graham returned to his home, but on each occasion he became involved in a shooting incident with police or Home Guardsmen. One Home Guardsman was shot and fatally wounded, so that he died the following morning; another, who went to his aid, was shot from ambush and died instantly.

These two new deaths led to the evacuation of women and children from the area, and further reinforcements were flown in. The order was given that Graham should be taken 'dead or alive'.

On the twelfth day of the manhunt a police officer from Auckland, using high powered binoculars, sighted him a mile away. Closing in on him with great care, Sergeant Quirke shot him without warning from a distance of twenty-five yards. The fugitive was then captured and taken to hospital, where he died the following day.

The volunteer who had been shot on the same day as four police officers from Hokitika — a fifty-four-year-old agricultural inspector — died from his injuries seventeen months later.

Murder of Inspector Walls, 1912

OCTOBER
9

On the evening of 9 October 1912, Countess Sztaray, of South Cliff Avenue, Eastbourne, set out in her brougham to meet friends for dinner at the local Burlington Hotel. After driving some distance her coachman told her that while waiting outside the house he had seen a man crouching on the roof of her porch. Assuming that a burglary was about to take place, the Countess then ordered the coachman to take her back, so that she could telephone the police. Inspector Arthur Walls, who happened to be in the neighbourhood, arrived at the house a few minutes later.

The intruder was still on the roof of the porch, unsure whether he had been seen. Walls immediately put an end to his uncertainty by ordering him to come down. But the man produced a revolver and fired two shots, wounding the police officer so seriously that he died shortly afterwards. In the confusion which followed, the murderer managed to escape, leaving a soft felt hat on the porch roof. The coachman, by this time, had driven off without seeing the man's face: he afterwards claimed that the shots had made the horse 'restless'.

The hat was traced to the shop where it had been bought, but the salesman had sold many others of the same type and had no idea who had bought that particular one. As it was the only clue to the murderer's identity, the police were not very hopeful of catching him. But then a young man named Edgar Power informed them that his friend John Williams, a professional burglar, was the person they wanted.

Williams, according to Power, had arrived in Eastbourne on 2 October in the company of his mistress, Florence Seymour, with whom he was living and who was expecting his child. He had since left for London on his own, using money which Power had given him, as he was afraid of being arrested for the crime. The murder weapon had been buried somewhere on the beach at Eastbourne.

Power, who was in love with Florence himself, agreed to take part in a plan to bring the culprit to justice. In accordance with this, he asked Florence to show him where Williams' revolver had been buried, so that it could be moved to a safer hiding place, and while she was doing so, police officers arrived on the scene and arrested them both. Florence was then terrified into making a statement about the evening of the murder, saying that Williams had left her sitting on the sea-front near South Cliff Avenue shortly before 7 p.m., and that he had later returned without his hat, saying that he had lost it. She went on to admit that the gun had been buried the following day.

John Williams, who had a criminal record, was lured into a trap in London with Power's help, arrested and charged with murder. The son of a Scottish clergyman, his real name was George Mackay, but it was under the name of Williams that he was tried — at the Lewes Assizes in December 1912 — when he was also referred to in the press as the 'Hooded Man' as a result of being hooded when he was taken to and from the courthouse. He did not have a strong defence and, although Florence changed her evidence in the hope of helping him, he was convicted and sentenced to death.

Florence gave birth while Williams was in the death cell, and was allowed to take the child to see him on the day before his execution, but a request that the couple should be allowed to marry was refused.

The execution was carried out in January 1913, when Williams was twenty-nine years old.

Execution of Susan Newell, 1923

On 10 October 1923, Susan Newell, a married woman aged thirty, was hanged at Duke Street Prison, Glasgow, for the murder of a thirteen-year old newspaper boy the previous June. The crime had been committed in the room which she and her husband rented in the nearby burgh of Coatbridge, and her husband had also been tried on the same change. He, however, had been acquitted, as it was clear that he had not been in Coatbridge when the murder took place.

Mrs Newell and her husband were a quarrelsome couple, and two days before the crime she had twice struck him on the head. The following day there was a disagreement between them when John Newell went to attend his brother's funeral, and he spent the night at his father's house. The day after that — the day of the murder — he was in Glasgow from midday till 9 p.m., and on arriving back in Coatbridge at 10.30 p.m., went to see his sister. He then went to the local police to complain about his wife assaulting him.

The murder was committed while Janet McLeod, the culprit's eight-year-old daughter by a former marriage, was playing in the street outside the house. The boy, John Johnston, came round with the evening papers, and Mrs Newell, who had been given notice to quit, called him into the room and strangled him, for no apparent reason. Janet returned to the room shortly afterwards and saw the 'little wee boy' lying on the couch, dead. She later helped her mother to put the body into a bag.

The next morning Susan Newell and her daughter set out on foot towards Glasgow, pushing the bundle on a hand-cart, covered with a bed rug. A lorry-driver stopped and offered them a lift, and Mrs Newell helped him to lift the cart onto the vehicle. But she became excited when they arrived in Glasgow, and when they lifted the cart down between them, she fell and upset it. She then became angry, told the driver that she did not need his help, and put the bundle back onto the cart. The driver went on his way, puzzled.

But a woman looking out of her kitchen window had noticed first a foot and then a head protruding from the bundle; she told her sister, and the two women began following Susan Newell and her daughter through the streets. Mrs Newell eventually left the bundle in a courtyard, but by this time a policeman had been called and she was arrested as she tried to make her escape. On being questioned, she said that the boy had been killed by her husband.

Janet McLeod also told the police that John Newell was the person responsible, but on being called to give evidence at her mother's trial she admitted that this was a lie; she had said it because her mother had told her to, she informed the court. Newell, by this time, had been able to prove that he was in Glasgow when the murder took place, and had been formally acquitted when the judge decided that he should not have been brought to trial.

Susan Newell was sentenced to death after an attempt to prove her insane had failed, and this sentence was carried out in spite of a unanimous recommendation of mercy from the jury. On the morning of her death she showed no fear, and one witness said afterwards that she was the bravest woman he had ever seen. She died without confessing her guilt, and refused to allow the hangman to pull the white cap over her face before the trap-door was opened.

Train robbery and murder in Oregon, 1923

OCTOBER 11

On 11 October 1923, three gunmen held up a Southern Pacific express train in the Siskiyou Mountains, in Oregon, killing four members of the crew. The victims included the brakeman and the fireman, who had both been ordered to uncouple the mail coach after it had been dynamited and set on fire. The murderers fled from the scene, leaving behind a revolver and a pair of overalls, in addition to their detonating equipment.

The manhunt which followed was unsuccessful, and although a garage mechanic was regarded with suspicion, the police asked Dr Edward Heinrich, a Californian criminologist, to assist them. Heinrich's microscopic examination of stains, hairs, fibres and wood dust on the overalls found at the scene of the crime provided information which not only cleared the garage mechanic but also led to the arrest of the real culprits.

The overalls belonged to a left-handed lumberjack who had worked among fir-trees of a particular type, said Heinrich. He was aged between twenty-one and twenty-five, not more than 5 feet 10 inches tall, weighed about 165 pounds, and was fastidious in his personal habits. This information, together with other pieces of evidence which came to light, led police officers to the home of Hugh, Roy and Ray D'Autrement, three brothers living in rural Oregon who had all worked as lumberjacks. All three of them had disappeared, and further evidence was obtained linking them to the crime. But it then took four years to catch them.

Hugh D'Autrement was finally arrested in the Philippines, and his two brothers — who were twins — were found in Ohio. On being brought to trial, they were all convicted and sentenced to life imprisonment. Two of them were eventually released — Hugh in 1958, Ray in 1961 — but the third died in a mental institution.

The case helped to establish Heinrich as a pioneer of forensic science.

Disappearance of Arthur Johnson, 1956

OCTOBER
15

On the night of 15 October 1956, Arthur Johnson, a fifty-three-year-old unmarried farmer, was seen alive for the last time as he drove home in his van through the bleak fenlands near the village of Farcet, in Huntingdonshire, about ten o'clock. Later, when it was learnt that he had disappeared, police officers found his jacket and spectacles inside his farmhouse and bloodstains out in the yard. His van — with a lot of blood inside it — was discovered on a rough track about two and a half miles away.

Johnson, a secretive man, had had the reputation of being rich. Although his sitting-room at Crowtree Farm had a damp, musty smell caused by dry rot, police carrying out a search of the place found many small sums totalling over £80, in addition to a little under £17 in a safe. But three bands which had been used as wrappers for bundles of banknotes were also discovered, indicating that a far larger amount was missing. It therefore seemed likely that Johnson had been murdered for the sake of money.

It was clear, too, that the person responsible had driven Johnson's car to the place where it was abandoned — and, as the area was full of fields bounded by ditches and dykes, with only narrow tracks between them, it would have been almost impossible for a stranger to do this in the darkness. For this reason, the police assumed that the culprit was somebody who knew the area well, and before long they began to suspect Morris Arthur Clarke, a twenty-seven-year-old lorry driver who lived in Peterborough, about seven miles from Johnson's home.

Clarke had known the missing farmer and had actually lived at Crowtree Farm while his wife was Johnson's housekeeper. When he left in January 1954, Johnson had lent him £100 to enable him to start a business, but this was not successful. By September 1956 he had debts of over £1000 which he could not pay, and at 5.25 p.m. on the day of Johnson's disappearance he was confronted by one of his creditors over a cheque for £200 which his bank had refused to cash. But the following morning he paid £200 in notes into the bank; then, an hour later, he paid a debt of about £33 to somebody else.

When Clarke was questioned he said that he had been at work on the night in question, and that he had saved all this money without his wife knowing about it. But he had no alibi for the period between 9.55 p.m. and 1.30 a.m., and twenty ten-shilling (50p) notes taken from a bureau at his home — as well as other notes found in a pocket of his blazer — all smelt of dry rot. Even so, there was not enough evidence to justify an arrest.

Ten days after his disappearance Johnson's body was found floating in a dyke about three miles from his farm. He had been battered over the head with a blunt instrument, and his right leg had been broken. A bloodstained stick found in a barn at Crowtree Farm appeared to be the murder weapon.

Clarke continued to deny being the culprit until the police obtained a warrant to search his house, and found — in his loft — another £641 in musty-smelling notes and an old purse full of sovereigns (£1 coins) and half-sovereigns. He then confessed and was charged with murder.

On being brought to trial, Clarke was convicted and sentenced to death, the judge remarking that the circumstances of his crime were so dreadful that he should not count on 'some other sentence being substituted'. However, the sentence was commuted to life imprisonment.

Disappearance of Gay Gibson. 1947

OCTOBER
18

On the morning of 18 October 1947, one of the female passengers of the ocean liner *Durban Castle*, then off the coast of West Africa, was reported to be missing. Gay Gibson, a twenty-one-year-old actress — her real name was Eileen Isabella Ronnie Gibson — was travelling from Capetown to Southampton, but had not been seen since the previous night. As it seemed that she had fallen overboard, the captain ordered the ship to be turned back so that a search of the seas could be made. But there was no sign of her, so it was assumed that she had been eaten by sharks.

It was not long before foul play was suspected. It was already known that shortly before 3 a.m. the two bells of Miss Gibson's cabin had been rung, summoning both the steward and the stewardess. When a watchman went in response to them a man opened the door a few inches and said, 'It's all right.' He then closed the door in the watchman's face. Later, about 7.30 a.m., a stewardess found the bed in that cabin to be more disarranged than usual and also noticed some stains on the sheet and pillow case.

When James Camb, the deck steward, was belatedly named as the man who had been seen by the watchman, he denied having been in the cabin at that time. The following day he agreed to have a medical examination, and was found to have scratches on his shoulders and wrists; he claimed that these had been self-inflicted as a result of a heat-rash. When the ship reached Southampton he was held for questioning by the police.

He then admitted that he had been in Gay Gibson's cabin during the early hours of 18 October, and said that the missing actress had died after having a fit while he and she were having sexual intercourse. He had tried unsuccessfully to save her by means of artificial respiration, and then, being 'terribly frightened', had pushed her body through the porthole, he claimed. He was unable to explain the ringing of the cabin bells.

The thirty-one-year-old steward was charged with murder and brought to trial at the Winchester Assizes in March 1948. The prosecution alleged that he had strangled Miss Gibson because she resisted his advances, and in support of this produced evidence of blood and saliva on the bedclothes, as well as the scratches on the prisoner's body.

A pathologist appearing for the defence unexpectedly strengthened the case against the prisoner by admitting the presence of traces of urine, which the government pathologists had not noticed, on one of the sheets of the dead woman's bed. But perhaps Camb's failure to call for assistance on the night in question weighed most heavily against him. He was found guilty and sentenced to death.

It was later revealed that Camb had assaulted three other women — none of whom had reported him — on different occasions aboard the *Durban Castle*.

Though his appeal was dismissed by the Court of Criminal Appeal, his sentence was commuted to life imprisonment in view of the fact that the House of Commons had just voted for a five-year suspension of the death penalty.

Released on licence in September 1959, James Camb changed his name and got himself a job as a head waiter. But after a few years of freedom he began to get into trouble again — for sex offences against schoolgirls — and his licence was revoked. He therefore went back to jail to continue serving his life sentence.

Mrs Knowles fatally injured. 1928

OCTOBER
20

One of this century's strangest cases of alleged murder began on the afternoon of 20 October 1928, when Mrs Harriet Knowles, the wife of a district medical officer in the Gold Coast territory of Ashanti (now in (now in Ghana), received a gunshot wound from which she died three days later.

Mrs Knowles and her husband were part of the territory's white community. They had given a lunch party that day at their bungalow in the Bekawi district, and afterwards retired for their usual afternoon rest. They were still in their bedroom at 4.30 p.m., when Sampson, their native houseboy, heard the sound of a shot.

Sampson, knowing that Mrs Knowles and her husband often quarrelled, ran to the home of Thortref Margin, the District Commissioner, and reported what he had heard. Margin, who had been one of the couple's lunch-party guests, promptly drove to the bungalow to find out what had happened. But Dr Benjamin Knowles, coming to the door with just a towel wrapped round him, denied that an accident had taken place and said that everything was all right. Margin therefore left, and saw no need to take any further action.

That evening, after being out for some hours, Margin returned to his house and found a message from Sampson, stating, 'Missie cry very much'. This put him in a difficult position, for he was now sure that something unfortunate had happened, but had no real grounds to justify another visit. All he was able to do was send the medical officer a brief note, saying that Sampson had 'got the wind up' and pointing out that if Knowles needed his assistance he had only to ask for it. Knowles did not reply.

The next day, after hearing Margin's story, Dr Howard Gush, the colony's surgeon, visited the couple. Knowles showed him bruises on his leg, which he said had been caused by blows with an Indian club during a 'domestic fracas' the previous afternoon. His wife, who had been shot in the left buttock, was seriously ill; the bullet had passed out of her body on the right side of the abdomen. Surprisingly — in view

307

of what her husband had said — she told Gush that this had been the result of an accident. She had been examining her husband's revolver while he was asleep and it had gone off when she unintentionally sat on it, she said.

Gush ordered her to be taken to the hospital in Kumasi (the capital of Ashanti), where — in her husband's presence — she made a statement on oath, claiming once again that her injury had been caused by accident. But the remarks which Knowles had made to the surgeon, and other things which he said later, all suggested that he had shot her. Indeed, he and his wife had come close to quarrelling on this point as a result of Knowles telling her, on two occasions, to tell the truth. When Mrs Knowles died during the early hours of 23 October, her husband was charged with her murder.

Though Knowles was a Scotsman in a British colony, he was tried under Ashanti law, which allowed no legal representation or trial by jury. The prosecution was conducted by the Commissioner of Police; the prisoner was allowed to cross-examine witnesses and give evidence himself. It was for the judge to decide whether the prosecutor had proved his case.

Sampson gave evidence against his former employer, telling the court that just before the shot he had heard Knowles shout, 'Show me!' Other witnesses gave evidence of the prisoner's suspicious behaviour and apparently self-incriminating remarks, and experts argued that a bullet found in a wardrobe was the one which had killed Mrs Knowles, having been fired by the accused as he lay on the bed. Mrs Knowles' account of what had happened was dismissed as a false statement intended to protect her murderer.

Knowles now claimed that his wife had told the truth in saying that she had discharged the gun accidentally, and claimed that he had been treating her himself to prevent her being questioned. He challenged Sampson's evidence, saying that it was after the gun had been fired that he had shouted, 'Show me!' He also claimed that the bullet found in the wardrobe had been fired by his wife on an earlier occasion, and that a second one found on the floor was the one which had caused her death.

The judge, in his summing-up, said that he found the ballistics evidence 'very confusing'. He nonetheless concluded by saying that the evidence against the prisoner was 'overwhelming'. Knowles was therefore found guilty and sentenced to death — a sentence immediately commuted to life imprisonment by the Governor of Ashanti.

Knowles appealed to the Judicial Committee of the Privy Council on both legal and constitutional grounds, and his conviction was quashed because the trial judge had misdirected himself in failing to consider manslaughter as a possible verdict. The constitutional question which had been raised — that of whether a British citizen in a British colony was entitled to trial by jury — was left unanswered.

Following his release, Knowles made no further revelations about what had happened on the afternoon of his wife's fatal injury. He died four years later, in 1933.

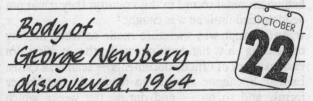

Body of George Newbery discovered, 1964

OCTOBER
22

On 22 October 1964, George Newbery, a sixty-year-old taxi-driver, was found dead by the side of a farm track seven miles outside Southampton. He had suffered head injuries caused by several blows with a rusty iron pipe — which was later discovered in some nearby bushes — but had still been alive at the time of being left there. His taxi was found abandoned near a rough part of Southampton called Six Dials, not far from his home, and splashes of blood on the inside showed that he had been sitting at the driving-wheel when the attack took place. His assailant had struck him from the offside rear seat.

The police began house-to-house inquiries in the Six Dials area, and also questioned the crews of ships about to leave the country, but nobody seemed able to help them. Other taxi-drivers said that they had seen Newbery on the evening of 21 October, and a tramp came forward to say that he had seen him lying at the roadside about 11.15 p.m. — at which time, according to the pathologist, he must have been close to death. But this was all the progress that was made during the first eight days, and it looked as though the police were going to be unable to solve the crime.

It was then found that £3 had been withdrawn from the dead man's Post Office Savings Account on the afternoon following the murder, and that greasy fingerprints had been left on the withdrawal form. The fingerprints did not match those of any Post Office employee who might have touched the form, so the police were sure that they belonged to the person who had made the withdrawal. But, as that person had no criminal record in this country, they could not be identified until he was caught.

An attempt was therefore made to trace him by comparing his handwriting with the writing on various types of official documents — seamen's cards, Labour Exchange application forms, driving-licence forms, and so on — and during the weeks which ensued 100,000 such documents were checked. But this was also to no avail. By the end of the year the police still had no idea who had killed George Newbery.

But then an unemployed cable-maker named John William Stoneley was caught trying to break into a Southampton garage. Stoneley, aged twenty-one, appeared in court the following day, but was released on bail, having said that he was about to get married. However, a fingerprint check revealed that he was the person who had made the £3 withdrawal from Newbery's Post Office account, and he was quickly re-arrested.

Stoneley at first denied knowing anything about the affair, but later asked for pen and paper and wrote out a long, self-piteous statement. In this, he said that on the evening in question he and another man, George Ernest Sykes, a twenty-three-year-old dairyman, had taken the taxi to the place where the body was found, and had there attacked the driver and taken his wallet. Only one blow had been struck with the iron pipe, he claimed, and the victim's wallet had been removed from his pocket unintentionally. Moreover, he (Stoneley) and Sykes were not responsible for Newbery's death, because it 'was caused by him not getting help'.

The confession, such as it was, led to Stoneley and 'Bill' Sykes being jointly charged with murder. They were tried and convicted at the Winchester Assizes, Stoneley being sentenced to death and his companion to life imprisonment. The solving of the crime was a personal triumph for Detective Chief Superintendent Walter Jones, the Head of Hampshire's CID. It was his fortieth successful murder investigation in twelve years.

Stoneley's sentence was afterwards commuted to life imprisonment and a few months later he married a girl of nineteen in a church on Dartmoor — the bride being given away by the prison welfare officer and the groom having another prison officer as his best man. After the ceremony the couple were allowed only thirteen minutes together before Stoneley went back to jail.

Murder of Albert Anastasia, 1957

OCTOBER
25

On 25 October 1957, Albert Anastasia, a notorious New York Mafia boss, entered the basement barber's shop at the Park-Sheraton Hotel in Manhattan for a quick haircut. While he was sitting back in the chair, with his head against the rest, two other men appeared in the shop and opened fire on him with automatic pistols. He died from multiple gunshot wounds.

Anastasia, an Italian by birth, had entered the United States illegally during the First World War. In the 1920s he had been a small-time mobster in Brooklyn, but later became head of one of the five Mafia families in New York City, controlling a powerful organization of racketeers and professional killers. He was believed to be responsible for scores of murders, and for this reason was called the 'Lord High Executioner'.

In 1940 a gunman named Abe Reles, belonging to a Brooklyn gang known as 'Murder Incorporated', made a long confession, giving details of many crimes which he and his associates had committed. His information led to convictions in a number of murder cases, and Anastasia, who had strong ties with this gang, had to go into hiding.

But the 'perfect' case which had been prepared

against him by William O'Dwyer, the Brooklyn District Attorney, fell apart in November 1941, when Reles — who was supposed to be under police protection — hurtled to his death from a sixth-floor hotel window.

His death was never satisfactorily explained, and it was commonly believed that he had been murdered. O'Dwyer remarked that his case against Anastasia 'went out of the window with Reles'.

Anastasia's own murder, which caused a sensation, was clearly the work of professional killers, who had managed to take him by surprise while his bodyguard was away on an errand. Afterwards, having discarded their guns, the two men disappeared into the busy streets. They were never apprehended.

Although the crime was never officially solved, Joseph Valachi, a member of the Mafia for thirty years, later claimed that Vito Genovese, the head of another New York family, had been behind it. According to Valachi, Genovese had ordered the murder because he had discovered that Anastasia was plotting against *him*, and other Mafia leaders had tolerated this violation of the organization's rules because Anastasia was himself out of favour by this time.

Valachi's story is to be found in *The Valachi Papers* by Peter Maas, published in 1968.

Just before five o'clock on the morning of 29 October 1936, a gold-miner on his way to work near the Witwatersrand town of Brakpan found two smouldering corpses lying in a shallow water trench running alongside the road. Spiros Paizes, a thirty-one-year-old Greek café proprietor, and his assistant, Pericles Paxinos — also a Greek — had both been murdered, and their bodies had been thrown into the trench before being soaked with petrol and set on fire. A cartridge case lay in a pool of blood on the asphalt road, and signs of a desperate struggle were found near the wire fence a short distance away.

The post-mortem revealed that Paizes had been shot in the head and neck, and that Paxinos had suffered a fractured skull as a result of being struck with a heavy blunt instrument. The motive for the murders was at first not known, but it was soon discovered that both men had been involved in illicit gold-trafficking. Paizes, it was also learnt, had been one of five men who left the nearby town of Benoni by car on the night in question, travelling towards Brakpan. He had been to Benoni to see a young woman who acted as a go-between in his deals, and had had £900 in his possession at that time. The woman did not recognize any of his companions, all of whom waited for him in the car.

The police began tracing and questioning Paizes' 'clients', and became convinced that one of the people responsible for the murders — the 'Torch Murders', as they were called — was Andries Stephanus Du Plessis, a twenty-year-old criminal whose activities included housebreaking and gold-running. On the night of 2 November the house in which he lived in Strubenvale, near Springs — a few miles from Brakpan, in the opposite direction — was surrounded in readiness for a raid. But by that time another three people had been killed, this time in Sandspruit, a railway siding ten miles from Volksrust, on the main line from Johannesburg to Durban. And Du Plessis was not at home.

Samuel Berman, who ran a store and filling-station, had just finished eating his evening meal in the company of his sister-in-law Essie Liebowitz and her husband Barney, who worked for him, when the front door was flung open and a masked gunman entered. Ordering Liebowitz to his feet, the man shot and killed him; he then shot Berman as he tried to escape and Mrs Liebowitz after she had locked herself in a bedroom with her baby. Finally, he forced his way into the store, opened the safe with keys taken from Liebowitz's pocket, and removed money, foreign coins, documents and a watch. Two native servants, who were washing dishes in the kitchen when the gunman entered, had by this time managed to leave the scene unharmed.

Du Plessis was arrested when he arrived home at 2 a.m., and the keys to Berman's store and safe were found in his possession. Bloodstains and a cartridge case linking him to the 'Torch Murders' were found in his car; so, too, were various items taken from Berman's safe and a helmet similar to one worn by the Sandspruit gunman. Moreover, he was identified by a native at a filling-station, who had sold petrol to him shortly after the first crime.

Du Plessis was brought to trial in Johannesburg on 15 March 1937, and elected to be tried by a judge and assessors. He admitted having been present at both crimes, but accused others of being responsible for what had happened in each case. The 'Torch Murders', he said, had been committed by two men to whom he was merely acting as chauffeur, because Paizes had caught them trying to swindle him over the sale of some gold bars. The triple murder in Sandspruit had also been the work of one of these men, and had taken place while he (Du Plessis) and a third man remained outside the store.

The trial ended on 31 March, the prisoner being found guilty of all five murders and sentenced to death; the accusations which he had made against the other three men — one a prosecution witness — were dismissed as false. Du Plessis then remained in the death cell for two and a half months while his case was considered by the Governor-General-in-Council, and was hanged on 17 June 1937 after an unsuccessful attempt to kill himself by slashing his wrists with a razor blade. He died without divulging the real names of other people known to have been involved in the murders.

Murder of Ruben Martirosoff, 1945

NOVEMBER
1

About 6.30 a.m. on 1 November 1945, the body of Ruben Martirosoff, an Armenian with a long criminal record, was found in a stationary car in Chepstow Place, Kensington, west London. He had been shot in the back of the neck as he sat at the driving-wheel, then moved to the back seat and robbed of all his valuables except a few pounds in a pocket on which he was lying. A felt hat was afterwards put over his face, concealing an exit wound above his right eye.

His death was thought to have occurred between two and four o'clock in the morning.

Martirosoff, known to his associates as 'Russian Robert', was a thief, a receiver of stolen property and a black-marketeer; he had five convictions in England and others in France and Germany. His wife, who identified his body, told police that he had gone out about eleven o'clock the previous night, intending to meet a Polish naval officer whose name she did not know. She said that her husband regularly carried large sums of money around in connection with his dealings.

It was learnt that at 1 a.m. a wartime constable had seen the car standing in Kensington Park Road, not far from Chepstow Place, and three men — one in the uniform of a foreign naval officer — walking away from it; the same witness had seen the men return and drive away in the car about twenty minutes later. Inquiries in the West End, where the same three men had been seen in a night-club between 11.15 and 11.45 p.m., revealed that one of them was Martirosoff and another a Pole named Marian, known to be in the handbag-making business.

As Marian's whereabouts were unknown, the police kept watch on a flat occupied by a Spaniard in the same line of business, with whom he was believed to be acquainted. Soon a Polish seaman called there to deliver a suitcase and, on being questioned, said that Marian had sent him. With this man's help, Marian was arrested the same afternoon on a street corner in the East End, and articles known to have been owned by the dead man — a wallet, a lighter and a wrist-watch — were found in his possession. He gave his name as Marian Grondkowski.

Further items which had belonged to Martirosoff — a signet ring and another two watches — were discovered at his lodgings in Ilford, Essex, which he shared with a friend named Henryk Malinowski; a naval officer's uniform (both men were deserters) and two automatic pistols were also found there.

Malinowski was arrested at the home of a widow whose two daughters were friendly with him. 'I saw you pick up Grondkowski,' he told police officers. Then, after being cautioned, he went on, 'I was there but I do not shoot. Grondkowski kill him.' A wallet containing four £5 notes was found in his pocket; the wallet was identified by Mrs Martirosoff as yet another of her husband's possessions.

Grondkowski and Malinowski both made written statements, each blaming the other for Martirosoff's murder but admitting to having robbed him and shared the proceeds. Later the Polish seaman who had led police to Grondkowski revealed that he had overheard the two prisoners planning not only to kill and rob Martirosoff but also to rob his wife. The case against them was further strengthened by fingerprint and ballistics evidence.

Arrested and charged within forty-eight hours of the crime, Grondkowski and Malinowski appeared for trial at the Old Bailey in February the following year. Both were convicted and sentenced to death, and on 2 April 1946 they were both hanged.

An earlier murder of which Grondkowski was suspected — that of a London taxi-driver shot dead at the wheel of his cab just a fortnight before Martirosoff's death — was never officially solved.

Death of Jacques Mesrine, 1979

Jacques Mesrine, who was killed in a police ambush in Paris on 2 November 1979, was a daring and resourceful criminal responsible for many robberies and murders. His death was a great relief to the French police, and the officers concerned were so overjoyed at it that they hugged and kissed each other, and even danced in the street. It was a fitting end to a remarkable career of crime, and one which Mesrine, who loved danger and craved publicity, would almost certainly have welcomed.

Born in Clichy in 1937, Mesrine began to associate with criminals while still a teenager and turned to burglary and safe-breaking after finishing his military service in Algeria. He was sent to prison for the first time in 1962, and by 1968 was one of the most wanted robbers in the country. He then went to Canada with a female accomplice, Jeanne Schneider, with whom he was later arrested for the kidnapping of Georges Deslauriers, a millionaire, and the murder of an elderly widow named Evelyne le Bouthillier.

Mesrine at this stage declared that he had committed several other murders but would have been incapable of the one with which he had been charged. Shortly afterwards he and his accomplice escaped from prison, Mesrine having attacked a guard and stolen his keys. They were, however, recaptured and brought to trial, when both were given prison sentences for kidnapping Deslauriers but acquitted of the murder of Mme le Bouthillier.

Mesrine served only a year of his ten-year sentence before leading a spectacular escape which made him a celebrity in Canada. After a bank robbery in Montreal he and one of his accomplices intended returning to the prison to release other prisoners, but had to abandon the plan after a gun-battle with police. A few days after that two forest rangers were shot dead when they discovered Mesrine with two associates near Montreal. Mesrine went on to commit several more robberies in Canada, then went to live off the proceeds in Venezuela.

Eventually he returned to France, where he was arrested on 8 March 1973, following a dozen more armed robberies. He escaped from the courthouse in Compiègne by holding up the court — with a gun which had been left in a lavatory for him — and using the judge as a shield. He was not recaptured for several months, and in the meantime committed further robberies of banks and factories.

But he then spent three and a half years in La Santé prison before being brought to trial, and during that time wrote an autobiography, *The Killer Instinct*, published in 1977. This gave details of various murders, but also revealed that an earlier claim to have killed thirty-nine people had been a lie. Mesrine's trial finally began three months after the book's publication, and resulted in a twenty-year prison sentence. The following year he escaped yet again.

Remaining at large for the next year and a half, he on one occasion robbed a casino in Deauville and on another tried unsuccessfully to kidnap the judge who had given him his twenty-year sentence; he came close to being arrested both times. He also gave interviews to journalists and wrote an open letter to the French police, deploring the conditions which existed in top-security prisons.

At the time of his death Mesrine was living in a luxury apartment in Paris, in the Rue Belliard. The police discovered his whereabouts and, knowing that he had sworn not to be taken alive, decided against making a raid. When Mesrine came out of the building accompanied by his latest mistress they even allowed the couple to get into his BMW car, which had been parked nearby, and drive off unchallenged.

But when Mesrine stopped at a road junction, a lorry pulled up in front of his car and another behind it. Before he had time to realize what was happening, four policemen climbed out and opened fire on him, shattering his windscreen. A police car then drew up alongside him, and the officer in the passenger seat leaned out and shot him in the head, killing him instantly.

Mesrine's mistress was also found to have been shot, but later recovered from her injuries.

President Giscard d'Estaing, who regarded the Mesrine affair as an affront to national dignity, was immediately informed of what had happened.

Human remains found at Brandy Cove, 1961

NOVEMBER
5

On 5 November 1961, three pot-holers exploring a disused lead mine at Brandy Cove, on the Glamorgan coast, found the skeleton of a woman who had been murdered forty-two years previously. The woman was Mamie Stuart, a twenty-six-year-old former chorus girl whose mysterious disappearance in 1919 had led to an unsuccessful police investigation.

The body had been hidden behind a thick slab of stone fifty feet underground, after being sawn into three pieces. A wedding-ring, an engagement-ring, a black butterfly comb and a rotted sack were found in the same cavern.

The remains were identified at Cardiff's forensic science laboratory, where transparencies of the skull were projected onto photographs of the ex-chorus girl, and the rings were identified by an elderly woman who had known Mamie Stuart intimately. At the coroner's inquest which followed the jury found not only that the dead woman had been murdered, but also that the evidence pointed to a man named Everard George Shotton being the person responsible for the crime.

Mamie, who came from Sunderland, had met Shotton, a marine surveyor of Penarth, near Cardiff, in 1917. They were married the following year, and lived in furnished rooms in Swansea from February to July 1919, when Mamie went back to stay with her parents for a while. Then, in November 1919, they were together again, living in a furnished house which Shotton had rented, five and a half miles from Swansea, near the village of Newton. But when Mamie's parents wrote to her there, the letter was returned by the Post Office, marked, 'House closed'.

In March 1920 police in Swansea were shown a portmanteau which had been left unclaimed at a local hotel for some months. Inside they found a second portmanteau, containing two dresses and a pair of lady's boots — all of which had been cut to pieces — together with various other items, including a piece of paper on which the address of Mamie's parents had been written. The bag had been left by a man who had stayed at the hotel on his own, but the clothes inside it had belonged to Mamie.

During the same month Mamie's handbag, containing a ration card and about £2 in cash, was found in the front bedroom of the house which Shotton had rented.

George Shotton's marriage to Mamie Stuart was

322

found to have been a bigamous one, for another woman whom he had married twelve years earlier was still his legal wife. The police officers involved in the case found him living with this woman — and their little son — in a house at Caswell Bay, only a mile and a half from Newton.

On being questioned, Shotton admitted having lived with Mamie, but denied marrying her. He said that he had not seen her since early in December, when they parted after a quarrel.

The police, who suspected that Mamie had been murdered, were not satisfied with Shotton's answers. Continuing their inquiries, they found that he was a jealous and suspicious man, and that Mamie — who had a lover — had sometimes shown herself to be frightened of him. Yet they searched the house in which the couple had lived, and dug up much of the surrounding countryside, without finding any trace of her.

Finally, Shotton was arrested and brought to trial for bigamy. He pleaded not guilty, claiming that Mamie had gone through the ceremony of marriage with somebody impersonating him. But he was convicted and sentenced to eighteen months' hard labour.

Although Shotton admitted that he was the man who had left the portmanteau at the Swansea hotel, the police made no further progress on the case until the discovery of Mamie's remains in 1961.

But one of the twenty witnesses who then gave evidence at the inquest — an eighty-three-year-old retired postman — claimed that one afternoon in 1919 he had seen Shotton lift a heavy sack into his van outside the house which he had shared with Mamie, and drive off in the direction of Brandy Cove.

George Shotton was not there to deny this, as he had by this time been dead for three and a half years. He had died in a hospital in Bristol, at the age of seventy-eight, on 30 April 1958.

On 8 November 1980, three men and a woman — all alcoholics — lured a casual park worker named Donald Ryan to a maisonette in Camberwell, south London, where the men attacked and battered him, evidently for the sake of whatever money was to be found in his pockets. Not satisfied with knocking him 'semi-conscious', however, they went on to immerse him in a bath of scalding water, and then — while he was still alive — started to dismember him with an electric carving-knife, a saw and a machete.

Before long the remains of Donald Ryan, a former amateur boxer, were ready for disposal. The trunk and limbs were taken out and hidden in nearby streets; the head was left in the kitchen of the maisonette — in a refrigerator — and later put out in the dustbin. But when the group went to a local public house, the three men still bloodstained, their appearance gave rise to suspicion and shortly afterwards the police were informed.

The culprits were arrested on various charges, including murder, and when they were later tried at the Old Bailey the evidence was so shocking that four members of the jury were ill. The trial ended with the three men being convicted of murder and the woman of unlawful disposal of the body. The men were given life sentences, the judge recommending that John Bowden, a twenty-six-year-old Londoner, should serve at least twenty-five years, and that Michael Ward, a Camberwell grave-digger aged twenty-eight, and David Begley, a forty-one-year-old porter from Walworth, should each serve at least fifteen years.

Bowden already had a criminal record. By the time he was twenty-four he had spent a total of five years in jail for crimes which included robbery, blackmail, burglary, assault, wounding and carrying offensive weapons. Since then, in association with the other members of the group, he had regularly attacked helpless down-and-outs during the course of robbing them. But his behaviour on the evening of Ryan's murder was such that the trial judge in January 1982 remarked, 'Bowden is a man who obviously enjoyed inflicting pain, and even killing. There never was a more horrific case of murder than this!'

On being sentenced, Bowden shouted at the judge, 'You old bastard! I hope you die screaming of cancer!'

After the trial his parents described him as 'a good boy, gentle and kind', who had only become violent as a result of being kept in solitary confinement on an earlier occasion. 'He was never the same afterwards,' said his father.

A year later, at Parkhurst Prison on the Isle of Wight, Bowden and another prisoner took the assistant governor hostage at knife-point, and only released him when the Home Office agreed to investigate certain grievances of theirs.

Murder of Arthur Baker, 1902

On 10 November 1902, Kitty Byron, a twenty-four-year-old milliner's assistant, stabbed her lover, Arthur Reginald Baker, to death in a London street. The crime took place during the early afternoon and was witnessed by a number of bystanders. Kitty afterwards burst into tears and threw herself onto her victim's body as he lay on the ground. 'I killed him willingly, and he deserved it,' she said to the policeman who arrested her. She was later tried for murder at the Old Bailey.

Kitty had been living with Baker in lodgings in Duke Street, Portland Place, for several months prior to the crime. Baker, a stockbroker, was already married, but gave Kitty to believe that he expected a divorce and would then marry her. But he drank heavily and there were frequent quarrels between them. Finally, when their landlady asked them to leave, he said that Kitty would go if he could keep the room.

On hearing about this after Baker had left for work on the morning of 10 November, Kitty was greatly distressed. She went to the City, buying a knife on the way, then sent him an express letter from Lombard Street Post Office, saying that she wanted to see him immediately. Before long he joined her at the post office, and an argument started between them, which continued as they walked out into the street. It was then, in Post Office Court, that Kitty pulled the knife from her muff and began to stab him.

Baker was generally disliked, and his fellow Stock Exchange members provided funds for Kitty's defence. When she was tried before Mr Justice Darling in December 1902, her counsel asked for a verdict of manslaughter, appealing for sympathy on her behalf, but the prisoner seemed hardly aware of what was going on. She was found guilty of murder and sentenced to death.

But public feeling was strongly in her favour, and 15,000 people signed a petition for a reprieve. Shortly afterwards her sentence was commuted to life imprisonment, and this was eventually reduced to ten

years. She served only six years before being transferred to a benevolent institution for women.

Murder in the Peak District, 1927

NOVEMBER
11

On the morning of 11 November 1927, a brutal
murder was committed at the New Inn, a public
house near the village of Hayfield, in Derbyshire's
Peak District. The victim, thirty-six-year-old Mrs
Amy Collinson — the landlord's wife — was alone
there at the time, as her husband Arthur had a
daytime job in Glossop, four miles away. It was not
until he returned home at 6 p.m. that the body was
discovered.

Amy Collinson had been knocked unconscious with
two blows to the head, then her throat had been cut
with a knife from the kitchen. This had happened in a
downstairs room, and the culprit had afterwards
taken £40 from a cash-box in the couple's bedroom,
leaving £10 behind. He had been able to find the
cash-box without difficulty and so was suspected of
being a local man who had worked out its location
from overhead noises while drinking there.

The Derbyshire police began interviewing the
pub's regular customers, and before long George
Frederick Walter Hayward, a thirty-two-year-old
unemployed commercial traveller living in a nearby
cottage, emerged as a suspect. 'Jerry' Hayward was
heavily in debt, owing £70 to a soap firm for which he
had formerly worked, £50 in rent arrears, and further
sums here and there. But, although his dole money

was only twenty-five shillings (£1.25) a week, it was learnt that since the murder he had manged to repay £4 which he owed to a furniture firm, and that his wife had been better off than usual.

Hayward admitted that he had been to the pub on the morning of the murder. He said that he had called in there to buy some cigarettes before catching a bus to New Mills — about three miles away — to collect his dole, and that Mrs Collinson had been all right at that time. However, bloodstains were found on his hat and tie, £35 was found hidden in the chimney at his hillside cottage, and a bloodstained length of lead piping discovered on top of a disused cistern at the New Inn was found to have been cut from the outlet of his kitchen sink.

Hayward was arrested and charged with murder. At his trial in Derby in February 1928 he claimed that Amy Collinson had committed suicide because of financial difficulties which she had often told him about, but in view of the medical evidence this was impossible to believe. He was therefore convicted and sentenced to death, his execution taking place at Bagthorpe Jail, Nottingham, in April the same year.

The New Inn was later renamed The Lantern Pike.

Death of Ernest Wilson, 1957

NOVEMBER 12

On the morning of 12 November 1957, Ernest Wilson, a seventy-five-year-old retired engineer, died at his council bungalow in Windy Nook, Felling-on-Tyne, County Durham, apparently from natural causes. Only a fortnight earlier he had married a widow of sixty-six, and it was she who called his doctor to Windy Nook, saying that her husband was very ill. This was an understatement, for Mr Wilson had, in fact, died some hours previously. But the doctor knew that he had suffered for many years from myocardiao degeneration of the heart, and so recorded the cause of his death as cardio-muscular failure due to this condition.

That evening Mrs Mary Elizabeth Wilson, who was now a widow again, called on Mrs Grace Liddell, a friend living in Hebburn-on-Tyne, in the same county, and asked if she could stay the night with her. She made no mention of her husband being dead, and on being asked if she was having any trouble with him, replied that he was 'badly' and had been seen by a doctor. Mrs Liddell put her friend up for the night, and went back to Felling with her the following morning. But when they arrived at the bungalow Mrs Wilson — who seems to have been quite a humorist in her own way — gave her the door key and invited her to go in first, remarking, 'When you get in you'll get a shock!'

Mrs Liddell entered the bungalow and found Mr Wilson's body laid out on a trestle table. Mrs Wilson then said that her husband had died in hospital, and seemed not to be put out when Mrs Liddell intimated that she did not believe this. Later the same day Mrs Wilson, a dumpy, ginger-haired woman with glasses, went to the hotel where she and her late husband had had their wedding reception, and told the bar manager that Mr Wilson was ill in hospital.

Mrs Wilson had been married three times. Her first husband, a retired chimney-sweep named John Knowles, had died in August 1955, after forty-three years of marriage, and his wife afterwards went on living in the same house — this one was in Hebburn — with their lodger, John Russell, who was believed to be her lover. But Russell died only five months later, leaving her a small sum of money, and in September 1956 she married Oliver Leonard, a retired estate agent. Mr Leonard, like his successor, died only a fortnight after the wedding.

None of these deaths had been regarded with suspicion at the time, and in all likelihood that of Ernest Wilson would not have been, either. But the extraordinary behaviour of Mrs Wilson could only serve to draw attention to her, and the gossip which ensued prompted a police investigation. The bodies of Ernest Wilson and Oliver Leonard were both exhumed and found to contain phosphorus, and on 11 December Mrs Wilson was accused of murdering them.

She stood trial on these charges at the Leeds Assizes in March 1958, when she was described by the prosecution as 'a wicked woman who married in succession two men and then deliberately poisoned them in order to get the paltry benefits she hoped she might obtain'. It was alleged that the substance administered in each case had been rat or beetle poison.

The trial lasted six days, much of that time being taken up with the evidence of expert witnesses. The prisoner did not go into the witness box herself, and after retiring for just under an hour and a half the jury found her guilty of both murders. She was therefore sentenced to death, but this sentence was commuted to life imprisonment after a last-minute reprieve. She died in Holloway Prison, at the age of seventy, on 5 December 1962.

The bodies of John Knowles and John Russell had been exhumed while she was awaiting trial, and these were also found to contain phosphorus. But as no evidence could be produced to show how it came to be in either of them an open verdict was returned in each case.

Body of Judge's daughter found, 1952

During the early hours of 13 November 1952, the body of Patricia Curran, the nineteen-year-old daughter of an Ulster High Court judge, was found beside the drive of her home in Whiteabbey, a village near Belfast. There were a large number of wounds on her face and body — thirty-seven, in fact — and it seemed at first that she had been blasted with a shotgun. But it was later discovered that they were stab-wounds, caused by a frenzied attack with a thin-bladed knife.

The dead girl, a student at Queen's University, Belfast, had attended lectures the previous day, and had been reported missing when she was not back indoors several hours later. Her clothes were torn, indicating that her murderer had intended to rape or sexually assault her, but her college books were found neatly stacked nearby, as though she had placed them there herself. She had apparently walked home from the village bus stop on purpose, for although she normally telephoned for a car when she arrived there, she had not done so on this occasion.

The police questioned Patricia Curran's friends and fellow-villagers, and the judge appealed for information which might help to solve the crime. During a check of airmen and civilians at the nearby Edenmore RAF station suspicion fell on Leading Aircraftman Iain Hay Gordon, a twenty-one-year-old Scotsman who had tried to arrange an alibi for himself for the evening of 12 November.

Gordon was a friend of Desmond Curran, the dead girl's brother, and had been to the family's home many times. It was learnt from Desmond that he was

331

obsessed with the murder and had expressed surprise that the victim had been stabbed so many times, as 'the fourth blow killed her'. It was also learnt that he had asked Desmond whether there was any reference to him in Patricia's diaries.

Arrested in January 1953, Iain Gordon eventually admitted the crime. He said that on the evening in question he had met Patricia by chance in White-abbey, and escorted her home at her own request. As they walked along the drive leading to the house he wanted to kiss her and she reluctantly allowed him to do so after putting her books and handbag down on the grass. But then, he said, he 'could not stop kissing her', and stabbed her with his service knife because she resisted his advances.

When Gordon appeared for trial at the Belfast Assizes in March evidence of schizophrenia was produced and the jury, after retiring for just under two hours, returned a verdict of guilty but insane. He was ordered to be detained during Her Majesty's pleasure.

Bill McCullough's body discovered, 1981

NOVEMBER
18

On the morning of 18 November 1981, Muriel McCullough, a fifty-two-year-old former beauty queen and businesswoman, telephoned her local police in the village of Ailsworth, Cambridgeshire, and said that her home appeared to have been burgled the previous night, while she was staying with a friend in Cheshire. Shortly afterwards PC Alan Gregory arrived at the house and found her in a nervous state, unwilling to go upstairs with him to investigate. He therefore went up on his own and found Mrs McCullough's husband lying dead in the master bedroom. Bill McCullough, who was four years his wife's junior, had been shot in the head.

PC Gregory was suspicious, for Mrs McCullough's behaviour in refusing to go upstairs and check her jewellery did not seem to be that of a woman who really believed that the place had been burgled. So, instead of telling her what he had discovered, he merely said that her husband was ill in bed. Even then, she remained downstairs instead of going up to see him — and afterwards, on being told the truth, she remained silent for a few moments, then finally shouted, 'Bill! Oh, my Bill! I want my Bill!'

The unimpressed constable reported his suspicions and, although Mrs McCullough was able to prove that she had been in Hale, Cheshire, 150 miles away, at the time of her husband's death, a close watch was kept on her movements. Before long the police learnt that she had had dealings with two Liverpool crooks, James Collingwood and Alan Kay, and that these two men had since been demanding money from a friend of hers named Joe Scanlon, who had helped her to make contact with them.

Scanlon later told the police that he believed Mrs McCullough had wanted to meet Collingwood so that she could arrange to have her husband beaten up. But when Collingwood was questioned he admitted that he had killed McCullough, saying that Mrs McCullough had agreed to pay him £8000 to do so, and that she had given him £1000 in advance, together with a plan of the district and details of the house. Kay had merely driven him there and waited outside while he (Collingwood) entered through an unlocked side door and shot McCullough as he slept.

333

Muriel McCullough had been married twice and had two children by her first marriage. Her first husband had died as a result of a heart attack and she had married his successor on 31 December 1980. But McCullough, an insurance executive, soon proved to be a heavy drinker, a debtor and a wife-beater. Moreover, he had a life insurance policy by which his wife stood to gain over £110,000 in the event of his death.

On being charged with murder, Muriel McCullough said that she had only hired Collingwood and Kay to beat her husband up. 'You have no idea what it's like when your husband beats you,' she told a senior police officer. 'I wanted him to have a taste of his own medicine, and I thought they would give him a good bashing. I wanted him to know what it's like on the receiving end.'

In November 1982 she stood trial with Collingwood and Kay at Birmingham Crown Court, the prosecution describing her as 'a tough, scheming liar' who had 'successfully kept the police at bay' for six weeks. Collingwood, having denied the offence, suddenly changed his plea to guilty, telling the court that Mrs McCullough had hired him to kill her husband but then failed to pay the bulk of his agreed fee. Muriel McCullough and Alan Kay continued to deny the offence but were both found guilty. The three prisoners were all given sentences of life imprisonment.

On the afternoon of 19 November 1924, Sir Lee Stack, the Sirdar, or Commander-in-Chief, of the Egyptian army and Governor-General of the Sudan, was shot and fatally wounded by ambushers while driving through the streets of Cairo. The attack took place as his car slowed down at a tramway — when all three of its occupants were injured — but the chauffeur was able to accelerate and drive away from the scene. The culprits pursued the vehicle for fifty yards, firing as they ran, then wounded a policeman before making off in a taxi which they had had waiting nearby. The Sirdar died the following day from shock and internal haemorrhages.

The attack was immediately thought to be the work of terrorists. Sydney Smith, a forensic scientist then heading a department of the Egyptian Ministry of Justice, found that the bullet which had killed the Sirdar bore a scratched groove, which linked the murder to several other crimes. Later it was learnt from informers that those responsible for it were members of a nationalist group led by Shafik Mansour, a Member of Parliament who had been charged in connection with the murder of a prime minister in 1910, and the attempted murder of another prime minister in 1914, but managed to escape conviction each time.

As there was no evidence against any of the members of this group, a police spy was used to trick two brothers named Enayat into attempting to flee the country. When they did so, they were arrested, and four automatic pistols and a quantity of ammunition were found in their possession. These were examined by Smith, who fired test shots from two of the guns and then compared the bullets and cartridge-cases with others from the scene of the crime. He was thus able to demonstrate that both guns had been used in the attack and that one of them was the murder weapon.

On being confronted with this evidence, the Enayat brothers — one aged nineteen, the other twenty-two — made confessions which implicated six other members of their group, including Shafik Mansour and an engineer named Mahmoud Rachid. All were arrested, and tools which had evidently been used to convert ordinary bullets into dumdum, or expanding, bullets were found at the engineer's home. This discovery was regarded as an important one, as the Enayats had had dumdum bullets and others had been used in the attack.

Shafik Mansour, a lawyer by profession, at first denied having been involved in the crime. Then, after hearing that the Enayat brothers had confessed, he began to feign madness. But eventually he admitted that he had incited the other prisoners to murder Sir Lee Stack, and that he had been similarly involved in a number of earlier political murders. At the end of May 1925 he and his fellow conspirators were brought to trial in connection with the shooting.

The prosecution produced evidence of four confessions — for Mahmoud Rachid had also made one — and although Shafik retracted his, claiming that he had made it while in a trance, this made no difference to the outcome. The ballistics evidence presented by Sydney Smith was impressive enough to be accepted without question by the defence, and the prisoners were all convicted.

They were sentenced to death, and seven of them, including Shafik Mansour, were afterwards executed.

In the case of the eighth, the sentence was commuted to life imprisonment.

Disappearance of Kathleen Heathcote, 1963

On the night of 21 November 1963, Kathleen Heathcote, a twenty-one-year-old shop assistant, failed to arrive back at her home in Mansfield, Nottinghamshire, after going to visit her fiancé in Selston, six miles away. She had, in fact, caught the bus from Selston, and was seen to leave it at the Stockwell Gate stop in Mansfield — about 400 yards from her home — at 11 p.m. But she had then disappeared after setting off along a lane leading to Princess Street, where she lived.

When she was reported missing it was immediately suspected that she had been the victim of a crime, and police began making routine inquiries in the Mansfield area. A number of items belonging to her were found on a piece of waste ground over which she had taken a short cut, and people living nearby remembered having seen a stranger looking through their windows on the night in question.

It was also learnt that on the following day — before the girl's disappearance was reported — a policeman had given a lift in his patrol car to a frightened-looking motorist whose own vehicle was stuck in the mud at this point.

Before long Ronald Evans, a twenty-two-year-old colliery electrician living in the village of Shirebrook, four miles away, was questioned, and a search of his home resulted in the discovery of further items belonging to Kathleen, including keys from her handbag. On being confronted with this evidence, Evans, a married man, confessed that she was dead and that he was the person responsible. His story was both strange and macabre.

He had, he said, been drinking on the evening of 21 November, and saw Kathleen crossing the waste ground where he had parked his car. Although it was raining, he attacked her, threw her to the ground and raped her while she was unconscious. But afterwards, as she was coming round, she kept groaning and he became worried about her. He therefore dragged her to his car and placed her on the back seat, intending — or so he claimed — to take her to the nearest hospital.

When he found that the car was stuck in the mud, he dragged her out of it — still groaning — and pushed her into the boot before going to telephone a breakdown service. But he waited in vain for a service van to appear and eventually left the car where it was and took a taxi home.

The following day he returned and found Kathleen dead in the boot, her body stiff and cold. It was then, after Evans had closed the boot door, that the policeman arrived on the scene and offered to help him find a breakdown van. The car was pulled out of the mud shortly afterwards and Evans drove it home with the body still in the boot.

On the evening of 22 November he left his pregnant wife and his mother at a bingo hall and drove thirty miles to the Ladybower Reservoir — on the High Peak mountain range — where he stripped all the clothes from the corpse and threw it into the water, disposing of the clothes separately. He then returned to the bingo hall in time to drive his wife and mother home.

On 28 November — the day after Evans had been

charged with murder — frogmen began searching the reservoir for the missing girl's body. The following day they were joined by deep-sea divers from the Royal Navy, and finally, on 1 December, the body was found in the submerged village of Ashopton, which had been flooded when the reservoir was built nearly twenty years earlier.

In March 1964 Ronald Evans was brought to trial at the Nottingham Assizes. He admitted that he had raped Kathleen Heathcote when she was unconscious and in a serious condition, and agreed that he could have helped her instead of leaving her to die in the boot. The judge told him that he had murdered 'a decent and modest young lady', and sentenced him to life imprisonment. But that was not the last that was heard of him.

On being released on licence eleven years later, he went to live in Bristol. The police there knew that he had murdered a shop assistant, but not that it had been a sex crime. So when a series of sex offences began there shortly after his arrival, he was not regarded as a suspect. But one night in 1978 a police-woman acting as a decoy was attacked in a dark street. She fought back, calling over her radio for help, and the offender, now known as the 'Beast of Bristol', was arrested. It was Ronald Evans.

In July 1979 he appeared for trial at Bristol Crown Court, and pleaded guilty to four charges of indecent assault against women — in each case forcing the victim to take part in a sexual act by means of threats. This time he was sentenced to nine years' imprisonment, but also ordered to resume the life sentence which had been imposed on him in 1964.

Bodies of two schoolgirls discovered, 1941

On 22 November 1941, the bodies of two girls were found in a wood in Buckinghamshire, during a search of the district by local police and volunteers. Doreen Hearne, aged eight, and Kathleen Trendle, six, had both died from stab wounds in the neck, each having been manually strangled to the point of unconsciousness beforehand. There was no indication that either of them had been sexually assaulted, though the skirts of both had been pulled up under their arms. The motive for the crime was therefore unknown.

The two girls had been reported missing three days earlier, after leaving their school in the village of Penn — about half a mile from their homes. Other children said that they had seen them being taken for a ride in an army lorry, and in Rough Wood, where their bodies were discovered — some four miles from the village — there were tyre marks and a large patch of oil which had been left by a vehicle. There was also a khaki handkerchief with the laundry mark 'RA 1019' among the items found at the scene.

Some of the children who had seen the lorry were able to describe it, and one boy remembered its military identification marks. The police were thus able to trace it to Yoxford, in Suffolk, where it was found to have oil leaking from its rear axle. The laundry mark 'RA 1019' was found to have been allotted to the driver of the vehicle, twenty-six-year-old Harold Hill, of the 86th Field Regiment, Royal Artillery.

The regiment had been in Hazlemere, a few miles from Penn, on the day in question, and Hill fitted descriptions of the man who had given the two girls a lift. His spare uniform — which he had been soaking — had bloodstains on it, and he was unable to explain how his handkerchief had been left at the scene of the murders. A claim that he had lost his army knife some months previously was later found to be a lie.

Harold Hill was charged with murder and brought to trial in January 1942. In spite of the absence of any discernible motive for the crime, he was convicted and sentenced to death. His execution took place in April the same year.

Murder of Edith Drew-Bear, 1934

NOVEMBER
25

On 25 November 1934, two men in Brighton, Sussex, reported hearing shots and screams on the East Brighton Golf Course, between Preston and Moulscombe. Police officers went to investigate, and found the body of Miss Edith Constance Drew-Bear, a twenty-one-year-old cinema attendant, in a water tank. She had been shot several times in the back and head — though none of the wounds had been fatal — and a silk scarf had then been tied tightly round her neck before she was immersed. Her death had been caused by strangulation.

Inquiries led to the arrest of Percy Charles Anderson, a motor mechanic also aged twenty-one, to whom Miss Drew-Bear had been closely attached. Anderson had been with her on the day in question, and had afterwards boarded a bus dripping wet and without his boots, jacket or waistcoat. The police found a bottle containing an irritant poison — a mixture of ammonia chloride and zinc chloride — in his pocket; they also found a number of weapons — a home-made pistol, a sheath-knife and a loaded stick — in his rooms, together with the empty container of a second pistol and bullets identical to those taken from the young woman's body.

Anderson said that he and Miss Drew-Bear had quarrelled, and that he had then gone for a swim in the sea to cool himself. He also said — or so it was later alleged — that the quarrel had started because the deceased accused him of smiling at another girl. But he could not remember what had happened after he went for a swim, as his mind had gone blank at this point.

At his trial at the Lewes Assizes in March 1935 a plea of insanity was made on his behalf. A Brighton doctor told the court that Anderson's black-out could have occurred as a result of an epileptic condition producing a state of maniacal excitement. Persons affected in this way could commit the most brutal acts of violence, being at the time perfectly oblivious of the injuries they inflicted on others and the damage that they themselves sustained, the doctor declared.

But the judge — Lord Hewart, the Lord Chief Justice — advised the jury that the onus was on the defence to prove insanity, as under the law every man was presumed to be sane until the contrary was proved. In order to meet this requirement, the defence had to show that at the time of committing the crime the prisoner had been labouring under 'such a defect of reason, from disease of the mind, as not to know the nature and quality of (his) act' — or that 'he did know it, but did not know that what he was doing was wrong'. In the case of Anderson it was difficult to see 'even a scintilla of evidence' of such a disease, the judge remarked.

Though no real motive for the crime had emerged, the jury took only forty minutes to return a verdict of guilty, and Anderson was sentenced to death. Following the dismissal of his appeal, he was hanged at Wandsworth Prison on 16 April 1935.

Murder of Colin Saunders, 1969

On 26 November 1969, Colin George Saunders, a thirty-five-year-old homosexual who worked as a chauffeur for a car-hire firm, was murdered by a young drifter from Liverpool with whom he had shared his bed-sitter in Bromley, Kent, for the previous five weeks. Stanley Wrenn, aged nineteen, attacked him in the early morning while he was still asleep, striking him twice with an iron gas-ring, then stabbing him a great many times with a knife which he had bought especially for the purpose. The crime was committed partly for the sake of money and partly out of malice, Wrenn having discovered that Saunders had infected him with gonorrhoea.

About four hours after the murder had taken place Wrenn left the house with about £12 in banknotes, some coins, Saunders' car-keys and driving licence, and a suitcase containing clean shirts and other stolen items. He got into the Humber belonging to Saunders' employers but reversed it at speed, causing a collision with another car. He then had to return to the house, pretending that he was telephoning the police, while the other driver waited in the street. A few minutes later he went out and told the other driver that the police were on their way.

But while he stood talking to him, another employee of Saunders' firm arrived on the scene and asked Wrenn what he was doing. Wrenn replied that he was 'taking the car round for Colin', and the newcomer helped him by moving the vehicle off the road. He then gave the keys back, telling Wrenn that he and Saunders were to go to the firm's office at eleven o'clock to see the manager. Finally, he spoke to the other driver before leaving.

Wrenn went back to the house once again, threw the keys down in the bed-sitter and shortly afterwards left for the third time, telling the driver who was still waiting that Saunders was getting up and that he (Wrenn) was going to the firm's office. This was not to the other man's liking, but he continued to wait in the expectation that the police would arrive at any moment. Wrenn, in the meantime, made his way to the nearest railway station and caught a train to London.

After waiting in the street for some hours the offended driver went to the house himself. One of the other occupants let him in, and they went into Saunders' room together. Finding the body, they called the police.

The room was in chaos, with clothes from the wardrobe strewn on the floor and splashes of blood in several places. There were two single beds, and the body lay on one of them, covered with bedclothes and a dressing-gown. The two murder weapons, both bloodstained, were found nearby; the gas-ring was later found to have been taken from another room in the same house.

There was no mystery to solve. The crime had been committed in a casual manner, and Wrenn gave himself up just as casually the following day, after he had been named in connection with it in an evening newspaper.

Appearing for trial at the Old Bailey on 24 March 1970, he pleaded guilty and was sentenced to life imprisonment. He was released in June 1980, when he was thirty years old.

Beryl Evans reported dead, 1949

On 30 November 1949, Timothy John Evans, a semi-literate van-driver aged twenty-five, walked into a police station in Wales and reported the death of his nineteen-year-old wife, whose body he claimed to have hidden in a drain at their home in the Notting Hill district of London. When police officers investigated the matter, they found that Beryl Evans was indeed dead — not in a drain but in a small wash-house — and so, too, was the couple's fourteen-month-old daughter Geraldine. Both deaths had been caused by strangulation.

Evans at first confessed to the murders, but later withdrew his confession and blamed John Reginald Halliday Christie, an older man who lived in another flat at the same address. Christie, a former wartime special constable, had known that Beryl was pregnant for the second time and offered to carry out an abortion for her, said Evans. He had afterwards said that she died during the course of this, and advised Evans to leave London for a while, saying that he would arrange for Geraldine to be unofficially adopted by a childless couple he knew. Evans, according to this account, had believed his daughter to be still alive when he reported his wife's death.

Evans was charged with both murders, and tried at the Old Bailey. Christie, who gave evidence against him, denied having had anything to do with the crimes, and seemed to have no motive for either of them. The trial was only for the murder of the child, but evidence concerning the death of Beryl Evans was admitted, as it was assumed that the two murders had been committed by the same person. On being found guilty, Evans was sentenced to death. He was hanged on 9 March 1950.

But three years later, on 24 March 1953, a West Indian tenant to whom Christie had sub-let his flat found the bodies of three other women in a kitchen cupboard which had been papered over. This shocking discovery was followed by others, the body of a fourth woman being found under floorboards in the same flat and the remains of a further two in the back garden. The four women whose bodies were found in the house — Christie's wife Ethel and three prostitutes — had all been murdered since Evans' execution. The other two had been killed and buried several years earlier.

Christie was arrested and admitted responsibility for all six of the murders, later adding that he had killed Beryl Evans as well. He already had a criminal record from many years earlier — one of his convictions being for assaulting a woman — but no importance had been attached to this when he appeared against Evans, as he had not been in trouble since 1933. At his trial at the Old Bailey — for his wife's murder — he pleaded insanity, but was found guilty. He was hanged at Pentonville Prison, at the age of fifty-five, on 15 July 1953.

Christie was a sex murderer. His last four victims — his wife and the three prostitutes — had all been strangled with ligatures, but the bodies of the three prostitutes also showed signs of carbon monoxide poisoning and sexual intercourse. Christie confessed that he had invited the women to his flat, and had used coal gas to make them lose consciousness so that he could strangle and rape them. He was, in fact, a necrophile.

But in view of his claim to have murdered Beryl Evans — though not Geraldine — and general disbelief in the possibility of two stranglers having lived in the same house at the same time, there were demands for an official inquiry into the question of whether the execution of Timothy Evans had been a miscarriage of justice. John Scott Henderson, a senior QC, was appointed by the Home Secretary to hold such an inquiry, and his report — published on the day of Christie's execution — concluded that Christie's confession to the murder of Beryl Evans had been false and that there could be no doubt that Timothy Evans had killed both Beryl and Geraldine.

In spite of this, many people believed that a miscarriage of justice *had* taken place, and during the early 1960s, following the publication of a book by Ludovic Kennedy, there were demands for a fresh inquiry. Eventually one was held under the direction of Sir Daniel Brabin, a High Court judge, who, in October 1966, reported his findings. These were that while Timothy Evans had probably not murdered his daughter — the crime for which he had been hanged — he probably *had* murdered his wife. The report led to Evans being granted a posthumous free pardon, but was received with scorn by people who had been campaigning for a review of the case.

'It took thirteen years for officialdom grudgingly to admit what was obvious in 1953 to all but the wilfully blind; that there were not two stranglers of women living in 10 Rillington Place, but one,' wrote Ludovic Kennedy in 1970.

But Professor Keith Simpson, one of the three pathologists who examined the exhumed body of Beryl Evans after Christie's arrest, tells us in his *Forty Years of Murder*, '(The) Brabin report upheld the coincidence, and it never seemed to me very far-fetched. Coincidences are far more common in life than in fiction.' He also draws attention to the lack of evidence of a sexual motive in her case and points out that — unlike the other women murdered in the same house — she was beaten up before being killed. The injuries which she received were, in his opinion, 'alien to Christie's style of murder'.

Death of James Pullen, 1933

On the evening of 1 December 1933, James Pullen, a senile old man of eighty-five, died from coal-gas poisoning at the home of his daughter and son-in-law just outside Bath, in Somerset. His son-in-law, thirty-two-year-old Reginald Ivor Hinks, was in the house with him at the time, and it was he who raised the alarm. He said that shortly after speaking to Mr Pullen in the sitting-room, he had found him lying on the kitchen floor, with his head in the oven and the gas turned on. His account suggested that his father-in-law had committed suicide.

This account was challenged at the inquest on Mr Pullen's body, initially by the dead man's own doctor, who had been called to the house on the evening in question. Dr Scott Reid, who had attended Mr Pullen for five years, said that as the dead man had suffered from senile degeneration of the brain, he would have been incapable of turning on the gas taps. Dr Reid also said that he had found a bruise on the back of the dead man's head — the result of a blow severe enough to have stunned him.

Following this sensation, two other witnesses — a pathologist and a police surgeon — both said that the bruise to which Dr Reid had referred had been caused while Mr Pullen was still alive. Then two more — a fireman and another doctor — told how they had been called to the house on the night preceding his death, when Hinks claimed that the old man had fainted or collapsed in his bath. On this occasion, according to Hinks, Mr Pullen's head had gone under the water and his face had turned black. But the old man had seemed unperturbed, and the doctor had found no evidence of inhaled water or shock. 'I thought the son-in-law must have simply got excited and was exaggerating,' the doctor said.

Hinks' wife Constance, to whom he had been married for less than a year, said that her husband had always been kind to her father and had looked after him since the end of June. She was asked about the incident which had occurred on 30 November, and told how she had helped to lift her father into a sitting position in the bath after her husband had called her to the scene. Her father had been 'practically himself' by the time the ambulance arrived, she said.

Questioned about her father's business affairs, Mrs Hinks said that he had owned four cottages, and had also owned a shop in Dorking, Surrey, until it was sold about August. He had given her £900 which he had received for the shop, and she had given it to her husband, who had used part of it to buy the house in which her father had died. Mrs Hinks also said that her father had made a will, leaving everything he owned to her.

Finally, a police constable told how he had gone to the house on the evening of 1 December and found two firemen giving Mr Pullen artificial respiration in the kitchen. The officer said that Hinks, who was wearing pyjamas and a dressing-gown, was very excited; he talked a great deal about his wife and said that he wanted Mr Pullen to be moved before she returned home. When asked what he had done when he found the old man with his head in the oven, he replied, 'I could see what had happened and I caught hold of his two feet and pulled him out. You might find a bruise on the back of his head where it hit the floor.' In a statement made later, he said that he had tried to revive the dead man by warming and massaging his heart.

The inquest, which had opened on 5 December, had already been adjourned several times, and was adjourned again after the constable had finished giving his evidence. When it was resumed on 19 January the jury returned a verdict of wilful murder against Hinks, and the coroner committed him for trial. Appearing at the Somerset Assizes, he was convicted and sentenced to death.

Hinks was a petty criminal with a record of fraud. He had married Constance after meeting her only a few weeks earlier, while he was working as a vacuum-cleaner salesman, and there could be little doubt that he had married her for the sake of the inheritance which she expected to receive at her father's death. Having done so, he had murdered her father for the same reason — and for this crime he was hanged in Bristol on 3 May 1934.

Constance, at the time of their meeting, had been a divorcée with one child, her first husband having divorced her on grounds of adultery. In January 1935 she gave birth to another child, in respect of which she later sought an affiliation order against a man living in Camberwell, south London. The man denied having been intimate with Mrs Hinks, and the order was refused.

During the early hours of 2 December 1925, Lock Ah Tam, a respected member of England's Chinese community, shot and killed his wife and two daughters at their home in Birkenhead, Cheshire. The crime was committed in a fit of rage after a family dinner party which had been held to celebrate the twentieth birthday of Tam's son Lock Ling. Tam afterwards telephoned the police and told them what he had done. The following February, at the Chester Assizes, he was convicted of murder.

Tam, a native of Canton, had settled in England after arriving as a ship's steward in 1895, at the age of twenty-three. He had afterwards risen to a position of prominence among his fellow countrymen, becoming the representative of organized Chinese dock workers in Europe and president of a Chinese Republican organization, as well as founding a seamen's club in Liverpool. At this time he was known to be prosperous, good-natured and charitable, and often helped the police to deal with problems which had arisen among Liverpool's Chinese population.

But in 1918 Tam suffered a head injury as a result of being struck with a billiard cue by a Russian sailor who had been invited to the club. He then began to drink excessively and was sometimes violent, particularly after an unsuccessful commercial venture in 1924 had led to his being declared bankrupt. His wife Catherine, a Welshwoman, stood by him loyally, but confided to a friend that she thought he was going mad.

On the night of the party Tam was in a good mood

until after the guests had left, when he suddenly began speaking angrily to his wife, stamping his feet and gesticulating. He stopped when Lock Ling intervened, but not long afterwards Margaret Sing, the maid, saw him loading a revolver. Shortly after that Tam got out his sporting-gun and shot his wife and youngest daughter; he then used the revolver to shoot his other daughter. By this time his son had run from the house in terror.

At his trial Tam was defended by Sir Edward Marshall Hall, who argued that his client had been in a state of unconscious automatism, caused by an epileptic fit, and was therefore insane at the time the murders were committed. But the jury was unconvinced by this and took only twelve minutes to reach a verdict of guilty. Tam was hanged at Walton Prison, Liverpool, on 23 March 1926.

Body of Margaret Brindley discovered, 1958

DECEMBER
3

On 3 December 1958, a lorry-driver stopped at a bridge over the River Ray, near the A41 road between Aylesbury, Buckinghamshire, and Bicester in Oxfordshire, intending to get water for his radiator. But on going down to the edge of the river, he found the body of a young pregnant woman. Margaret Brindley, a twenty-year-old prostitute, had been savagely battered, and her face was unrecognizable. However, she had been arrested for soliciting in London's Hyde Park only a few days earlier, and so could be identified from her fingerprints.

352

Margaret had moved to London after leaving her home in Wolverhampton, Staffordshire, when she was eighteen, and for the last ten months of her life had lived with a Turkish Cypriot named Eyyup Celal — the man who had persuaded her to go on the streets. Celal told police that he had taken Margaret to Paddington Station on 30 November so that she could go back and stay with her parents, to await the birth of her child. He also said that on 2 December — when it was believed that Margaret's murder had taken place — he had spent the whole day with another prostitute named Dorothy Johnson.

When Dorothy Johnson was questioned, she said that Celal had spent the night of 1 December with her, but not the following day. Another girl, Maureen Kelly, revealed that she and Margaret had been in Hyde Park together on the night of 1 December — and that Celal had seen them there about 9.30 p.m. It was also discovered that Celal had been seen driving along the Aylesbury to Bicester road on 2 December.

Forensic evidence linked Celal even more strongly to the crime, for a bloodstained metal bar found at the scene bore traces of paint identical to that which had been used on a door at his home, and lipstick on one of his monogrammed handkerchiefs — also found at the scene — was of the same type as a smudge left on his face by Dorothy Johnson on the morning of 2 December. Celal's car was found to be bloodstained, though he had washed it since the murder.

The twenty-one-year-old Cypriot, known as 'Tony the Turk', was therefore charged with Margaret Brindley's murder. At his trial at the Old Bailey in February 1959 it was alleged that he had committed the crime because the victim, being pregnant, had ceased to be of any use to him. Although he denied having lived off Margaret's earnings, Celal was convicted of murder and given a life sentence.

On 15 August 1960, Margaret Brindley's mother

— a woman of forty-eight, also named Margaret — was found battered to death in a house in Dunstall Hill Road, Wolverhampton, where she had been living with another man — a Jamaican — after leaving her husband. Her murderer, another West Indian living in the same house, had beaten her to death with a shoe after being insulted when he asked her for some money which she owed him. He, too, was sentenced to life imprisonment.

Murder of Mme D'Audeville, 1890

DECEMBER
4

On 4 December 1890, René Sarrebourse d'Audeville, a bankrupt member of the French nobility, shot his estranged wife dead at the home of her wealthy parents, M. and Mme Heurteaux, at Nantes, in Brittany. Mme D'Audeville and her parents were having lunch at the time, and the culprit, entering suddenly, shot her in the mouth. He afterwards tried to shoot Mme Heurteaux, but her husband, a retired sardine merchant, managed to prevent this by striking his arm as he fired. Sarrebourse d'Audeville was charged with murder and brought to trial in Nantes the following March, the case exciting much public interest.

The prisoner, who was little more than thirty years of age, looked considerably older. He had led a dissipated life, spending most of his time hunting, fishing, drinking and gambling, and had married Heurteaux's daughter Félicie when he was twenty-seven for financial reasons. He then squandered the money from his marriage settlement within a short time, and finally went bankrupt as a result of speculating in stocks and shares which he could not afford. It was claimed that he had also ill-treated his wife and forced her to make a will in his favour.

In June 1890 Mme d'Audeville petitioned for a judicial separation, and was authorized to take up residence at her parents' home. The accused was left without any money at all and, being incapable of work, had to rely on friends for assistance. Then, in November, following various unsuccessful attempts to induce his wife to return to him, he bought a revolver and a double-barrelled shotgun and took rooms just a few yards from the Heurteaux residence. At the time of the shooting he also had a long, freshly-sharpened knife in his possession.

'In the room which I had taken, in the Rue Bonne-Louise, I heard roars of laughter going on between my wife and her parents,' he told the court at his trial. He said that as a result of this 'burst of merriment' he had forced his way into their presence, intending to take his own life.

But his father-in-law, on being asked whether he believed this, replied that the prisoner was 'much too great a coward' to do such a thing. 'The truth is that he was revenging himself by murdering her, because he had been deprived of the allowance I had always made her!' declared Heurteaux.

Further allegations were made by the prisoner's mother-in-law, who described him as 'a very evil man' and said that he had subjected her daughter to 'three long years of martyrdom' in his attempts to get his hands on the family fortune. Another witness, a former nurse to his children, said that the accused had dragged his wife about by the hair and beaten the children unmercifully. He had even threatened to throw the youngest one, aged four months, out of the window, this witness told the court.

Sarrebourse d'Audeville sobbed and moaned a great deal during the course of the proceedings, claiming that he had loved his wife and that the allegations of ill-treatment were all false. Three doctors testified that he was in such a condition of mind that he could not be considered responsible for his actions, and a friend's written deposition stated that the prisoner had fallen into a state of melancholy and hinted a lot about committing suicide after an attempted reconciliation with his wife had failed. By this time he had owned only a small iron bedstead and one or two chairs, and claimed that he was dying of hunger and cold.

Several other friends of the prisoner told the court that they regarded him as a scatter-brained fellow, easily excited but by no means evil, and the defence claimed that he was at the very least 'on the borderline of insanity'. But the jury took only half an hour to find him guilty, without extenuating circumstances, and he was sentenced to death. The sentence was later commuted to hard labour for life by the French President.

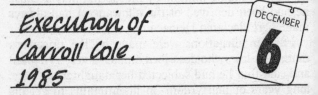

Execution of Carroll Cole. 1985

DECEMBER 6

On 6 December 1985, Carroll Edward Cole, a forty-seven-year-old drifter convicted of the murders of five women, was executed in Carson City, Nevada. The execution was carried out by means of a lethal injection, the condemned man being strapped to a table in the jail's converted gas chamber for the drugs to be administered. Cole thus became the fiftieth person to be put to death in the United States — but the first in Nevada — since the reinstatement of the death penalty nine years earlier.

Cole was a native of Sioux City, Iowa, but had been brought up near San Francisco. He had been dishonourably discharged from the navy for stealing two pistols and since then had been arrested for a variety of offences, including an unsuccessful attempt to kill his first wife by setting fire to a Dallas motel. His record also showed that he had been in mental hospitals in four different states, one of them following a suicide attempt in 1967.

Cole was arrested in December 1980 in connection with the murder of Wanda Fay Roberts, a thirty-two-year-old woman whose body had been found in a Dallas car park three weeks earlier. He then confessed that he had killed eight women during the previous nine years, and hinted that he may have killed many others as well. Some of the women he mentioned were known murder victims; others were not known to be dead or were believed to have died from natural causes. He later claimed that he had killed thirty-five women altogether.

The reason that some of these deaths had been put down to natural causes was that the victims had been hopelessly drunk at the time. 'The women had high levels of alcohol in their blood and were probably comatose or unconscious when Cole killed them,' one detective involved in the case explained. 'It doesn't take much to choke to death a person in that state and not leave any marks. Cole just might have found the way to commit the perfect murder.'

His second wife, Diana Faye, whom he had married in 1974, was one of his victims. Her body was found in their apartment in San Diego two days after Cole's arrest — by which time, according to the coroner's estimate, she had been dead for about a week. Her murder was followed by that of forty-three-year-old Sally Thompson in Dallas on the night of 30 November. Both of these women had been drinking heavily just before they died, and both were at first thought to have died of natural causes.

Carroll Cole showed little interest in the charges that were brought against him, and was unperturbed at the possibility of being executed. 'I have been in and out of institutions all my life,' he said. 'I know I'm sick. I just can't help myself. I just want the killing to stop.'

He was tried in Dallas, where he was convicted of three murders and given three life sentences, to be served concurrently. In this case he said that he had been 'repulsed' by what he called the loose morals of the victims, and said that he had killed them because they reminded him of his mother. 'I think I kill *her* through them,' he said.

Three years later Cole was brought to trial in Las Vegas for two more murders, this time pleading guilty and requesting the death penalty. When his wish was granted, he smiled and said, 'Thanks, Judge!' He later told a reporter who interviewed him on Death Row, 'I know I'll kill again if I get out of prison. So why prolong the life of a despicable person who acted as the judge, jury and executioner to the people he murdered?'

Shortly before his death Cole gave permission for his brain to be used for the purposes of research. He spent his last hours playing poker with the prison chaplain, and swallowed Valium tablets to steady his nerves before the execution was carried out.

Body of Thomas Meaney discovered, 1950

On the morning of 8 December 1950, William Donoghue, a forty-two-year-old bus conductor living in a block of flats near London's Waterloo Station, was found standing in the doorway of his own flat, staring at a body which was lying on the landing outside. The body was that of an older man, and lay face down in a pool of blood. Donoghue, who appeared dazed, kept muttering to himself, 'Is it a dummy or a body? Take it away!'

The police were informed, and a constable arrived on the scene. Donoghue, on being questioned, said, 'If that is a real man, I done it!' He then went on to say that the man had come home with him the night before. 'I thought he was joking with me,' said Donoghue. 'He was lying on the bed, making gurgling noises. I must have struck him with the bayonet and dragged him out on the landing.'

Later, at Southwark police station, Donoghue made another statement, giving more details of what had happened. The dead man was sixty-three-year-old Thomas Meaney, a friend of his who had worked as the driver of a Black Maria. Donoghue had met him at one of the local public houses the previous evening, and stayed drinking with him until closing time. Then, as they were both heavy drinkers, they went to the flat together and drank a bottle of gin which Donoghue had bought during the course of the evening. Eventually Meaney fell asleep on the bed and Donoghue dozed off leaning on a table.

Not long afterwards Donoghue woke up and tried to get into bed. He was far from sober by this time,

359

and had forgotten that Meaney was there with him. So when he found him lying asleep on the bed, he thought it was a dummy which somebody had left there for a joke.

He pulled his friend off the bed, and Meaney fell to the floor without protest, 'like a sack of coal'. While he lay there Donoghue stabbed him repeatedly with a Second World War bayonet which he normally used as a bread knife. Even then, when he saw his friend's blood, Donoghue did not realize what he had done — he merely assumed that the blood was red juice from a tube and that it had been used to trick him. He therefore dragged Meaney out onto the landing, then returned to the flat and went to bed.

It was not until he woke up several hours later and found blood all over the floor that he had any inkling of what had really happened.

Incredible though this story must have seemed, the police officers who investigated the affair could find no evidence to disprove it. Donoghue and Meaney had been friendly towards each other as they left the pub, and there was no reason to suppose that they had quarrelled afterwards. Donoghue had no injuries to suggest that there had been a struggle, and appeared to have had no other motive for killing his friend. Moreover, the dead man — who had been stabbed sixteen times in the head and neck — had no injuries to his hands, as he would have had if he had tried to protect himself.

No blood sample was taken from Donoghue at the time of his arrest, so his blood alcohol reading was not measured. But Meaney's was found to have been at a dangerously high level, at which one is ordinarily incapable of forming a felonious intent. And as Donoghue had been the drunker of the two when they left the pub together, it was possible that his blood alcohol level had been even higher than Meaney's at the time of the stabbing.

At any rate, when he was brought to trial at the Old Bailey in February 1951, the Principal Medical Officer at Brixton Prison gave his opinion that Donoghue — 'a quiet, inoffensive and respectable little man', according to his counsel — *had* been drunk enough to believe that he was stabbing a dummy rather than a human being. As a result of this, the Director of Public Prosecutions decided that there was insufficient evidence to proceed on a murder charge, and the prosecution accepted a plea of manslaughter. Donoghue was accordingly sent to prison for three years.

Execution of Alpha Otis Stephens, 1984

DECEMBER
12

On 12 December 1984, Alpha Otis Stephens, aged thirty-nine, was electrocuted at the Diagnostic and Classification Centre in Jackson, Georgia, following his conviction for murder ten years earlier. The execution took place shortly after midnight, the condemned man being strapped into the electric chair at 12.15 a.m. He declined to make a final statement, and watched intently as he was being prepared. It was noticed that he was trembling and biting his lips.

At 12.18 he was given a charge of 2000 volts — at which his head rolled slowly and his chest heaved. But when the electricity was switched off two minutes later he was seen to be breathing, and six minutes after that — when it was safe to enter the execution chamber — doctors examined him and pronounced him still alive. The warden therefore ordered that a second jolt be given, and at 12.28 a.m. Stephens' chest heaved once more and his head again rolled. When the charge was cut off for the second time at 12.30 he was dead.

Stephens, known as 'Sonny Boy', had been sentenced in 1974 for the murder of a builder named Roy Asbell during the course of a robbery. A plea for mercy had been rejected only a few hours before the sentence was carried out.

Though described as 'macabre' and 'disturbing' by witnesses, the use of the second jolt when the prisoner was found to be breathing was 'standard procedure', according to a prison spokesman.

At an execution in Alabama in April 1983 three charges were needed before the condemned man, John Louis Evans, was pronounced dead. During the first the electrode on his left leg burnt through and fell off; then, when the second was given, a puff of smoke and a burst of flame erupted from his left temple and leg, but doctors said that they were still not certain that he was dead.

Evans' lawyer afterwards complained that his client had been 'burnt alive' and 'tortured ... in the name of vengeance and in the disguise of justice'.

Kidnapping of Marion Parker, 1927

DECEMBER
15

On 15 December 1927, Marion Parker, one of the twelve-year-old twin daughters of a Los Angeles bank personnel officer, was abducted from her school by a youth pretending that her father had met with an accident. Her father, Perry Parker, afterwards received a number of ransom notes and telephone calls from a youth calling himself 'The Fox', and letters from his missing daughter — begging him to co-operate with the kidnapper — were also received. The ransom demanded was $1500.

Parker got the money ready in $20 gold certificates, as instructed, and drove to the place where he was to meet the kidnapper. However, he was followed by a police officer, and the culprit, realizing this, failed to appear. The next day, 17 December, he drove to a different location — having received further orders in the meantime — and waited in his car until another stopped alongside it. The driver of this second car, a youth with a handkerchief over the lower part of his face, then pointed a sawn-off shotgun at him and demanded the money.

Parker saw that the youth had a bundle which looked like a child with him, and was told that it was Marion and that she was asleep; he then handed over the money. At this, the youth said that he would leave the child further along the road, and told Parker not to move until he had done so. He then left the bundle a short distance away and drove off quickly. A moment or two later Parker was horrified to discover that his daughter was dead and that her forearms and legs had been cut off. The bundle contained the upper part of her body.

The kidnapper made good his escape, but his car, a Chrysler coupé which had been stolen in Kansas City, was found abandoned a few hours later. It was not taken away for examination for two days, as it was hoped that the culprit might return for it, but he did not. In the meantime the child's limbs, wrapped in towels and newspapers, were found in Elysian Park, in the same city.

Shortly after this somebody suggested that a youth named Hickman, a former employee of the same bank as Parker, might be the person responsible. Hickman, a messenger, had been convicted of forging cheques, and Parker had interceded on his behalf — with the result that Hickman was put on probation instead of being sent to jail. But thumb-prints found on one of the ransom notes — and also on one of the abandoned car's mirrors — were identified as his, and a search was started for him.

William Edward Hickman, aged nineteen, was arrested in Oregon on 22 December, with almost the whole of the ransom money in his possession. He was taken back to Los Angeles on Christmas Day, and soon confessed that he was guilty of the murder of Marion Parker. He had kidnapped her because he needed money to pay college expenses, then strangled her because he feared discovery, he said. He had then dissected her body so that he could put it into suitcases.

A search of the apartment which Hickman had occupied at the time resulted in the discovery of further evidence, including clotted blood in pipes in the bathroom. Shortly afterwards he made a further confession, revealing that on Christmas Eve, 1926, he and another youth named Welby Hunt had held up a Los Angeles drug-store and murdered the druggist, Ivy Toms. Welby Hunt was therefore arrested, and he also confessed, stating that he and Hickman had committed a number of other hold-ups as well.

Hickman was brought to trial for the murder of Marion Parker in January 1928, pleading not guilty by reason of insanity. But a note which he had passed to another prisoner, stating his intention of putting on an act of some sort to impress the jury, fell into the hands of the district attorney and was used against him. He was convicted and sentenced to death.

The trial of Hickman and Welby Hunt, for the murder of Ivy Toms, began the following day — 16 February — and in this case both prisoners were convicted of first-degree murder and sentenced to life imprisonment.

Hickman's execution, by hanging, had been scheduled to take place on 27 April 1928, but due to various appeals it was not carried out until 19 October the same year. During his months on Death Row he became a Catholic and spent much time reading his Bible, but was treated with contempt by many of his fellow-condemned. When the execution was finally carried out at San Quentin Prison, a mishap occurred, and he died from strangulation rather than a broken neck.

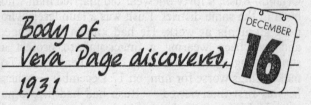

Body of Vera Page discovered, 1931

DECEMBER 16

On the morning of 16 December 1931, Vera Page, a girl of eleven, was found strangled among the shrubs of a garden about a mile from her own home in London's Notting Hill district. She had been criminally assaulted and then murdered elsewhere — probably soon after her disappearance on the evening of 14 December — and the state of decomposition of the body suggested that it had been kept in a warm place, such as an inhabited room, in the meantime.

It was found, too, that although there had been rain during the night before its discovery, only the back of Vera's coat, where it had touched the ground, was damp. So the body had clearly been lying outside for only a short while.

The child had been strangled manually, and a cord had afterwards been tied loosely round her neck, perhaps to enable her murderer to carry her body over his shoulder. A finger-stall, smelling strongly of ammonia, was found in the crook of her right arm, its size indicating that it had been used by a man. There was also soot and coal-dust on her face and clothes, and candle-grease on her coat.

Inquiries in the area led to the discovery of a disused coal-cellar under the pavement of Stanley Crescent, near which Vera Page had last been seen alive, and where it was now believed that the crime had been committed; and a woman told police that during the early morning of 16 December she had seen a man pushing a bundle on a wheel-barrow near the place where the body was found.

Before long suspicion began to centre on Percy Orlando Rush, a forty-one-year-old married man who lived in the same district. Rush was a launderer, who used ammonia at work. He had known Vera Page, and had been wearing a finger-stall to protect a suppurating wound not long before her death. To make things worse for him, on 17 December — when he was first interviewed — Rush had had a pyjama cord in his pocket; this could have been the cord which was tied round Vera's neck after death.

But the evidence against him was far from conclusive. Bandages and lint from his home were not identical to those found in the finger-stall, and it could not be stated definitely that the grease on the child's coat was the same as that of candles in his possession. Moreover, the woman who had seen the man with the wheel-barrow was unable to identify him.

At the inquest which followed, Rush gave evidence, denying that he had had anything to do with Vera's death. He said that he had started to walk home from work — a journey which took him two hours — only a short while before the child was seen alive for the last time, and claimed that he had discarded his finger-stall two days earlier. The coroner, having questioned him at length, pointed out the possibilities of coincidence, and the jury returned a verdict of murder by some person or persons unknown.

The crime was never solved.

Body found in mineshaft, 1948

DECEMBER
20

On 20 December 1948, a Coal Board official looked down a disused mineshaft at Walton, near Wakefield in Yorkshire, and saw a body floating in water 130 feet below. He informed the police and it was brought to the surface with the use of grappling irons, but the head, both forearms and one leg were missing. The pathologist who carried out the post-mortem was therefore able to say only that it was the body of an elderly woman who had been five feet tall, and that it had been immersed for some years.

The missing parts were later found under the water by a mine rescue worker, and the pathologist was then able to estimate that the woman had been over seventy years of age. It was still not possible to determine the cause of her death, but it seemed unlikely that she had fallen down the shaft by accident, as the opening had been covered with heavy boards — which, in any case, had been put back into position afterwards. So the police naturally regarded her death as a possible murder, and it was not long before they discovered her identity.

A check of missing-persons lists revealed that Emma Sheard, a woman of seventy-five, had disappeared from her home in Chevet Terrace, just a hundred yards from the mineshaft, seven years earlier. The house which she had owned was still occupied by her great-niece, Winifred Hallaghan, who, on being seen by police officers, admitted not only that the body in question was that of her great-aunt, but also that she (Mrs Hallaghan) had killed her.

Mrs Hallaghan, a nursing orderly, said that she and her husband had both been living at the victim's house in 1941. There had been a great deal of tension between her great-aunt and herself at the time, and the old woman had infuriated her by saying that Mr Hallaghan was having an affair with somebody else. 'We had a row and I hit her with the flat of my hand, and she fell against the sewing machine and cracked her head,' Mrs Hallaghan told the police.

She went on to say that she had disposed of the body during the early hours of the following morning after wheeling it to the old mineshaft in a pram, and explained the old woman's disappearance to neighbours by saying that she had 'wandered away'. In 1943, however, she had forged her great-aunt's signature on a house conveyance document, transferring the property in Chevet Terrace to herself.

Although Mrs Hallaghan was arrested for murder, the charge was withdrawn during the committal proceedings. But in March 1949 she appeared for trial at the Leeds Assizes on a number of other charges — three of forgery as well as one of manslaughter — and was convicted on all of them. In passing sentence, the judge told her, 'I do not doubt that you have suffered greatly over the years, but this court must not let any such consideration interfere with the course of justice.' He sent her to prison for five years.

Murder of Ernest Key. 1938

On the morning of 24 December 1938, Ernest Percival Key, a jeweller aged sixty-four, was found unconscious and covered in blood in the back room of his shop in Surbiton, Surrey. He had been attacked during the course of a robbery and stabbed about thirty-one times in the head, face and neck. He died on the way to hospital.

A bowler hat which had been left at the scene of the crime was examined by the county pathologist, Dr Eric Gardner. From the evidence of its size and hairs found attached to it, he was able to give police officers some useful information about the owner's appearance before the arrival of the Home Office pathologist, Sir Bernard Spilsbury.

The hat was found to belong to William Thomas Butler, an unemployed driver aged twenty-nine who lived with his wife and two children in Teddington, about three miles from the shop. Butler had a criminal record for house-breaking, and it was discovered that shortly after the murder he had had hospital treatment for cuts on his hands, using a false name and address and claiming that he had injured himself in an accident with a wood-cutting machine. He had actually cut his hands by stabbing the old jeweller with an unguarded dagger or knife.

Charged with murder, William Butler was brought to trial at the Old Bailey on 15 February 1939. The trial lasted two days, the prisoner claiming that he had killed in self-defence and was only guilty of manslaughter. He was, however, convicted of murder and sentenced to death, his execution taking place at

Wandsworth Prison, London, on 29 March 1939.

Dr Gardner's part in the solution of this crime was exaggerated in an English newspaper article, and exaggerated even more in a German one. As a result of this publicity, Scotland Yard received a request from the German police for information about 'the clairvoyant, Erich Gardner', who could solve a murder case merely by looking at a hat.

Execution of George Loake, 1911

DECEMBER
28

On 28 December 1911, George Loake, a sixty-four-year-old unemployed engine driver, was hanged at Stafford Jail for the murder of his estranged wife Elizabeth. The crime had taken place on 7 August previously, at a house in Warwick Street, Walsall, where Elizabeth was staying with a family named Dolloway. It followed an unsuccessful attempt at reconciliation on her husband's part — the last of a number which he had made since their parting several weeks earlier.

Loake, a widower with nine children, had married Elizabeth Newitt, a divorcée eighteen years younger than himself, eight years before the tragedy occurred. At the time he had been a jovial and well-liked man, and he and Elizabeth had been happy together until the summer of 1909, when he was involved in an accident during shunting operations just outside Walsall.

As a result of this accident, he suffered internal injuries and began to complain of blinding headaches; he also became sullen, took a morbid interest in knives and started to drink heavily. Eventually, in March 1911, he was sacked for leaving his engine unattended while he went off to buy alcohol.

After working for the London and North Western Railway Company for over fifty years Loake then found himself with no prospect of obtaining work elsewhere, and no right to the pension which he would otherwise have been entitled to on reaching retirement age. As he and his wife were forced to spend their savings, they soon had nothing left, and in June 1911 they were evicted from their home in Portland Street, Walsall. It was at this point that Elizabeth left him and, taking the two children from her first marriage, went to stay with the Dolloways.

By this time Loake's behaviour was becoming progressively worse. He had repeatedly assaulted his wife during their last few months together, and now, living in a lodging house, he made frequent threats of suicide — one of them when he visited his daughter Maud the day before the murder. The effect of this was that his children were all wary of him and unwilling to offer him a home.

On 7 August — Bank Holiday Monday — Loake went to see Elizabeth about 10.30 a.m., and spoke to her in the living room of the Dolloways' house. When a quarrel started and she turned to leave the room he suddenly grabbed her from behind and began stabbing her with a knife which he had had concealed inside his coat. His wife screamed, struggled and managed to leave the house — only to die in a nearby courtyard while a doctor was examining her. A post-mortem revealed that she had six knife wounds about her face and neck, as well as others in her left hand and forearm.

Loake had been arrested after an unsuccessful attempt to cut his own throat and was brought to trial at the Staffordshire Assizes in November. One of the witnesses who appeared against him was eleven-year-old Tommy Dolloway, who had been watching the scene in the living room unobserved when the attack took place. He had afterwards run upstairs and locked himself in his bedroom until he felt that it was safe to emerge.

The defence claimed that the prisoner was guilty only of manslaughter, because he had not intended to kill his wife and had been of unsound mind at the time. But the jury took only sixteen minutes to find him guilty of murder, and the judge told them that they could not possibly have come to any other conclusion. Loake then listened in silence as he was sentenced to death.

During the next few weeks his appeal was heard and dismissed, and the Home Secretary, who had received petitions for a reprieve, decided against recommending the use of the royal prerogative to spare his life. On the morning of 28 December a small crowd of little more than a dozen people waited outside the prison for news that Loake had been hanged.

Shooting of Ruth Hadley. 1908

DECEMBER
29

On the bitterly cold night of 29 December 1908, Edward Lawrence, a rich Wolverhampton brewer, called on a Dr Galbraith, claiming to have shot a woman. Galbraith accompanied him to his home, but refused to go inside until a colleague agreed to go with him. Finally, when the two doctors entered the house together, they found a young woman lying on the dining-room floor, fatally injured. Ruth Hadley, an attractive barmaid, had been shot in the right temple and had a slight wound in her right arm. She died shortly afterwards.

Lawrence, a married man who was well known locally, had been having an affair with Ruth for some time, and had left his wife and children for her. He also had a craving for drink and, under its influence, was inclined to become violent. His wife had obtained a decree nisi on account of a brutal assault which she had suffered at his hands — as well as his adultery — but had never had the decree made absolute. More recently, Lawrence had been fined for assaulting a policeman with his teeth.

In the room in which the shooting had taken place a meal for two people was found on the table, almost untouched. Prior to the arrival of the police Lawrence, in his customary drunken state, made various remarks which appeared to be an admission of guilt, but later his attitude changed and he declared that Ruth had shot herself. Moreover, the revolver which had been used was found to contain four undischarged and only one spent cartridge, suggesting that Lawrence had reloaded it, in the hope of giving the impression that only one shot had been fired.

Lawrence was charged with murder and in March 1909 appeared for trial in Stafford, where prosecution witnesses told the court that he had shot at Ruth and threatened her on earlier occasions. It was also revealed that Ruth had left Lawrence in September 1908, returning to him just before Christmas, and that he had had another mistress in the meantime. Another witness, a servant girl who had seen the couple quarrelling on the night of Ruth's death, said that Lawrence had accused Ruth of being drunk, and that she had denied this, making as if to throw a cruet at him. The servant added that when she left the room she heard the key turn in the lock and knew that it was Ruth who had turned it.

Edward Marshall Hall, defending, produced witnesses to prove that Ruth had been as violent as his client, that she had attacked or threatened Lawrence on many occasions, and that, on returning to him in December 1908, she had been maddened by the knowledge that he had had another woman in her place. He then called the prisoner, an educated and well-spoken man, to give his own account of her death.

Lawrence told the court that on the night in question, when he accused her of being drunk, Ruth had thrown crockery and fire-irons at him, and he had told her to leave his house for ever. He had then gone to his bedroom to fetch the revolver — which he invariably kept under his pillow — and had fired it in order to frighten her. Afterwards, he said, he had gone back to the bedroom and hidden the gun under his mattress, unaware that he had wounded her slightly in the arm. But Ruth had then gone to the bedroom herself, found the gun, and returned to the dining-room, apparently intending to kill him. During the course of a struggle which took place at this point she had accidentally been shot dead.

The court listened to the prisoner's story in silence, and found it to be unexpectedly credible, even to the extent of being corroborated by minor details given by other witnesses — of the disarranged state of the bedroom, for example. The judge, who had previously been hostile to Lawrence, was suddenly won over to his side and later, following a dramatic speech by Marshall Hall, summed up in his favour.

The jury, after retiring for only twenty minutes, returned a verdict of not guilty, and the judge, in discharging the prisoner, said that he had received a 'most terrible lesson'. 'If you will turn over a new page in your life, you may yet have a happy time with your lawful wife and children, and then, perhaps,

God will forgive you for the life you have led,' Mr Justice Jelf continued. 'I earnestly trust that what I have said to you will bear fruit in your heart and in your life.'

The case thus gave Marshall Hall his greatest victory in a murder trial — at least in his own opinion. But three days later Edward Lawrence was in trouble again, this time for assaulting another man in a Wolverhampton inn.

Murder of Grigori Rasputin, 1916

During the early hours of 30 December 1916 (or 17 December, according to the Gregorian calendar), a dissipated monk with remarkable healing powers was murdered by a group of conspirators in Petrograd (now Leningrad). The crime, which the victim had foreseen, showed the inability of the Tsar to maintain order and so was far-reaching in its effects. But it was the monk's powers of survival which made it the most famous murder in Russian history.

Grigori Efimovich Rasputin, a man of peasant origin aged about forty-five, was ungainly, drunken and lecherous, but exercised great influence at the Russian court through having several times saved the life of the Tsar's son Alexei, a haemophiliac. This influence enabled him to interfere in the affairs of both Church and State, securing appointments for his own nominees and exasperating others. He was also suspected of being the centre of a pro-German conspiracy which was undermining the war effort.

On the night of 29 December Rasputin was lured to the home of Prince Felix Yusupov, the instigator of the conspiracy. Yusupov, aged twenty-nine, was married to the Tsar's niece and had invited the 'Holy Devil' to a midnight supper on the pretext that the Princess was ill and wanted him to treat her. In fact, the Princess was not in Petrograd at the time, and Yusupov entertained Rasputin alone in an attractively-furnished room of the palace cellar, giving him cakes and wine poisoned with potassium cyanide.

The poison had no apparent effect on Rasputin, even though he consumed a large amount of it, and after an hour and a half Yusupov went to see his fellow conspirators in an upstairs room, to ask them what he should do. On being given a revolver, he returned to the dining-room and shot his guest in the back. Dr Lazovert, a Polish physician, then entered the room and pronounced Rasputin dead. But this proved to be a mistake, for shortly afterwards the victim of the crime opened his eyes, struggled to his feet and lunged at Yusupov's throat.

The terrified Yusupov ran upstairs, calling out a warning to his friends. Vladimir Purishkevich, a member of the Duma, then pursued Rasputin from the palace, firing shots at him in the snow-covered courtyard. The monk fell to the ground with bullets in his chest and shoulder, and Yusupov and Purishkevich, who were both hysterical by now, kicked and battered him as he lay there. Finally, the conspirators bound Rasputin with ropes and pushed him under the ice of the River Neva. Even so, when his body was recovered two days later, his lungs were full of water and one arm was almost free, showing that he had still been alive at the time of his immersion.

The news of Rasputin's murder was received with approval by Petrograd society and the Tsar, Nicholas II, could not punish the culprits without causing widespread offence. Yet his failure to do so served only to show that his power, which depended on fear rather than loyalty, was far from invincible. In murdering the court favourite with impunity, Prince Yusupov and his friends — one of whom was the Tsar's cousin — ensured the downfall of the Romanov dynasty.

Rasputin's powers of survival have been the subject of some speculation, and the failure of the poison — 'enough potassium cyanide to kill a monastery of monks', according to Yusupov — has naturally been seen as quite extraordinary. In this connection, however, the late Professor Keith Simpson pointed out that cyanide is more or less harmless until it comes into contact with the gastric juices, so that if the victim suffers from chronic gastritis — 'as Rasputin probably did' — he could swallow many times the fatal dose without being affected by it.

Murder of Grace Adamson, 1975

DECEMBER 31

On the evening of 31 December 1975, Mark Rowntree, a youth of nineteen with an urge to kill, was wandering round Bingley, in Yorkshire, with a long-bladed knife hidden in his shoulder-bag. He was on the look-out for a suitable victim, and before long stopped outside the home of Mrs Grace Edith Adamson in Old Main Street. Mrs Adamson, a widow of eighty-five, was knitting as she watched television, and as her curtains were undrawn, Rowntree could see her through the window.

Selecting her as the person to be killed, he rang her

doorbell and waited, holding his knife in readiness. When she came to find out who was there he induced her to open the door by saying that he was 'the police'. He then rushed into the house and stabbed her seven times, two of the wounds piercing her heart. Afterwards he left the scene of the crime, buried the weapon locally and went to a public house for a glass of beer.

Three days later Rowntree again felt the urge to kill. He bought himself another knife, and that evening made his way to the nearby village of Wastburn, where he attacked sixteen-year-old Stephen Wilson at a bus stop. The victim, with three stab wounds in his chest and stomach, ran away screaming and managed to get help. He died after being admitted to hospital, though not without giving an account of what had happened. Rowntree, in the meantime, had swum across a river — this was during a snowstorm — hitched a lift to a taxi-rank and taken a taxi back to his lodgings in Bradford Road, Shipley.

The police were now able to issue a description of the person they believed to have killed both Mrs Adamson and Stephen Wilson, saying that he was about twenty-two years old, 'with black shoulder-length hair, wearing a black jacket and carrying a shoulder-pack'. A few days later they interviewed the taxi-driver who had picked him up while he was soaked from swimming the river and thus discovered his address — but not in time to prevent him committing two more murders.

These took place on 7 January, eight days after he had killed Mrs Adamson, and the victims on this occasion were Mrs Barbara Booth, a twenty-four-year-old prostitute, and her son Alan, aged three. Rowntree had previously met Mrs Booth through a contact magazine, and on feeling once again the urge to kill, went to see her at her home in Burley, Leeds. There, having pretended that he wanted sexual intercourse, he stabbed her eighteen times, using the same knife he had used to kill Stephen Wilson. He then killed her son, who had been hiding in a corner, as he feared that the boy would be able to identify him.

Rowntree returned to his lodgings later the same day and found the officer in charge of the investigation waiting for him; he was taken into custody and admitted the four crimes. Claiming to have been driven by an insatiable desire to kill, he said that he had set himself a target of five murders, in order to beat Donald Neilson, the 'Black Panther' (see vol 1, 14 January), whom he admired.

It was learnt that Rowntree, as a baby, had been adopted by a middle-class couple. He had been sent to a public school and had qualified to go to university, but had then left home and gone to work as a bus conductor. He was found to be schizophrenic and to have been motivated by a desire for revenge as a result of being rejected by members of the opposite sex.

Rowntree appeared for trial on four charges of murder at Leeds Crown Court in June 1976. He denied murder in each case but admitted manslaughter, pleading diminished responsibility. The prosecution accepted these pleas, and the judge told the prisoner, 'It's clear from the medical evidence that at the time you committed these terrible crimes you were suffering from this severe mental illness.' He ordered that Rowntree be sent to Rampton Hospital, a top-security psychiatric establishment, for an indefinite period.

TRUE CRIME DIARY

James Bland

A gruesome gallery of shocking murders

One hundred and eighty real-life modern murder stories, quirky, gory, ingenious, bungled, or just plain horrifying, arranged in diary form for the delectation of all true crime addicts.

4 January 1964: the Boston Strangler's last victim found naked, trussed, raped and strangled with a New Year greetings card against her right foot.

15 May 1948: June Anne Devaney, aged three years and eleven months, found raped and murdered a hundred yards from the Blackburn hospital where she had been recovering from pneumonia.

23 July 1943: invalid Archibald Brown, of Essex, blown to pieces by an anti-tank mine attached to the seat of his wheelchair.

23 November 1910: Dr Crippen hanged at Pentonville prison for the murder of his second wife. He had poisoned her, and concealed her dismembered remains beneath the cellar floor of their home.

29 December 1969: Muriel McKay abducted from her London home. The body was never found, but two Trinidadian brothers, Arthur and Nizamodeen Hosein, were convicted of her murder – it is popularly believed that she was fed to the pigs on Arthur Hosein's farm.

True Crime Diary

FUTURA PUBLICATIONS
NON-FICTION/CRIME
0 7088 3264 4

DR CRIPPEN'S DIARY

An Invention

By Emlyn Williams

Neither novel nor biography, DR CRIPPEN'S DIARY is a dramatic mixture of true crime and inventive fiction by the bestselling author of BEYOND BELIEF.

Interpreting known facts through his knowledge of criminal psychology, Emlyn Williams has created the journal Crippen *could* have kept, from his twenty-first birthday to his last hours. Following the fate of his monstrous wife and his young lover, Ethel Le Neve, it brings to life one of the most notorious murderers of the twentieth century.

Ingenious and convincing, Crippen – seen for decades as a vicious murderer – emerges as a tragically misunderstood character, tried beyond endurance.

FUTURA PUBLICATIONS
CRIME/FICTION
0 7088 3929 0

ACTS OF MURDER

Jonathan Goodman

True life murder cases from the world of
stage and screen

From the stage-door stabbing of London's foremost
matinee idol by a very mad and very bad Scots actor who
believed that he had been denied his due recognition by
the star's unscrupulous machinations, to the trail of terror
wrought by the mysterious Charles Pearce, the Paganini of
crime, and the suspicious demise of Groucho Marx's
favourite 'ice-cream blonde' in her Hollywood garage,
these tales will thrill the mind and chill the blood.

'Fascinating . . . Irresistible for nostalgiacs of crime or
showbiz.' *Daily Mail*

FUTURA PUBLICATIONS
NON-FICTION/CRIME
0 7088 3603 8

A TANGLED WEB

Sex Scandals in British Politics and Society

H. Montgomery Hyde

No event seizes the public imagination, fills the pages of the press and the conversations of the gossips like a Sex Scandal; the greatest and the most powerful brought low by the most interesting of subjects.

And here there is much to satisfy even the most salacious of curiosities, an informed, informative and entertaining chronicle of lecherous lords, perverted politicians, seducing celebrities and discreditable diplomats. From Lord Melbourne's enthusiasm for flagellation to the public revelations about Cecil Parkinson and his private secretary, via Parnell, Profumo and Lambton, Wilde, Driberg and Thorpe, the author unravels the tangled web of sexual intrigue with lucidity and wit.

'This disgustingly entertaining book' *Books & Bookmen*
'this book has all the scandalous details' *Today*

FUTURA PUBLICATIONS
NON-FICTION
0 7088 3256 3

All Futura Books are available at your bookshop or
newsagent, or can be ordered from the following address:
Futura Books, Cash Sales Department,
P.O. Box 11, Falmouth, Cornwall TR10 9EN.

Please send cheque or postal order (no currency), and
allow 60p for postage and packing for the first book
plus 25p for the second book and 15p for each additional
book ordered up to a maximum charge of £1.90 in U.K.

B.F.P.O. customers please allow 60p for
the first book, 25p for the second book plus 15p per
copy for the next 7 books, thereafter 9p per book

Overseas customers, including Eire, please allow £1.25
for postage and packing for the first book, 75p for the
second book and 28p for each subsequent title ordered.